The Asbury Theological Seminary Series in Christian Rev~~~~~~~~~~~

This volume is published in collaboration with the Center for the Study of World Christian Revitalization Movements, a cooperative initiative of Asbury Theological Seminary faculty. Building on the work of the previous Wesleyan/Holiness Studies Center at the Seminary, the Center provides a focus for research in the Wesleyan Holiness and other related Christian renewal movements, including Pietism and Pentecostal movements, which have had a world impact. The research seeks to develop analytical models of these movements, including their biblical and theological assessment. Using an interdisciplinary approach, the Center bridges relevant discourses in several areas in order to gain insights for effective Christian mission globally. It recognizes the need for conducting research that combines insights from the history of evangelical renewal and revival movements with anthropological and religious studies literature on revitalization movements. It also networks with similar or related research and study centers around the world, in addition to sponsoring its own research projects.

Aaron Perry's timely anthology on *Developing Ears to Hear: Listening in Pastoral Ministry, the Spiritual Life, and Theology* represents a definitive discussion of a neglected theme in Christian spirituality that has important links to the Pietist and Wesleyan traditions. These are movements of revitalization that recovered the element of personhood as central in theological focus and in spirituality. Appearing within the context of this series makes sense, since at the heart of every movement of revitalization there has been the recovery of a capacity to hear God's personal and loving address, in Jesus Christ and by the witness of the Spirit, to persons in need of that decisive intervention in their lives. Reverberating from that encounter, the fruit of listening is transformative for the whole matrix of one's interpersonal relationships. The diversity of perspective represented among the contributors to this volume invites the reader to enter a robust discussion and reappropriation of this neglected theme. To that end, we are pleased to offer this study as congruent with the mission of the center and its research objectives.

J. Steven O'Malley, PhD
Director, Center for the Study of World
Christian Revitalization Movements and
General Editor, The Asbury Theological Seminary
     Series in Christian Revitalization

Developing Ears to Hear:
Listening in Pastoral Ministry,
the Spiritual Life, and Theology

Br. Raymond Escott, N/OSB
2016

Aaron Perry, Editor

Asbury Theological Seminary Series:
The Study of World Christian Revitalization Movements in
Pietist/Wesleyan Studies (No. 5)

EMETH PRESS
www.emethpress.com

Developing Ears to Hear:
Listening in Pastoral Ministry, the Spiritual Life, and Theology

Copyright © 2011 Aaron Perry
Printed in the United States of America on acid-free paper

Library of Congress Cataloging-in-Publication Data

Developing ears to hear : listening in pastoral ministry, the spiritual life, and theology / Aaron Perry, editor.
    p. cm. -- (The Asbury Theological Seminary series in world Christian revitalization movements in Pietist/Wesleyan studies ; no. 5)
  Includes bibliographical references and index.
  ISBN 978-1-60947-020-3 (alk. paper)
  1. Listening--Religious aspects--Christianity. I. Perry, Aaron Jenkins.
  BV4647.L56D48 2011
  248.4--dc23
                        2011023874

Contents

Section 4. Listening and Theology

Abbreviations

CEV	Contemporary English Version
ERV	English Revised Version
ESV	English Standard Version
KJV	King James Version
NASB	New American Standard Bible
NET	New English Translation
NIV	New International Version
NKJV	New King James Version
NRSV	New Revised Standard Version
RSV	Revised Standard Version

Foreword

Our age has been aptly referred to as the *information age*. We live in a world where we have more information at our fingertips than any generation in history. The problem is that somewhere in the wake of this explosion of information we lost the capacity to listen. Information is pouring out into the world like a broken fire hydrant. *Google* is as familiar to us as baseball, or grandmother's home-made apple pie. But, it seems that listening—truly listening—has become a scarce commodity, or like an endangered species; it is occasionally spotted, but rarely actually seen or experienced. Whether it is the latest round of the "worship wars" in the churches, or in the congressional halls of Washington D.C., we find a lot more talking than listening and a lot more speaking than hearing.

This is a book about listening. It is about active, engaged listening which discovers, in the process, many wonderful redemptive moments which can bring healing, hope, and a renewed sense of direction and purpose in our relationships. The authors are all practiced in listening, whether it be listening in worship, listening to those we are discipling, or really listening to the Word of God through the practice of *lectio divina*. It seems that in every area of the church's life and ministry we have too much talking, teaching, and instruction, and not enough listening, reflecting, and contemplating. This creates too many one-way streets and dead-ends and not enough joyful exchange, collaboration, and genuine growth. This is compounded by the fact that what teaching we do receive is often shallow, self-referential, and fails to resonate with Apostolic Christianity. This may explain why we have stopped listening. Even the gospel message has, for some, begun to sound like just another form of commodification and market-ing, rather than the proclamation of the glorious, transforming news of Jesus Christ. It seems that everyone, on both sides of the pulpit or the kitchen table needs to cultivate the art of serious reflection and active listening. In short, this is a book for everyone.

The collective message of this book is that the church of Jesus Christ needs what we might call a period of '*selah*.' The word *selah* occurs throughout the Psalms. The precise meaning of the word *selah* is unknown. However, most believe that it signifies some kind of musical pause or interlude. This is precisely what this book envisions. We need time to pause and to listen. Like any healthy heart, we must have a proper balance between the active pumping of blood (diastolic) and the brief period of rest (systolic) where the blood is being re-oxygenated and prepared to be pumped out in ways that give life and nourishment. Much of the church today has lost the capacity to pause and to listen and to be re-oxygenated in a way which is essential for long-term vitality.

This collection of essays is a prescription for a new period of health and vitality for the church. In the summer of 386 A.D., a young Augustine had just completed a book on the life of one of the great listeners in the history of the church, the famous desert father, St. Antony. After reading about the life of St. Antony, Augustine wept. You may recall that his whole life at that time was given over to the art of speaking. He was skilled in rhetoric and had become a teacher in Milan. However, Augustine had not really taken time to cultivate listening. The life of St. Antony deeply moved Augustine and he went into a back garden to think, to pray, and to listen. Suddenly, Augustine *heard* something. This great orator, skilled in speaking and rhetoric, began to really *listen*. It was a sing-song voice of a young child who kept repeating the phrase, *tolle lege,* meaning "take up and read." Augustine listened. Augustine heard. He picked up the Scriptures, was gloriously transformed, and the rest is one of the great chapters in the history of the church. Who knows what might happen if the people of God began to listen again?

Timothy C. Tennent, Ph.D.
Professor of World Christianity
President, Asbury Theological Seminary

Acknowledgments

Writing extensive acknowledgements is never wise as human memory will so often fail, forsaking even the most deserving of acknowledgement. Thus, the following should only be taken as symbolic of the many people deserving thanks.

I am grateful for the leadership and congregations of Calvary Community Church and Centennial Road Church for inspiring, encouraging, and supporting me in this writing project. Thanks go to each and every contributor, including those who were forced to withdraw along the way. Thank you for providing me the necessary encouragement to see your valuable work through to completion.

Thanks go to my wife, Heather, for listening to my ideas about listening and for graciously walking with me in developing the practice. Thank you, as well, to my parents, Ellard and Kathryn Perry, and Ken and Beth Morgan.

Two chapters have been previously published, at least in modified forms. Chapter 8, "Listening to God, Shaped by the Word" by Edith Humphrey, was originally presented at the 2006 AWESOME conference, a support network for ordained evangelical Anglican women. It was subsequently published in *Anvil* 24:1 (2007). The concluding chapter, "Becoming the Church Who Listens: Listening, Narrative, and Atonement," was originally published in a modified form in *Wesleyan Theological Journal* 43:1 (Spring 2008). I am grateful to include these pieces of work here.

JNTRODUCTJON

Have You Ears to Hear?

Aaron Perry

The tragedy is that our eternal welfare depends upon our hearing and we have trained our ears not to hear.[1]

~A.W. Tozer

Introduction

He who has ears to hear, let him hear (Luke 8:8b NIV). The sobering words come at the end of Jesus' parable of the sower. They challenge those who could simply shrug off Jesus' cryptic invitation to a new movement. They invite the intrigued who listened just at the edge of the crowd. They offend the skeptics who opposed the sower himself. All kinds of ears heard the words, but what ears would *hear* the message?

Have you considered those who did not hear? Is it not likely that some who heard Jesus employ this parable only heard it that single time and in an unhearing moment lost a potential future because they did not listen? What lives took a turn for mediocrity because they did not truly hear? What names are now known only to God because their hearts were, at least in that moment, *hard*? Evidently hearing—truly hearing—matters a great deal.

Even now your ears are picking up sounds—cars humming past your home, computers whirring in the background, the trudging steps of a passerby—but what message evades your ears? Have you ears to hear? What has gone unheard, drowned out by noise of schedule, busyness, hard-heartedness? What has gone unheard because of a refusal to *listen*?

1

Have you ears to hear? The challenge comes to Christians and Christian leaders once again—not inconsequently those in whom faith communities have discerned a call. But listening can feel like a waste of time. Listening can even add to busyness. It can make us late. Listening can drain even the most devoted and caring pastors. Yet, if Jesus' challenge still applies to his hearers, then pastors and Christian leaders must live into their vocation by considering freshly what it means to listen, by developing listening skills, and by devoting themselves to becoming listeners.

Have you ears to hear? What people will you face today who only want a listening ear? What people will step in and out of your neighborhood, in and out of your ministry who will only listen to you once you have listened to them?

These questions are not meant to discourage or overwhelm. They are meant to entice. They are meant to draw open the ear even to listen to this book. This book aims to develop ears to hear by being practical and formational. In reading, you will have opportunity to practice a sort of listening and in reading you will be challenged to explore what being a listener means. To help explore the variety of ways that listening is necessary and practical in Christian service and leadership, I will introduce several fields in which it is important for Christian leaders to listen and to become listeners. But first, let's ask a more basic question.

What Does it Mean to Listen?

Have you ears to hear? Are your ears and your heart picking up the messages that your followers are speaking, writing, texting, and emailing? Perhaps the reason for missed messages is less sinister. Do we even know what it means to listen? Even if all hearts are open and ears are ready to hear, is it fair to ask what it really means to listen? Does listening in the digital age mean the same thing as it meant to previous generations? Does one listen to a text message in the same way one listens to a living voice?

Approaches to listening are partly determined by critically accepted or assumed models of communication. Models that emphasize the individual in speaking will emphasize the individual in listening.[2] Other approaches to listening, however, have emphasized the dynamic, social construction of meaning that takes place in the midst of conversation.[3] In other words, listening doesn't just let the other communicate her thoughts, but provides an opportunity for those thoughts to be shaped and developed. This means that even in writing this chapter, as I give thought to how readers will engage these words, my own thought is being formed. The same phenomenon is enabled by listening.

So, what does it mean to listen? Listening has over fifty active and working definitions.[4] But let's consider listening in a new way. Philosopher Jean-Luc Nancy describes listening as an action that discovers a secret. While ears may pick up all kinds of sounds, it is only by listening that hidden messages are captured.[5] Sometimes these messages are cryptic: a person wants a hidden word to be heard. Other times, the messages are hidden even to the speaker. These lurking messages, hidden even to the speaker, mean that listening is straining toward a *self*.

Consider this lurking self in this way. Have you ever been in an argument when, from your own mouth, to your own surprise, out popped an opinion that you didn't know you held? Where did it come from? How did it develop? *Who* gave it to you? That opinion is evidence of a self, and such selves are there to be found by listening. Sometimes you will only know another person by having ears to hear them. Listening, then, means to enter a type of (even unintentional) sharing.[6] To listen does not mean torturing another for information, but only discerning what self lurks in and beneath another's speech.

Think of listening as entering that type of space created by sound. Sound, including the sound of speech, penetrates, opens in and around, moves toward and away from the hearer.[7] Do you remember the last time you were in a meaningful context of musical sound—a rock concert, a worship service, the opera, or another event? Did you get lost in the music? Did you find yourself simply surrounded by the wondrous sound? Yet, the music was also entering your body through your ears. It went inside you even as you were inside it.

This experience of music—to be in the space of sound and to be filled with sound—tells us that there is a double opening in the practice of listening. Listening, when we think of sharing, is a double opening that provides the context for relationship. Take a moment and, in complete silence, try to listen. Complete silence is hard to achieve, but try to eliminate any unnecessary noise. Listen closely. Keep listening. Did you notice the silence inside yourself? Did you hear your heartbeat? This is what Jean-Luc Nancy calls the echo chamber of the self. This chamber is what lets you know there is an opening in you to hear the other.[8] You are not just a person who listens; you are created as a listening object. (Notice that this doesn't just mean those with the physical ability to hear, as the heartbeat can be *felt* when one is 'listening' for it!) Listening is about moving "toward the opening of meaning"[9] that is sound even as the listener is open.[10]

Does this philosophical discussion of listening help *open* your mind to listening? Does Nancy's discussion around openness—that when you listen you open yourself and you are found in an openness—help expand your appreciation for the practice? Does the notion that as one listens, one strains toward a meaning, otherwise secret but now made public, help influence the importance and difficulty of something like *confession*?

This reflection makes listening feel complicated. Yet in *complicating* what it means to listen, we are given the opportunity to begin thinking about listening, and even the world, in a new way. When we look at the amazing phenomenon of listening, the world can become like new. Messages are mixed into the world all around us! What might God himself be speaking to those with ears to hear? With this new world before us, let's turn our attention to other fields where listening is emerging as an important practice and idea.

Listening and Leadership

"We live in an era of intense conflict and massive institutional failures, a time of painful endings and of hopeful beginnings."[11] That is the start of Otto Scharmer's massive book, *Theory U: Leading from the Future as it Emerges.* Scharmer does with leadership what Nancy has done with listening: he makes it more *complicated.* Through interviews, conversations, and other forms of listening,[12] Scharmer sought to learn not only what leaders do and how they do it, but the inner source from which leaders operate.[13] In the process he discovered a social field theory (Theory U) and a social technology (the principles and practices of "presencing").[14]

Let's unpack Theory U and "presencing." The following diagram of Theory U gives us a start.[15]

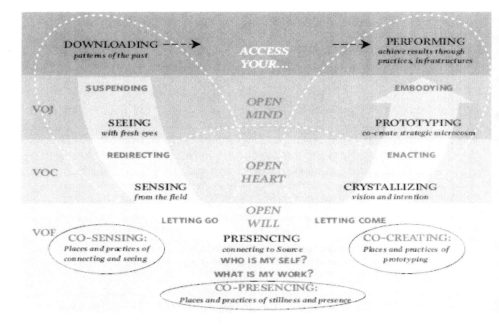

Exploring such a complex diagram would take us too far away from our focus, so let me give a brief description. The left side of the U describes the process of deep observation. Scharmer discovered that leaders ceased a simple downloading of information, and instead saw and *planned to see* from different perspectives.

The right side of the U is about the new project, product, organization, or whatever else that emerges from the movement of presencing. Once one has let go of fears, one can *let come* the future that desires to emerge. This gesture allows the crystallizing movement, where ideas begin to take shape, before there is prototyping and performing.

While we might be tempted to see Theory U, especially in diagram form, as a mechanical, linear process, instead Scharmer urges his readers to see it as a whole.[16] Think of it like Albert Pujols hitting a home run or Michael Jordan dunking a basketball: while the action can be described sequentially, it is not a step-by-step process that guarantees success across all contexts. Theory U is this full theory of what happens in the social field.

At the bottom of the U is the movement of presencing. Presencing is what leaders do, perhaps only intuitively, when they are able to align all resources to the outcome that is best for all involved without manipulating resources (including money or people). Presencing is the ultimate way in which the social field theory, Theory U, happens. Presencing is what Albert Pujols and Michael Jordan do in their moments of athletic profundity. Scharmer calls this movement *presencing* because it means being fully *present* in the moment and *sensing* the future that wants to emerge. To place this in Christian terms, presencing is that movement of being used for exactly what God has made you at exactly the right time to enable God's desired future. This is not simply a moment, but a *movement*. There is an understanding of your role and your call. While we might be tempted simply to take these moments as they come—whether they last five minutes or a season—Scharmer's research suggests that the presencing movement is a technology; it's an invention that people can access with certain practices.

Think of it like this. Have you ever felt "in the groove"? It's the experience of knowing you are right where you are meant to be, doing exactly what you are meant to do. This description approaches what Scharmer describes as "presencing." This is the movement where there is meaningful change or meaningful attention to the moment and there is potential for something new. But how does one enter this presencing movement?

The presencing movement is being aware of the social field from multiple points of access. I grew up in a farming community. What impresses me to this day about farmers is that they *know* the land. They know its potential. They know its temperament. They know what it needs. They feel for the land when the seasons come late or early. To farmers, the land is almost *alive*. And what matters in the land lies beneath the surface, invisible to the eye. Scharmer uses this farming imagery to capture the conditions of the *social field*, the *soil*, in which possibilities grow.[17] Leaders are farmers who must tend to the potentiality, hindrances, energy found among the people the lead—among their *social fields*.

Just as the soil in a field would have different levels beneath the surface, so are there different levels in which we give attention to the social field. Scharmer calls these levels "field structures of attention." A field structure of attention is the place by which information, opinions, anticipations, expectations, etc., are accessed and processed. Scharmer believes there are four field structures of attention: I-in-me; I-in-it; I-in-you; I-in-now. Each of these points of access and process grow on the previous one. The I-in-me point, the most superficial level, is able only to access and process from within the self; I-in-it, one level deeper, accesses from the broader subject; I-in-you accesses from without the subject; I-in-now accesses from the self, from within, and from without the subject. These field structures of attention are important because the "essence of leadership is to shift the inner place [of operation] both individually and collectively."[18] Presencing is the deepest, most complex form of access; it is the I-in-Now movement.

Obviously this is quite abstract and risks moving away from our theme of listening. Fortunately, Scharmer clarifies the idea of the field structure of attention by describing the four field structures with practices of listening. There are four types of listening that correspond to the ways we pay attention to the social field:

> 1. Downloading listening (I-in-me): This listening confirms previous judgments; it says, "Yeah, I already know that."
> 2. Factual listening (I-in-It): This listening is open to new or contrary data; it says, "Ooh! Look at that!"
> 3. Empathic listening (I-in-You): This listening is open to the other as a person. It looks into the "story of a living being, a living system, and self."[19]
> 4. Generative listening (I-in-Now): This listening is open to the emerging field of the future. The listener's will is open to new understandings of the self and vocation in this listening. It says, "I am connected to something larger than myself."[20]

The practice of listening is not only important in Scharmer's research methods and explanation of his complex theory, but Scharmer also devotes an entire chapter to conversational actions (including listening) in his further explanation and enactment of the presencing movement. Conversation can create the necessary social field where deep access is possible.[21]

Conversations utilizing the deepest form of listening enable creation and a new world.[22] These practices of listening and conversation allow leaders to be open to the emerging future that is opening to them. Such a constructive and formative role for the practice of listening is also found in a recent development in Christian spirituality.

Listening and Christian Spirituality

Eat This Book, Eugene Peterson's exploration of spiritual reading of Scripture, believes that engaging appropriately with Scripture has serious implications for transformation in ways that resonate with our earlier discussion on listening.[23]

Listen to this description of reading from Peterson. He writes,

> *Hagah* is a word that our Hebrew ancestors used frequently for reading the kind of writing that deals with our souls. But "meditate" is far too tame a word for what is being signified. "Meditate" seems more suited to what I do in a quiet chapel on my knees with a candle burning on the altar. Or to what my wife does while sitting in a rose garden with the Bible open in her lap. But when Isaiah's lion and my dog meditated they chewed and swallowed, using teeth and tongue, stomach and intestines: Isaiah's lion meditating his goat (if that's what it was);

my dog meditating his bone. There is a certain kind of writing that invites this kind of reading, soft purrs and low growls as we taste and savor, anticipate and take in the sweet and spicy, mouth-watering and soul-energizing morsel words— 'O taste and see that the LORD is good!' (Ps 34:8).[24]

This is the kind of reading that changes a life because these are the kinds of words that are meant *"to get inside us*, to deal with our souls, to form a life that is congruent with the world that God has created, the salvation that he has enacted, and the community that he has gathered."[25]

Reading is not simply for the head; it is for the whole body, the whole life. This is why Peterson believes that reading is *eating*. This life-changing reading takes the words into the self that "are intended to do something *in* us."[26] These are words that are alive, as a voice.[27]

Isn't this approach to Scripture starting to sound like the complicated listening we discussed above? Think about the similarities between Peterson's approach to Scripture as eating and Jean-Luc Nancy's description of listening. For Nancy, the ear takes in the sound and the body becomes its echo chamber; for Peterson, the mouth takes in the word and chews, gnaws, mulls, and swallows. For both, there is an opening for the other in the self. These similarities reveal a deep resonance: Peterson emphasizes that Scripture is *originally* the living voice. God's word was spoken among the community before it was written down. The living voice of God enabled a community to believe, obey, and worship before the word was written.[28] Thus, the "primary organ for receiving God's revelation is not the eye that sees but the ear that hears."[29] Listening, serious listening, is the approach that enables the life-changing work of the voice of Scripture.

Listening and Hermeneutics

Part of the reason that Eugene Peterson has written on *spiritual* reading is because there are various ways to read Scripture. While this is somewhat counterintuitive—How can there be more than one way to read a text?—upon deeper inspection various readings of the same text is commonplace. In recently coauthored a book with my brother Tim. Not only did I read that manuscript more times than I care to remember, I also read it in a number of ways: I read it for flow; I read it for content; I read it for errors; I read it for spiritual encouragement. When I read for flow, I read to determine the pace of the text. When I read for content, I wanted to make sure the arguments held together and that our biblical exegesis was sound. When I read for errors, I *looked* (slightly different from reading!) for typos, grammatical errors, and incomplete sentences. When I read for spiritual encouragement, I let the text impact me. So, there are various ways to read a text.

Peterson has written a text on *spiritual reading*, because people can also read Scripture historically (What happened in the past?), homiletically (How can this preach to my people on Sunday?), and as literature (What ideas and issues does this text raise that address people across the ages?). The realization that texts can be read in multiple ways has led to the science of hermeneutics.

Hermeneutics is the study of interpretation. It often focuses in areas of religion, literature, and law, but the study can apply to other disciplines. Hans-Georg Gadamer (1900-2002), one of the most influential thinkers in hermeneutics in the 20th century, took very seriously the role of listening in hermeneutics, and his work is now being used to influence interpretation of Scripture. So, what has this to do with listening?

For Gadamer listening is about being addressed by the other as a self—to let the other "really say something to us."[30] Thus, Gadamer writes, "[A]nyone who listens is fundamentally open."[31] Picking up this idea for biblical hermeneutics, Merold Westphal calls this openness a "vulnerability to the voice of the other."[32] Such vulnerability is exactly what enables there to be a change when engaging Scripture. A vulnerable reader does not (simply) mine the text for meaning, as one mines a mountain for precious metals. A vulnerable reader allows the text to mine them; a vulnerable reader allows the text to ask the questions. The reader does not probe the text; the text probes the reader. In this practice, Gadamer suggests not that the reader *answer* the text, but that the reader learn to ask their own questions.[33] Thus, listening—whether in typical or atypical fashion—is a practice of interpretation that allows a conversation to develop.[34]

The reason this dynamic relationship with Scripture, especially using listening as a practice when engaging Scripture, is because language is God's mode of communication and that God's subsequent bestowal of language on humans means that humans can "respond, answer, converse, argue, [and] question" God.[35] God is the "intiator and guarantor of language *both ways*."[36] Now, if Scripture is a living voice, from the one who assures language both ways, then we can see how Scripture is a conversation partner to which we must learn to *listen*. Thus, as Scripture addresses people it shapes them as listeners because one grows in the capability of listening by practicing listening. Scripture both communicates with listeners and creates listeners with whom it can communicate, not in a linear sense, but in a context of relationship: in the space, we could say, created by its sound. So, listening helps to shape how we think about reading Scripture and how we interpret it.

Listening and the Political Moment

Listening is also emerging as a practice in the midst of changing political climates. One could point to Michael Ignatieff, leader of the Liberal Party of Canada, and his listening tours across Canada in January 2009, March 2010, and the summer of 2010, or to Hillary Clinton as she launched her 2008 campaign for the Democratic nomination as a *conversation.*

Listening has emerged as an essential practice in the changing globopolitical moment, as well. As the global village shrinks, so does the distance between various religions, which means so does the distance between faithful, passionate, and outspoken followers of these religions. How do Christians learn to navigate such a moment? How do Christians navigate these forthcoming (and present) confrontations of religious communities?

In the face of this time and through asking these questions, political theologians are beginning to utilize listening as a Christian practice. Writing of these forthcoming and existing clashes of community, Graham Ward says, "[I]f we are to reach any common understanding of ourselves, one another, and the threats and possibilities that pervade the cultures in which we are situated, it is only by being impolite and listening to one another's impoliteness."[37] What sets Ward apart from other proponents of dialogue and listening in the place of interracial and interreligious conflict is that this approach is grounded in the Christian faith.[38]

British political theologian Luke Bretherton unpacks listening as a constructive practice that cultivates a political sphere. Listening helps to overcome prior assumptions of agenda and political program. Bretherton believes that listening "creates a common realm of shared action and meaning."[39] With significant public space occupied by communities of various faiths, listening helps foster a conversation about how to act together that allows for "real politics."[40] Thus, churches have an opportunity to teach the discipline of listening as a *Christological* act, centered on the community's interaction with Scripture and each other as Jesus opens the church and the Scriptures, so that disciples of Jesus can foster political participation in his name. The question facing pastors, then, is how the shepherds of these flocks will shepherd congregations in the midst of political upheaval and turmoil.

This is the opportunity before the church: becoming a community that excels in the practice of listening and as a result creates opportunities for personal and communal transformation. Recall that Jean-Luc Nancy described listening as a practice that allows the other into you. Thus, as Christians listen, they are practicing a deep form of presence (as opposed to distance) in the world. As events, stories, and other experiences are shared with the church and are listened to, then, the church is able to attune itself to the world.[41] Just as a frequency dial tunes the listener in to the station, so does listening tune the listener in to the world. Why is this transformational? Because as Christians listen, what they hear can be presented to God and Christ can be present through his listening community.[42] This is the opportunity before you as a Christian and as a leader. Have you ears to hear?

Developing Ears to Hear

I trust this introduction has expanded your horizons of what it means to listen. The practice and study of listening is emerging across several fields with strong implications for this time. In such a spirit, the essays included in this book continue to offer introductions and expansions of listening across various fields.

These essays are arranged in three sections. The first section, *Why Listening?*, offers two essays which continue to open a space in which the topic of listening can be heard. Alan Mann, a British theologian and church consultant, offers a defense of listening by engaging culture and Scripture. Catholic theologian Stephen Webb reflects on silence and sound in the Christian life and in corporate worship, opening our ears to importance of reflection on the roles of sound and noise.

The second section discusses listening and pastoral ministry. Each contributor is a current or former pastor who writes from experience. Theologian Brent Peterson reflects on the practice of listening in developing kingdom ethics through worship and how does the pastor gives helps the church listen in various corporate worship practices. Michael Pasquarello then asks what role listening plays in the pastoral role of preaching and offers Martin Luther and Dietrich Bonhoeffer as exemplars of preachers who listened first. Pastor David Drury offers contemporary and ancient examples of leaders who utilized listening and different models of leadership to help pastors learn to lead as listeners. Counseling professor Anne Gatobu writes on the role of listening with the Holy Spirit in pastoral counseling, helping pastors to deepen their dependence of the person of the Spirit in serving as a listener. David Higle writes on the role of listening to adolescents in the process of discipleship. His essay gives practical instruction in providing spiritual care for students which is essential in North American communities experiencing extended adolescences. Finishing up the section, a very helpful, intentionally practical essay from Frederica Mathewes-Green is included. Her work, however, is not simply tips and tricks to effective listening, but continues to expand the definition of listening as she treats the body in listening, the role of the listener, and offers suggestions on improving as a listener.

Section three is *Listening and the Spiritual Life*. Edith Humphrey reflects on listening and the Word through the life of Mary, mother of Jesus, and the text of 2 Peter. This essay shows part of the benefit a listening approach to Scripture may yield. Daryl MacPherson writes on the role of listening in contemplative prayer. MacPherson explores helpfully the challenges a pastor might face through various seasons of trial, giving special attention to several ideas from St. John of the Cross. Nathan Crawford introduces readers to Julian of Norwich, Theresa of Avila, and Simone Weil and the practice of listening in loving God.

Section four covers *Listening and Theology*. Ephraim Radner leads this section with an essay especially for vocational theologians as he reflects on the life of listening that is the biblical *Job*. Next, Timothy Furry examines listening and Scripture, giving special attention to St. Augustine's hermeneutic of love. Ken Gavel concludes the section with a final reflection on listening and *lectio divina*. His work also serves well to develop a theology of the word, useful in contemporary hermeneutics.

Each essay aims to be formative and give opportunity to practice listening through highlighting personal experience. In conclusion, we explore listening, atonement, and the mission of the church. Listening is a practice that stems from the life of Christ and must be incorporated into our churches. The chapter tries to capture the spirit of the preceding essays by sending us into the world as newly developed, practiced, and formed listeners—both as individuals and as the church.

I challenge you to see this book as an opportunity to listen. Be critical, yet open to its ideas. Some of the essays will require more attention than others. They will not be understood the first time they are read. This will also be the case with people who come to you for help. To listen well will necessarily take (at least) two or three conversations. Yet, at the same time, let me encourage you to listen well to the essays which may read a little more quickly. Subtle graces are hidden in your short conversations, whether with these chapters or over a quick coffee with a live person. The variety of essays gives you opportunity to listen when it is easy and to listen when it is hard.

Of course, this book poses an opportunity that live listening does not: You can close this book and take a break without appearing rude. (Not so simple with either short or in-depth conversations!) In reading, learn the rhythms or your listening ability. When do you read well? What energy level is necessary for you to give your best effort to the other—whether in book form or as a living being?

Perhaps this challenge is best seen in light of Jean-Luc Nancy's thoughts on listening and openness. Recall that listening is dual opening: of the listener and of the speaker. This phenomenon of double opening is displayed in Luke's gospel. On the road to Emmaus, Jesus travels with two companions, whom he discovers are *talking* about everything that has happened (Luke 24:14 NIV). Yet in their discussions, they are downcast. They do not believe what the prophets have *spoken* (Luke 24:25 NIV), because they are slow of heart. Their hearts, their "inner commitments, dispositions and attitudes,"[43] are evidently *closed* to the work of God. They have not believed because they are not *open*. Yet Jesus explains what was *said* in the Scripture concerning himself (Luke 24:27 NIV). After Jesus breaks the bread and disappears from their sight, the two companions say to each other, "Were not our hearts burning within us while he talked with us on the road and opened the Scriptures to us?" (Luke 24:32 NIV). Notice Jesus' action with the Scriptures: he *opens* the Scriptures. Here is the first of the double opening of listening. Luke places the second just a few verses later. Jesus appears among the disciples and confirms that he is flesh and bones. Luke then says, "Then he *opened* their minds so they could understand the Scriptures" (Luke 24:45 NIV). Here is the second of the double opening for there to be listening: the Scriptures are opened and the disciples' minds are opened.

A Christian approach to listening can take its cues from this story. Just as in the story from Luke there is a phenomenon of double opening—of the self and of the text by Jesus, so also in this text there is an initial opening: the authors have opened themselves to you. As you enter this text, may Jesus open you to this initial opening thereby developing in you ears to hear.

Notes

1. A.W. Tozer, *The Pursuit of God* (Camp Hill, PA: Christian Publications, 1993), 71.

2. Michael W. Purdy, "Listening, Culture, and Structures of Consciousness: Ways of Studying Listening," *International Journal of Listening* 14 (2000), 47-48.

3. See, for example, Connie Fletcher, "Listening to Narratives: The Dynamics of Capturing Police Experiences," *International Journal of Listening* 13 (1999): 46-61; C.D. Hardin and E. T. Higgins, "Shared Reality: How Social Verification Makes the Subjective Objective," in *Handbook of Motivation and Cognition: The Interpersonal Context*

(ed. E.T. Higgins & R.M Sorrentino; vol. 3 of *Handbook of Motivation and Cognition*, ed. E.T. Higgins & R.M. Sorrentino; New York: Guilford Press, 1996), 28-84; Michael Purdy, "Listening and Community: The Role of Listening in Community Formation," *International Journal of Listening* 5 (1991): 51-67.

    4. See Ethel C. Glenn, "A Content Analysis of Fifty Definitions of Listening," *International Journal of Listening* 3:1 (1989): 21-31.

    5. Jean-Luc Nancy, *Listening* (trans. Charlotte Mandell; New York: Fordham University Press, 2007), 6. "Être à l'écoute, 'to be tuned in, to be listening,' was in the vocabulary of military espionage before it returned, through broadcasting, to the public space, while still remaining, in the context of the telephone, an affair of confidences or stolen secrets" (4).

    6. Nancy, *Listening*, 12.

    7. Nancy, *Listening*, 14.

    8. Nancy, *Listening*, 21.

    9. Nancy, *Listening*, 27.

    10. Nancy, *Listening*, 25.

    11. Otto Scharmer, *Theory U: Leading from the Future as it Emerges* (San Francisco: Berrett-Koehler Publishers, 2009), 1.

    12. Scharmer, *Theory U*, 19.

    13. Scharmer, *Theory U*, 7.

    14. Scharmer, *Theory U*, 17.

    15. Scharmer, *Theory U*, 45.

    16. Scharmer, *Theory U*, 44.

    17. Scharmer, *Theory U*, 8-9.

    18. Scharmer, *Theory U*, 11.

    19. Scharmer, *Theory U*, 12.

    20. Scharmer, *Theory U*, 11-13.

    21. Scharmer, *Theory U*, 291.

    22. Scharmer, *Theory U*, 298.

    23. Eugene Peterson, *Eat This Book: A Conversation in the Art of Spiritual Reading* (Grand Rapids, MI: Eerdmans, 2006).

    24. Peterson, *Eat This Book*, 2.

    25. Peterson, *Eat This Book*, 3-4. Italics added.

    26. Peterson, *Eat This Book*, 21.

    27. Peterson, *Eat This Book*, 11. Italics added.

    28. Peterson, *Eat This Book*, 85-86.

    29. Peterson, *Eat This Book*, 92.

    30. Hans-Georg Gadamer, *Truth and Method* (London, New York: Continuum, 2004), 355.

    31. Gadamer, *Truth and Method*, 355.

    32. Merold Westphal, *Whose Community? Which Interpretation? Philosophical Hermeneutics for the Church* (Grand Rapids, MI: Baker Academic, 2009), 115.

    33. Westphal, *Whose Community?*, 116.

    34. Westphal, *Whose Community?*, 117.

    35. Westphal, *Whose Community?*, 103.

    36. Westphal, *Whose Community?*, 103. Italics added. For readers interested in philosophy, hermeneutics, and theology, see Kevin J. Vanhoozer, *Is there a Meaning in this Text: The Bible, the Reader, and the Morality of Literary Knowledge* (Grand Rapids, MI: Zondervan, 1998). This text is also utilized in chapter 13.

    37. Graham Ward, *The Politics of Discipleship* (Grand Rapids, MI: Baker Academic, 2009), 22.

38. For an example of advocating dialogue in the midst of racial and religious conflict, see J. Martin Ramirez, "Peace Through Dialogue," International Journal on World Peace 24:1 (2007): 51-67.

39. Luke Bretherton, "Reflections on Graham Ward's *The Politics of Discipleship*," Online at http://www.calvin.edu/~jks4/churchandpomodocs/bretherton.pdf.

40. Bretherton, "Reflections on Graham Ward," 9.

41. Ward, *Politics of Discipleship*, 281. Recall how Scharmer described the open mind, will, and heart as three instruments to be tuned.

42. Ward, *Politics of Discipleship*, 282.

43. Joel B. Green, *The Gospel of Luke* (New International Commentary of the New Testament; Grand Rapids, MI: Eerdmans, 1997), 854.

SECTION 1

WHY LISTENING

Chapter 1

Why Listening? Considering Contemporary Culture, Christianity, and the Value of Listening

Alan Mann

Are You Listening?

Good, then I'll begin.

Once upon a time I thought about training to become a counselor. My previous employee, a social inclusion charity based in London, England had put all their staff through a personal strength finding program. Unsurprisingly for a writer, my strengths included *Learner*, *Input* (being inquisitive), and *Intellection* (the love of thinking). Rather pleasingly, however, two of my strongest attributes turned out to be *Developer* and *Empathy*. The person running the training day felt I needed to utilize these more, both in my professional and private life. Inspired by this revelation, I applied for a preliminary course in counseling, which took the title, *Being There: An Introduction to Christian Listening*. I was keen to pursue and develop some basic counseling skills, but I was not sure if there was enough mileage in the subject of *listening* (let alone *Christian Listening*) to fill twelve sessions. What could be so complicated about listening that it needed so much consideration? And why make a distinction between listening and Christian listening?

Author and training consultant, Annette Simmons, suggests that "most people who think they listen don't, or are doing it badly." She goes on to recall the words of one of her clients who defined listening as, "Waiting for my turn to talk."[1] Such a self-centered response is easily criticized. In truth, however, this honest answer is probably a fair reflection of the attitudes and inadequacies we all face when it comes to listening. Perhaps part of the reason is the self-evident reality that we live in an increasingly noisy world. From dawn until dusk, and even during the hours of darkness, we are bombarded with all kinds of sound vying for our attention, filling the space where there would otherwise be silence, human conversation, or at the very least the sound of our inner self. Faced with such an onslaught, it is all too easy to cope by tuning out. How many of us choose to cocoon ourselves (particularly via technology) from the hustle and bustle, and from those immediately in our presence, preferring the sound of our mp3 player or the comfort of text messaging? This withdrawing has been described as *urban trance*, an artificially created absence; a switching off and disengaging from our immediate surroundings, often by the use of further noise. To adapt something Jesus once said, many people have become ever hearing, but never really listening.[2]

Another way to cope with all the noise is simply to add to the cacophony, have our say, and let others know what we think, feel, and believe. I prefer talk radio to commercial music stations, which have as their staple content "The Phone In" when listeners are encouraged to call up and contribute their voice and opinion to a hot topic of debate. In all the years I've been listening to such programs, only once have I heard a contributor be humble enough to admit that their views had been changed by what they had heard. Is that because she was the only one who was ever truly listening? I hope not, but you do not have to listen long to talk radio to realize that most people are not really listening, they are simply waiting for their turn to speak. Indeed, they are encouraged to voice their opinion and to give their point of view. Presenters may intervene and say, "You can't all talk at once," or "Let them have their say, then you can make your point," but that is merely enforcing the idea that what really matters is getting your opinion out there, rather than valuing the insight of others enough to truly listen to them.

Naturally, it would be wrong for me to paint church as a whole with a similar brush, but I've been around long enough now, and worshiped in a number of traditions, to be concerned that Christians are not immune to the vagaries of the cultures in which we live. The church itself is too loud at times. Rather than listening, we shout at the world but get no response because no one is listening to us either. Certainly here in the United Kingdom, where I live and work, this is all too evident when one watches or listens to debates on current issues. If leaders of mainstream Christianity are asked for their opinion you can sense people switching off. The reason for this is almost certainly twofold. Firstly, people already know what their stance will be on the subject. Secondly, people perceive the responses that are given to the complex issues we face us in contemporary life to be outmoded and lacking the nuance necessary to be truly meaningful. The result is that audiences too often feel that Christians are not really listening but instead have come prepared only to speak "truth," that they fail to recognize as such. Our unique and vital voice simply dissipates into the air of a culture where everyone is vying for the attention of hurting ears. As is evident in these words of Dietrich Bonhoeffer, these are not new concerns.

> The first service one owes to others…consists in listening to them. Just as love of God begins in listening to His Word, so the beginning of love for [others] is learning to listen to them. It is God's love for us that He not only gives us His Word but lends us His ear… Many people are looking for an ear that will listen. They do not find it among Christians, because these Christians are talking where they should be listening.[3]

Of course, you may want to argue that speaking out and declaring God's truth is a fundamental role of Christian discipleship. After all, as Christians we have faith in a God who spoke as an act of creation; and as disciples of Jesus, we are called to proclamation (*kerygma*). But while affirming this biblical reality, we too often deny what should also be evident from Scripture—listening is vital to creative action, prior to affective proclamation, and necessary if we are to truly reflect the God in whose image we are made, and the Christ we follow. Indeed, listening is an important precursor to so much the church is involved in: evangelism, pastoral care, social action, cultural engagement, and prophetic challenge. More than that, only listening can transform us (and the story we are telling) so that we, and more importantly the gospel, have a greater chance of being heard above the clamor of our contemporary culture. Yet the problem remains, like the rest of the world we are far keener to tell everyone what we know and believe, rather than being prepared to listen to the story others are telling and so hopefully engage them in a truly mutual, meaningful and transformative conversation.

As I learned from the wise people who run the *Being There* counseling course, talking is easy; listening is the hard part. To truly listen you have to be fully present and available to others. You are not listening if you are preoccupied with your own agendas or simply waiting for the opportunity to butt in and have your say. Listening is also about the creation of a safe place for people to explore who they are. At times it may even demand our willingness to suffer with others, being there in their distress rather than avoiding, denying or minimizing their pain.[4] Echoing such sentiment, Mother Mary Clare has observed that listening "is not a passive affair, a space when we don't happen to be doing or saying anything and are, therefore, automatically able to listen. It is a conscious willed action, requiring alertness and vigilance, by which our whole attention is focused and controlled."[5]

God is…Listening

As Christians, if we are to listen well then we must learn to listen as God listens. That said, it is not always obvious that the God of Scripture is listening. Like us, God is perhaps better known for being vocal. Indeed, the biblical narrative opens with God creating through the act of speaking—"And God said…." Furthermore, depending on biblical translation and emphasis, God also 'calls,' and 'declares,' 'commands,' and 'demands.' No wonder we have had to live long with caricatures of the preacher pounding from the pulpit, "Thus *sayeth* the Lord!" With such a portrait, there is the very real danger that people perceive

God as nothing more than a ranting divine parent rather than One who listens to, and is concerned for, the creation he spoke into being.

Though this act of creation-by-speaking is chronologically prior to the rest of the biblical narrative, it is no more important (and arguably paradigmatically less so) than that of the Exodus motif. What is significant about this is that the Exodus starts with a God who listens and responds, rather than one who speaks or commands:

> After the death of the king of Egypt, the Israelites still complained because they were forced to be slaves. They cried out for help, and God heard their loud cries.... The Lord said: I have seen how my people are suffering as slaves in Egypt, and I have heard them beg for my help because of the way they are being ill-treated. I feel sorry for them, and I have come down to rescue them from the Egyptians. (Exod 2:23-24; 3:7-8 CEV)

We may not feel comfortable with the idea, but taken at face value the author of Exodus writes in such a way as to portray God as oblivious to what is going on in Egypt until he hears the cry that goes out from the people of Israel. Indeed, this very point is made by Walter Brueggemann when he writes, "It is the voiced pain of the slave community that evokes a response from Yahweh and moves Yahweh to active intervention."[6] Of course, we need to see the biblical narrative as a whole when forming our understanding of the character of God, for certainly there are times when God is portrayed as being far more proactive than he is in the early stages of the Exodus story. But rather than let that discussion distract us, it would be far more fruitful, challenging and personally character-forming to hold on to the fact that God not only hears (indicating that he is listening) but that he responds to what he hears in a way that is transforming, liberating and redeeming. Not only that, but the fact that God is constantly and intently listening becomes evident once the text is read more closely.

Perhaps due to the longevity of their slavery in Egypt, the cry that goes out does not directly address the God of their Fathers—the God of Abraham, Isaac and Jacob. It is nothing more than a primal, exhausted cry of an exploited and oppressed community whose ancestors once worshipped God in freedom. For whatever reason, God is not asked to hear their cry, and yet he does. Through the Exodus narrative we are given an image of a God who listens, not because he is addressed directly, but because listening is part God's being, who God is. Ontologically speaking, God is a listener. In the words of the Old Testament scholar, Deryck Sheriffs,

> God...is conscientized to respond to the oppressive situation by the cries of distress.... The spontaneous groans of [Exodus] 2:23 express pain rather than appeal to God for covenant protection. The next phrase speaks of a "cry for help," but God is not specified as the one addressed. Nevertheless, the cry reaches God and triggers a suzerain response.[7]

Through the Exodus, Israel comes to understand, recognize, and relate to God as one who listens and acts in response to hearing. As already acknowledged, the Exodus becomes paradigmatic for Israel. It should not surprise us, therefore, that post-Exodus Israel's cries are no longer vocalized in plaintive anonymity, instead they are specifically directed to the God of Israel, the God of their Fathers, who brought them out of the land of Egypt, out of the land of slavery.

> Please listen, LORD, and answer my prayer! I am poor and helpless. Protect me and save me because you are my God.... Please listen, LORD! Answer my prayer for help. When I am in trouble, I pray knowing you will listen. (Ps 86:1-7 CEV)

> I patiently waited, LORD, for you to hear my prayer. You listened and pulled me from a lonely pit full of mud and mire . . . I am poor and needy, but, LORD God you care about me, and you come to my rescue. (Ps 40:1-2, 17 CEV)

God's responsive-listening becomes a leitmotif of the biblical narrative. Through exodus and exile, occupation and oppression, God again and again proves to be a faithful and active listener culminating in what one could argue is the supreme act of responsive listening—the Incarnation. In Jesus, the God of the Exodus embodies listening. Jesus is the ultimate demonstration of the lengths to which God will go in hearing the needs of his world.

Observing the incarnation, Frank Lake, one of the pioneers of pastoral counseling, wrote, "God...has listened through his Son. Christ's saving work cost him most in its speechless passivity of dereliction. It is this which gives him the right to be called the greatest listener to all suffering. It is this which gives his listening its redemptive quality."[8] Therefore, no longer can God be accused of being distant, waiting to hear the cries of his people. God has become fully present and available to humanity. In the oft quoted words of Jesus, "God so loved the world that he gave his one and only Son" (John 3:16 NIV). But perhaps it is not too theologically, or biblically far-fetched, to suggest that one could equally say, God so *listened* to the world that he sent his one and only son, for as Philip Greenslade notes, God's love "is a *listening love*."[9]

That "God is love" (1 John 4:8 NIV) is one of the key theological revelations of the New Testament. But love can so easily be a slippery and abstract term. If one is to state that God is love, however, then not only does love define who God is, but God gets to define that love. So it is that Karl Barth, in his *Church Dogmatics*, observes that "All our further insights about who God is must revolve round this mystery—the mystery of His love. In a certain sense they can only be repetitions and amplifications of the one statement that God loves."[10] Therefore, through the Old Testament narrative, we are left in no doubt that this God of love is a God who listens. In the New Testament, that listening-love becomes physically present in the person of Jesus who then himself leaves his followers in no doubt that love can only be love as God intends it to be if it is expressed in liberating, redemptive, reconciling and healing acts towards others (for example, see Luke 4:18ff and Matt 25:34ff). What's more, such loving acts surely include listening, for time and time again Jesus gives ear to the plight of the vulnerable, the dispossessed, the sick and the marginalized. Indeed, according to the Apostle Paul, writer of that great hymn to the pragmatic nature of love, without the decency to be truly present and actively listening, we are again, simply waiting for our turn to talk, which makes us nothing more than clanging gongs and noisy cymbals—the antithesis of a Spirit-inspired divine love (see 1 Cor 13).

Finally, with the incarnation we become party to the almost paradoxical revelation that, not only does God listen to his people and his creation, but he listens to himself: "Jesus looked up and said, 'Father, I thank you that you have heard me. I knew that you always hear me'" (John 11:41-42 NIV). With these words Jesus echoes that post-Exodus expectation that we have seen in the words of the psalmists—Yahweh, the God of Israel, listens. But they also reveal in space and time what surely must be true in the endlessness of eternity—listening is fundamental to any understanding that God is a communal being. Again, this is reiterated by Jesus when he speaks of the post-ascension coming of the Third Person of the divine communion, the Holy Sprit, who "will not speak on his own; he will speak only what he hears" (John 16:13 NIV). So it is that Anne Long can suggest that, "Listening is at the heart of God for he is not one but three, a Trinity of Father, Son and Spirit."[11] And with that observation we come full circle to discover that even creation starts, not with speaking, but with a divine conversation at the heart of which is an active, mutual, loving listening— "Let us make…" (Gen 1:26 NIV).

Listening as Discipleship

For obvious reasons, we were not privy to any divine conversations that might have taken place prior to the creation. We are, however, made aware that those conversations led to us being made in the image of God—"Now we will make humans, and they will be like us" (Gen 1:26 CEV). As human beings we are in a very real sense, icons of the living God. What is more, through the Incarnation, we have been shown God's intention for what it means to be a fully-formed human being, and through the life, death and resurrection of Jesus, we are called to become, once more, authentic icons who live and move and have our being in God (see Acts 17:28 NIV).

Though it clearly cannot be the sum total of what it means to be human, due to this connection between our humanity and the image of God, it has to be recognized that to be human is to listen, not simply through our audible hearing, for not all people have access to this sense. All human beings, however, being earthed in creation *hear* that primal, primeval Word, which calls us to *listen* by being ourselves, earthed and fully present within creation. As the world's leading percussionist, Dame Evelyn Glennie demonstrates, listening is far more than audible hearing, for Glennie has been profoundly deaf since the age of twelve. For her, listening is about being present and responding to the moment in a holistic way. The absence of the sense of hearing has allowed Glennie to reassess what it means to be one who listens, and her insight challenges us all to consider, not only what it means to be a person made in the image of God, but also what it means to follow Christ in this world.

In first-century Palestine, the rabbi-disciple relationship was commonplace. Quite literally, disciples would follow their chosen rabbi, hanging on their every word, seeking wisdom and the right way to live, and, perhaps one day, to become a rabbi themselves, and have their own disciples. In Hebrew culture, however, Wisdom was never simply the ability to regurgitate the words of the teacher, to hold one's own in a philosophical debate, or to gain knowledge for the sake of knowledge. The evidence that one had listened to the rabbi, that one had 'got Wisdom' in the way that the book of Proverbs constantly rallies, was to demonstrate that one had heard with one's entire self, actively responding in line with that teaching. By implication, to follow Jesus, to claim to be his disciple, is to respond to the fullest revelation of divine Wisdom and not only 'hear' his teaching but also to 'hear' the plight of the world in which we find ourselves and respond to it. As the Apostle James encourages:

> Obey God's message! Don't fool yourselves by just listening to it. If you hear the message and don't obey it, you are like people who stare at themselves in a mirror and forget what they look like as soon as they leave.... God will bless you in everything you do, if you listen and obey, and don't just hear and forget. (Jas 1:22-25 CEV)

Building on the words of James, Anne Long notes the insightful observation that, "The word 'obedience' is derived from the latin *audire*, to hear. To obey is to then act upon what we have heard. We are not being truly attentive unless we are prepared to act on what we hear."[12]

Of course, this was not a new idea unique to the New Testament. At the heart of Israel's sense of religious identity is what we know as the *Shema*: "Hear, O Israel and be careful to obey.... Hear, O Israel: The LORD our God, the LORD is one. Love the LORD your God with all your heart and with all your soul and with all your strength. These commands that I give you today are to be upon your hearts" (Deut 6:3-6 NIV). Again, the connection between hearing and responding is evident, for to love God is not comprised of some fuzzy, ethereal emotional feeling, but a holistic, self-giving, active love for the world, which we see commanded and expressed throughout the Old Testament and perhaps best summarized by the words of the prophet Micah when he writes, "What does the LORD require of you? To act justly and to love mercy and to walk humbly with your God" (Mic 6:8 NIV). It should not surprise us, therefore, that Jesus' own teaching is in continuity with his Hebrew heritage, even if at times he has been noted to diverge from it. So it is that Jesus responds to the question, "Which is the greatest command," by effectively saying, "Listen Israel: Love the LORD your God with all your heart and with all your soul and with all your mind [and with all your strength]. This is the first and greatest command. And the second is like it: Love your neighbor as yourself" (Matt 22:15ff; cf. Mark 12:28ff).

Listening as Cultural Engagement

Though perhaps there might be an element of artistic license in the telling, or even questionable authenticity to the story, while I was gathering my thoughts on this subject I heard someone on the radio recount an anecdote from the heady days of the 2008 US presidential campaign. As we now all appreciate, President Obama is a great communicator and orator. However, there was a time when not all was going well with his path to the Whitehouse. Senator Obama (as he was at the time), was on the campaign trail, criss-crossing the United States in an attempt to sell his vision for a new America. No one could deny that the crowds were turning up, but the question remained, were they listening to Obama, and just as importantly, was he listening to them? Concerned that the Senator's erudite way of speaking was failing to connect with significant numbers of marginalized, blue collar voters, an advisor decided to approach Obama.

"Senator," began the advisor nervously, "for a number of weeks now, several of us have been worried that while your rallies are well attended, and we are getting excellent media coverage, we are not really reaching out to ordinary working Americans. While your heart is for them, and there is no doubting you want to see a real, positive, and lasting change, when it comes down to it, you are not really able to speak the language of the common people." To which (so it is claimed), Senator Obama responded, almost without hesitation, "Au contraire."[13]

This is a rather whimsical story. Lying at its heart, however, is a valuable observation. If your desire is truly to help people, to change their lives for the better, to empower them, to give them self-worth and dignity, or to transform, liberate, and heal them (in the most holistic sense of the word), then first and foremost you have to listen to them. You have to listen to their story, to understand who they are, how they see the world, and the kind language they use to describe it and themselves, for by such things reality is shaped and formed. As one writer has put it, albeit in rather hyperbolic terms: "We dream in narrative, day-dream in narrative, remember, anticipate, hope, despair, believe, doubt, plan, revise, criticize, construct, gossip, learn, hate and love by narrative."[14]

In recent years, the observation that, to a greater or lesser degree, we all construct and make sense of our identity and the world in which we live through stories has been used very effectively by those who work in the therapeutic and counselling professions. Though not a counsellor himself, George Stroup has typically observed that "it is no accident that when they are asked to identify themselves most people recite a narrative or story."[15] It is just such observations that have fuelled interest in the power of stories to change lives and to change the world around us.

Though stories can be life-affirming and liberating, the opposite is equally true, we can become trapped, disempowered, and shamed by our stories. They turn into prisons of meaninglessness that isolate, and alienate—something that is true for both individuals and communities. In order to address such debilitating stories in a meaningful and sufficient way, one requires alternative stories, or counter-stories that question the power or validity of the ones currently being told; ultimately, so it is hoped, constructing a new, redeemed and authentic identity.

A few years ago now, I took part in a conference in London. During one of the sessions, a fellow contributor began to share about his two adopted children. They had been born into a culture very different to his own, and had suffered unspeakable trauma and poverty in their formative years. Unsurprisingly, when he and his wife adopted those children into their own family they brought with them a story, and related emotional and physical behaviour, that was hard to deal with. In order to give these children any hope of a future it became obvious that they needed to build a new and more positive story of who they were. This, however, meant that my friend, his family, and the counsellors helping them needed to first listen with great intent to the stories which carried the children's identity. Only when everyone truly understood who these children were could a counter-story be offered through which they could begin to build a new, liberated and restored self-identity and become part of their new family who had a story of their own.

Though writing more for the business community, the observations of Annette Simmons have universal application, echoing those of the narrative therapists when she writes, "Listening to people helps them pour out a little of their current thinking so they can make room for new thinking. There are times when listening does all the work. When you deeply listen to someone, they listen to themselves and sometimes that alone is enough [for their life to change]."[16] And what is true of individuals is also true of our communities and the society in which we find ourselves. So, to return briefly to Barack Obama and the US Presidential Elections, one could argue that his success back in 2008 was down to the fact that he had learned to listen to the story his fellow Americans were telling at the time, and that through this he was able to envision them with a new story of who they could be, as individuals, communities, and as Americans. Indeed, it may not be too far fetched to suggest that, through mutual listening, the United States has begun to tell a new story about itself.

For me, as a cultural theologian, these stories of narrative therapy and political vision-building raise important questions about how we as the Church meaningfully and sufficiently engage the people and places we encounter. In her work, *Speaking in Parables*, Sallie McFague (as she is better known), suggests that "the purpose of theology is to make it possible for the gospel to be heard in our time."[17] I would suggest that this purpose stands or falls on our willingness and ability to listen. Our responsibility, as it has been since the paradigmatic intervention of the incarnation, is to discern the story/stories of the time and place in which we live, to understand the question behind the questions of our cultural and philosophical context and to engage them with a meaningful and sufficient story. After all, this is one of the purposes of incarnation, and it is at the heart of truly transforming encounters. This, however, is something unachievable unless we are willing to listen to the world in which we live, and equally, to listen with a critical ear to ourselves as Christians and as the-Church-at-large. For though we claim to hold God's truth within our corporate identity, the communication of that truth isn't as straight forward as simply repeating the anecdotes, sound bites, and sermons that we may have been fed. Truth needs translating into the language of the listener if it is to be heard. This is self-evident if there is quite literally a language barrier. It is less evident when one is talking about the understanding and interpretation of signs, symbols, metaphors and semantics—which are so often the grammar of biblical truth and the grammar of the cultural philosophies that underpin the stories people tell about themselves and the world in which they live. To quote the Catholic theologian Terry

Veling, the task of the Church is to pay "attention to God's concern for the world…listening and responding to the questions and issues that are circulating within our culture and society, within our own lives, within our parishes and congregations, our workplaces, our local neighbourhoods."[18] The real truth is each new frontier of Christian mission requires fresh theological pursuit. We are not called to rest on our laurels, to speak of, discuss, and implement the theologies of our forebears as if they are determinative for all contexts everywhere. Rather, we are called to be a listening community out of which ever-new expressions of our faith can emerge.

To return, almost to where we started, I would want to argue that it is both appropriate and challenging to suggest that, like post-Exodus Israel, the people of this world need to live with the knowledge that when they cry out the Church of Christ hears their cries and is both willing and able to respond. As Lucy Winkett wishes to say, listening to individuals and communities around us "reveals a variety of involuntary, visceral lamenting sounds in reaction to forces of destruction."[19] Therefore, wherever real needs exist, the church has a God-given, Christ-inspired mandate to listen and so be engaged: Asylum, poverty, people-trafficking, housing, education, employment, healthcare, youth issues, crime, marriage, community development, the environment, urban regeneration, international relief, trade justice, globalization, human rights, taxation, addiction, discrimination, care for the elderly, foreign policy, and metal health, and so the list goes on. "All listening begins and ends in God. The God who listens in infinite compassion is the God who creates in each of us the desire to listen to him, to his world, to each other, to ourselves so that, filled with his Spirit, we might continue his work here on earth."[20]

Notes

1. Annette Simmons, *The Story Factor* (Cambridge MA: Basic Books, 2006), 182.
2. Adapted from Matthew 13:14 (NIV): "You will be ever hearing but never understanding."
3. Dietrich Bonhoeffer, *Life Together* (London: SCM, 1954), 97-98.
4. These thoughts are based on course notes from *Being There: An Introduction to Christian Listening;* Network Counselling and Training, Bristol UK. Online: http://www.network.org.uk/
5. Mother Mary Clare, *Listening to God and Listening to Community* (Oxford: SLG, 1978), 4.
6. Walter Brueggemann, *Theology of the Old Testament* (Minneapolis: Fortress, 1997), 364.
7. Deryck Sheriffs, *The Friendship of the Lord: An Old Testament Spirituality* (Carlisle: Paternoster, 1996), 76-78.
8. Frank Lake, *Clinical Theology* (London: DLT, 1966), 14.
9. Philip Greenslade, *A Passion for God's Story*, (Carlisle: Paternoster, 2006), 89.
10. Karl Barth, *Church Dogmatics* (eds. G.W. Bromiley and T.F. Torrance; Edinburgh: T&T Clark, 1957), 2:2:283.
11. Anne Long, *Listening* (London: DLT, 1990), 175.
12. Ibid., 167.

13. The words portrayed in this conversation are the author's own based on his recollection of a story heard on a BBC Broadcast. They are for the purpose of illustration only and should not thought of, or used in a way that suggests they are original and authoritative.

14. Barber Hardy, *Towards a Poetics of Fiction: An Approach Through Narrative* (n.p., 1968), 5, cited in Alasdair MacIntyre, *After Virtue* (Notre Dame: University Press, 1981), 211.

15. G.W. Stroup, *The Promise of Narrative Theology* (London: SCM Press, 1984), 111.

16. Annette Simmons, *Story*, 182.

17. Sally TeSelle, *Speaking in Parables* (London: SCM, 1975), 1

18. Terry A. Veling, *Practical Theology* (New York: Orbis Books, 2005), xix.

19. Lucy Winkett, *Our Sound is Our Wound: Contemplative Listening to a Noisy World* (New York: Continuum, 2010), 48.

20. Long, *Listening*, 179.

Chapter 2

Silence, Noise, and the Voice of Jesus Christ

Stephen H. Webb

In 2004 I published a book, *The Divine Voice: Christian Proclamation and the Theology of Sound*, on the history of sound in Christian theology.[1] I called my method theo-acoustics and took as my subject what it means to be not only a hearer of the word but also a proclaimer of the Gospel. I began with the biblical observations that God spoke the world into being and that Jesus Christ is called God's Word. Believing is hearing in the biblical worldview, I pointed out, not seeing. Grace is as subtle (and invisible) as sound. The followers of Jesus knew his authority by his voice ("Never has a man spoken the way this man speaks!" [John 7:46 NASB]), and we still follow Jesus today by listening to the voices of those who proclaim him. Arguably, we do not know what we truly believe until we say it out loud. These were some of my themes.

More specifically, my book included personal confession (about my own difficulties with public speaking), philosophical speculation (about why we typically identify believing with seeing instead of hearing), historical investigation (about the role of the Reformation in elevating the spoken word as a medium of worship), and practical recommendation (about the proper use of music and the importance of reading the Bible out loud in worship). I even compared the church to a community theater where amateurs build a sense of closeness and intimacy by speaking their lines and performing their roles. The Church is a place where Christians rehearse the biblical story in the hope of learning how to inhabit more deeply their role as witnesses to the good news. I also talked about why churches should spend more time evaluating their soundscapes than their landscapes. The church is constructed of sound more than brick and mortar.

I wrote that book while I was losing my hearing, which was always in the background of every sentence. I knew I was drawn to think and write about the world of sound because I was being forced to retreat into a world of silence. Now that I look back at that book, however, I wonder how I could have put so much emphasis on the importance of hearing when my ears were becoming increasingly deaf. I also wrote that book while I was a Protestant. (I grew up in an independent church in the Campbellite, restorationist tradition, moved to the Disciples of Christ for many years, and then became a Lutheran.) I was frequently asked to preach at various churches back then, and so what it means to stand up and talk about Jesus Christ was often on my mind. In 2007 I was received into the Roman Catholic Church, and when people inevitably ask me what impact this change has had on my theological thinking, I look back to *The Divine Voice* and wonder how I would write that book differently today, now that my hearing is much lower and my liturgy must higher than it was several years ago.

I take as my central focus for this essay the way in which noise can blight our soundscapes as surely as pollution and trash cans scar our landscapes. Indeed, we live in an extremely loud world—our age is louder than any that has come before it. Historians write books exploring *The Audible Past* and sociologists write about *Audio Culture*. We are thinking about sound more than ever before, even as we keep trying to devise ways to escape its omnipresence. Perhaps we are thinking about sound precisely because we cannot escape it. Given that fact about our common situation, I want to ask two questions. What does it mean that we enter into church on Sundays from a world that is increasingly noisy and loud? And given that Roman Catholicism has a long tradition of honoring silence, and is generally depicted as a church that has a lower decibel worship than most Protestant churches, what can Protestants learn about sound and silence from Catholics (and vice versa!).

I should say from the start that I am not one of those converts who think that the Catholic mass is perfect, even if it is heaven on earth. Catholic churches have all sorts of problems these days, from keeping young people engaged to figuring out what to do with the music. Nonetheless, I feel more evangelical than ever before now that I am Roman Catholic. What I mean is that I have found an intimacy and immediacy in the mass that takes me right back to the worship services of my youth. I had to learn how to appreciate the mass, however, and its quietness was one of the things I had to grapple with the most.

That we live in a noisy world hardly needs much arguing. Open your door and walk down the street, or just stay in bed and crack a window. Noise was not invented by the industrial age—complaints about noise are almost as old as humanity itself—but machines and electronics have certainly magnified the problem. Perhaps most significantly, electric lights have turned nighttime into work time and blurred the boundary between the dominance of sight in the light of day and the heightened sensitive to soft sounds in the dark. Americans especially are known to love being loud—the very expanse and openness of our landscape requires it, and perhaps our political system too, since freedom is increasingly defined, it seems, as the right to be heard, no matter whether you have anything to say. Our loudness is something we often discover about ourselves when we travel abroad. People in other countries often interpret our noisiness as a form of brashness, but it could just be that we forget to lower the volume when we leave our sonically sizable country. Americans are also known for liking the latest gadgets and newest equipment, yet every advance we take toward figuring out how to reduce noise gives us at the same time new tools to make sounds louder. To escape the roaring racket, there are portable sound therapy machines that block out some kinds of sound and heighten others. Others choose to plug in every time they go out, thus enveloping themselves in sound cocoons, which turn the whole wide world into a personal miniature stereo system. We deafen ourselves in order to achieve a little bit of peace and quiet.

Noise, of course, is a relative term. What is disturbing to someone trying to sleep at night is an affirmation of life to someone else, just getting ready to party. I hear the cries of my baby in a very different way than the cries of *your* baby. Noise reminds us that we are not in control of our surroundings, which is surely why hell is often portrayed as the epitome of noise. Dante, for example, writes of

Tongues mixed and mingled, horrible execration,
Shrill shrieks, hoarse groans, fierce yells and hideous blather
And clapping of hands thereto, without cessation.[2]

Noise is the sound life makes when it is pushed to the limits. That is one definition of noise; other, more concise definitions include "junk sound," "ugly sound," "sound pollution," "excessive sound," and "unwanted sound." Just as dirt is matter out of place, according to the evocative definition by the anthropologist Mary Douglas, noise is sound that has seeped out of its intended space. And just as pollution can sting the eyes, noise can ruin the ears. Americans abuse their ears (or are the victims of sonic abuse) more than any other people, and the statistics on the growing rates of tinnitus and hearing loss are alarming. Who hasn't had a peaceful Saturday afternoon interrupted by a leaf blower that sounds like a Harley Davidson? Rock concerts often peak at more than 120 decibels (what is rock and roll if not controlled noise, or noisy sound?), which is almost as loud as an airplane taking flight or a chain saw buzzing in your hands. Rock and roll is a window into the American soul precisely because it embraces noise with so much fervor. Loud sounds can be painful (and have been used in warfare to frighten and paralyze the enemy), but they can also evoke excitement and joy at the prospect of surrendering to something so overwhelming. After all, sound is a matter of vibration, and loud sounds literally move and shake us, and not just in our ears. Experts recommend using hearing protection for exposure to sounds louder than 85 decibels, yet the entertainment industry keeps coming up with ways to supersize the sonic dimension of every enjoyable experience.

Lactantius, a fourth century North African Christian apologist, wrote on the temptations of the ear, a neglected topic given how easily we associate seduction with the eye instead. He does not mention Eve, but she was misled by what she heard, not what she saw. Lactantius belongs to a now almost forgotten moral tradition that admonished believers to guard what they hear as well as what they see and say. "Let nothing be agreeable to the hearing but that which nourishes the soul and makes you a better man."[3]

The solution to noise for many people is silence, but that is not an option for Christians. I am not saying that Christians should not seek solitude every now and then. A walk in the woods is restorative because we can let our ears slow down as they open up to new sounds. Indeed, if the book industry is any indication, silence is catching on in America, with book titles such as *In Pursuit of Silence, A Book of Silence,* and *The Quest for Absolute Silence.* Quiet time for prayer is an important part of spiritual health, but Christians should be a bit skeptical of this newest health trend. Indeed, too much silence can be just as distracting as too much noise. There are rooms or chambers built to approximate a zero decibel environment for therapeutic purposes, but sensory deprivation can also be an effective torture technique. Even those who use isolation tanks for recreational reasons often experience hallucinations and end up hearing voices or even feeling the presence of evil. Absolute silence at zero decibels is probably impossible to experience, and who would want to anyway? Absolute silence is death.

So, what are Christians to do? We cannot shut our ears as we can shut our eyes. Nonetheless, we can spend more time in the one place where sound is tempered by joy and always directed heavenward. As Lactantius advises, "If it be a pleasure to hear melodies and songs, let it be pleasant to sing and hear the praises of God."[4] The Church should be sonically different from the world outside its doors, giving us a space where we can find not just peace and quiet but also, and more importantly, the joyful noise of people worshipping the Lord.

Some religions treat silence as the origin of the universe and the ultimate goal of all spiritual practices, but nobody would mistake a church today for a meditation retreat. For one thing, churches seem to be getting louder all the time. For another, Christians are called to be vocal: "I believed, and so I spoke," wrote the Apostle Paul (2 Cor 4:13). Silence can and should be used in Christian worship to heighten our awareness of God, and silence is also important as an opportunity to dwell on personal sins that need to be turned over to God in private. Nevertheless, silence for Christians is not an end in itself. As the Psalmist writes, "Blessed is the people who know the joyful sound" (Ps 89:15 ERV). Churches were once known for the loudness of their bells (just as mosques are still known for the very public call to prayers), and the Bible says that the Day of Judgment will be announced by the blast of a trumpet. The Bible associates noise with God's triumph: Paul writes, "For the Lord Himself will descend from heaven with a shout, with the voice of the archangel and with the trumpet of God, and the dead in Christ will rise first" (1 Thess 4:16 NASB). Even nature is noisy as it longs for the same redemption promised to us (Rom 8:22).

New age religious movements promote and cultivate silence precisely because silence invites an inward turn where individuals can hear whatever they want and thus listen to gods of their own making. When Paul says that faith comes by hearing (Rom 10:17), he did not mean that we should listen to ourselves. Every one of us is lost, and we can find ourselves only by turning away to God. That turn is a matter of listening to what other Christians have to say. It is also a matter of listening to the Bible. Reading the Bible out loud in Church is not just a curious holdover from the days when many Christians were illiterate and thus needed to hear the Bible in order to have any chance of understanding it. Reading the Bible out loud, to each other and in the presence of the Holy Spirit, is what Christians do in order to be Christians. Singing, reading, praying and preaching are all sonic activities. Silence is well and good as a means of preparation for prayer and evoking the Word of God, but Christians are followers of sound, not seekers of peace and quiet.

The church is a hearing culture. My most vivid memories of my childhood church is the time, right before communion, that was set aside for silent reflection. My father was an elder at our church and often gave the communion meditation. The combination of his words and then his silence, as he led our speechlessness before the majesty of what Jesus had done to erase the misery of what we always do, was overpowering. We were invited to close our eyes and think of him, so that our inward turn was really an opening up to someone else. And it was all in preparation for receiving the bread and the juice—remembering with our bodies what Jesus did with his.

When I go to Protestant churches these days, there is not much silence, and I am fine with that. I like the upbeat energy. When I go to mass, it is like watching TV with the sound turned way down, and I end up wishing there was less quietness and more silence. Catholicism has long honored the religious value of silence—from the Carthusian monks who embrace nearly complete solitude to the Trappist branch of the Order of Cistercians who developed their own sign language to minimize the need to speak out loud—but many Catholic churches do not seem to know what to do with it these days. The mass moves forward so efficiently that there is not much space to slow down time, and when it is over, instead of leaving with the Holy Spirit in your heart you are left with a bunch of announcements that fill your head.

When I started attending mass regularly, in anticipation of being received by the Catholic Church, its quietness was its most striking feature. I must admit that I found the stillness a bit disturbing. Coming from a low-church background, where the songs and sermons were so emphatic, everything in the mass seemed so understated. Even after all the announcements and the simple words of dismissal ("The mass is ended") there was none of the social chattering and busy bustling that follows the end of a Protestant service. I had the same feeling, by the way, when I moved from Chicago, where I did my graduate work, to Crawfordsville, a small town in Indiana where I went to teach at Wabash College. I was so used to the noise of the big city that walking around this small town the first couple of nights rattled me with its quiet. Being on streets without noise was menacing, as if somebody had ordered everyone to hush when they saw me coming down the sidewalk. The silence made every sound stand out, so that I found myself suspicious of every creak or scuttle.

I learned to appreciate the quiet of the mass, but it took several months. I had to reorient myself to a new liturgical acoustics. And what I was witnessing at mass was much louder than what the mass used to be! In the celebration (a jarring word to Protestants in this context) of the traditional Latin Mass, the priest uses three vocal tones, low, medium, and high. The low voice is used for the prayers that inaugurate the consecration of the Eucharistic elements. The medium voice is used when the priest needs to be heard by the servers, and the high voice is reserved for the reading of the Gospels and the homily. With his back facing the congregation (because all the faithful faced the altar, which was traditionally attached to the chancel wall), the priest was speaking with the people, not to them. The altar (which Protestants call the communion table) was the place of a mystery so great that a silent awe was the most appropriate response. The words of consecration, in fact, were to be said in an inaudible voice. I have read that this practice originated in monasteries where priests celebrating the mass in the various side altars would lower their voices to avoid disturbing each other. Whatever its origins, the silence of these sacred words is not an affirmation of silence in general. The lesson instead is that the Word of God should be as intimate to us as our inner voices.

If the Latin Mass is any indication, we can formulate a law of Christian acoustics: the higher the liturgy the lower the decibels. What is the evidence for this law? First, rituals are a way of speaking through action, so that the more rituals a church has, the less it will be compelled to put everything into words. Second, tradition lets history speak with its own voice, which suggests that individual voices should harmonize and even blend in with the chorus of the Christian past. Third, a high ecclesial hierarchy means that the priest is not speaking for himself, and thus should use a tone more becoming of a servant than a leader. When the priest celebrant's chair in a new church is dedicated, for example, the bishop is the first to sit in it, as a reminder that the parish has a pastor only because the bishop cannot be everywhere in the diocese. Fourth, and finally, the mass climaxes with a sacrifice in which God is literally presented to the faithful. The hushed tones of awe, tinged with humility and even a bit of fear, are an appropriate response to a mystery that, in a way, can be tasted but not seen or heard.

Low-liturgy Protestant churches make sure you hear every word, loud and clear, because they put the focus on a decision that needs to be made here and now, which suggests that, as in a court of law, every word counts. Surely this is why Protestants are usually better than Catholics in designing acoustically accessibly spaces. My parish has a new church that is a feast for the eyes, but the impressive spatial heights lose the sound like vaporized liquid on a hot surface. There is a microphone, but the priests, deacons and readers speak into it as if they are looking down a bottomless well. Many Protestant churches encourage people to lift up their voices, which is sound's natural direction anyway. They do this with the use of screens, which keep congregants from looking down at hymnals, and electric instruments, which forces singers to raise their voices if they want to be heard. (Think of the way the nature of singing changed with the introduction of electronic guitars.)

As a hearing impaired person, I am grateful for every effort to deliver sound right into my ear. In mass, I often do not hear much of the sermon, and I am probably too complacent about that. The sermons are conversational, fatherly, and restrained, so I usually do not think that I am missing much. The words to the responsorial Psalm are never posted anywhere, and it seems to me that most of the congregation cannot make out what they are from the cantor, who is therefore forced to sing solo. It seems somehow un-Catholic of me to think about complaining. Besides, I am in a meditative mood, and everything earthly is so completely overshadowed by the communion that is yet to come. So I sit quietly and try to gather my wandering thoughts into a prayer.

I think the main reason I do not complain about the acoustics is that I have learned to be deeply at home in the quiet of the mass. I am not trying to argue here that Catholic sound management is inherently better than the Protestant variety. I can even imagine a future where some parts of the world will be known for their raucous masses while many Protestant churches will embrace the proclamatory potential that can be found in silence. But for me, for now, the quietness of the mass is good. The world is such a noisy affair that there is something to be said for worship that offers a transition from one decibel count to another. During the week I have to crank my aids to try to catch all the conversations going on around me, and the sound is never perfect, always precarious. I lean into people, wantonly violating their private space, to try to receive their words. At mass I can sit back and let the Word come to me. I can even say the right words at the right time without hearing with any clarity what anybody else is saying. The mass tells me to be patient and to be prepared, until the time comes to proceed with cupped hands to the place where I will open my mouth without making any sound. All I need to say is amen, and that sounds absolutely right.

Notes

1. Stephen H. Webb, *The Divine Voice: Christian Proclamation and the Theology of Sound* (Grand Rapids: Brazos Press, 2004).

2. Dante, *The Divine Comedy, 1: Hell* (trans. D.L. Sayers; New York: Penguin Books, 1949), 86.

3. Lactantius, "The Divine Institutes," *The Ante-Nicene Fathers*, (ed. Alexander Roberts and James Donaldson, 10 vols.; Grand Rapids: Eerdmans, orig. pub. 1886), 7:188.

4. Ibid., 188.

SECTION 2

LISTENING AND PASTORAL MINISTRY

Chapter 3

Listening and Ethical Formation in Worship

Brent D. Peterson

After the benediction had been given, the Pastor moved to the back of the sanctuary to greet her parishioners. Many offered cordial remarks and complementary words regarding her sermon. She glanced up and saw one of her young church elders approaching and he did not look pleased. "Pastor, we did not sing any songs that I liked today." The Pastor looked lovingly and compassionately at him and said gently, yet firmly, "It is a good thing worship is not about you." He was taken back a bit and could offer no response. The Pastor quickly followed by saying, "Why don't we have lunch this week and talk about worship?"

It is likely this conversation has played out thousands of times throughout the history of the Christian church. Too often conversations like this are premised around personal preferences regarding style, instrumentation, and the familiar. It would have been much quicker for the pastor to have responded to her congregant by asking, "Well, what songs do you like? I can see if we can include some of them in the next couple of weeks." The seduction of resolving the complaint from this young believer in this way might settle the present complaint, but in the end it leads to the further idolatry of Christian Worship.

Many Christian congregations in North America have just endured what has been infamously named the "Worship Wars." Many congregations, attempting to "connect" and "reach out" to their culture with the hope of being "relevant," developed worship services hoping both to attract new people as well as keep the saints happy. It was a daunting task and a great deal of relational and ecclesial blood was spilt in the process. With such motivation, too many worship services have been planned and executed without a strong theology of worship.

In this essay I will sketch a brief theology of worship by considering two primary questions: first, what is the purpose of Christian worship? Second, how do we know what we are doing in worship is Christian? Addressing these questions not only suggests certain practices, but also affirms how participating in communal worship is the primary activity that helps persons become more fully human. Exploring these questions begins to illuminate a Christian theology of worship this essay will propose. *Christian communal worship is the primary listening-healing encounter between God and the church. Christian communal worship is an event of embodied listening and thus heals and transforms the church to live out its renewed vocation as the body of Christ, to be joyfully broken and spilled out for the world.*

The Purpose of Christian Worship

The pragmatics of weekly worship and the demanding schedule for both pastors and volunteer laity often lead to a failure of addressing simple, yet crucial questions. Failing to address these questions explicitly steers pastors and lay leaders into situations that can become very destructive often undergirding idolatrous worship. The first question that must be addressed is so basic and assumed it is rarely considered. *What is the purpose and point of communal Christian worship?* Why does the church worship? Why does God gather the church on the Lord's Day? The answers to these questions speak into the spirit of this entire project. Communal worship is first and foremost about embodying God's worth. Worth-ship must always be about and for God. Turning it into anything "about me and for me" fails to appreciate fully the God who calls and gathers us together. God created us to be creatures that worship. When some hear that God created humans to worship the Creator, some may think God's gift of worship is nothing more than some manipulative narcissistic ploy to stroke an anemic divine ego. Conversely, the gift of worship provides creatures with the opportunity to be more fully human, to live more fully into one's creation in the image of God. The question is not *if we will worship*, but what will we worship. We have two worship options: God or self. The worship of self takes on many forms with many different practices, habits, and rituals. The worship of self develops from a vast spectrum of disease, ranging from grandiose egos and pride all the way to failing to have a proper pride and ego. Genesis 1 and beyond reminds us that creatures are to worship only that which is not created; hence, the only one worthy of worship is God. To give any created thing ultimate worth is the definition of idolatry and sin. God provides us with the gift of worshipping the Triune God, so as to free us from the emptiness of worshipping ourselves. In this way, as we worship God we are more fully human, doing what God created us to do. God created humans in God's image to love God, love themselves and others, and care for creation as an extension of the first three.

Listening to be More Fully Human

As creatures are gathered to worship, they are made present both to God, oneself, and others. Being present to God, oneself, and others involves not only praise, but also a posture of listening and transformation. Communal worship is the primary transforming encounter with God and the church. In this event of communal worship the church offers its praise to God along with a posture ready to listen, ready to encounter God's prophetic, comforting, and challenging Word. This entire spirit of listening is an act proclaiming that God is of ultimate worth along with a desire to be what God created humans to be.

Listening as Liturgy

Addressing how worship is liturgical helps to elucidate further how worship enables us to be more fully human. Some may think a worship service is liturgical if someone is wearing a robe and several candles are burning. In truth, all services are liturgical. The liturgy of Christian worship designates the activity and practices of humans in worship. Ironically, the idea of liturgy began outside Christianity in the politics and civic practices of Rome. "*Leitourgia* is classically understood with two related ideas, both from the realm of imperial politics. First, liturgy is a means by which a gathering of people are united and made a *polis*."[1] Alexander Schmemann writes that "the original sense of *leitourgia* was an action by which a group of people become something corporately which they had not been as a collection of individuals."[2] The liturgy of a worship service binds and unifies Christians together as the body of Christ. Liturgy also describes "the public duty of a citizen to the state. This service was often very costly in both time and money. This act or 'work' was not only for the benefit of the state but helped to confirm and further establish one's allegiance to the state as a compatriot."[3] In this way the liturgy is the work of the people confirming one's allegiance to a certain ideology. Similarly, a Christian worship service being liturgical celebrates the political nature of worship where Christians affirm and renew their allegiance to the kingdom of God and membership in the body of Christ.

Listening as Being Present

The liturgy of a communal worship service proclaims and praises God's worth providing persons an opportunity of being fully present, to God, oneself, and others. Unfortunately, too many persons come to worship not ready to listen, but seeking entertainment. Some come for a simplistic plastic hearing failing to be really present to God, oneself, and one another. For the sake of this essay, I want to distinguish between hearing and listening. The young elder came to hear the familiar; he came to hear words he liked to tunes he knew. He had not come ready to listen to God's transforming voice. Too often when persons come to hear rather than listen, they are not really present to God, themselves, or other humans.

We have all had too many occasions when we were sharing stories or problems with a friend and he was there in body but not spirit. He may have physically heard the words spoken, but he failed to listen deeply to what was being said. While worship is about and for God, in order to be for God liturgical leaders must pay attention to how persons are present to God, themselves, and others. Leaders must pay attention not only to the words and actions of the liturgy, but the arrangement of sanctuary furniture. Two practical questions: how are persons invited to encounter God in your service? Second, how are persons invited to be made present and encounter themselves and other persons in worship?

Listening that is Christian

As an act of worship, the church's praise proclaims God's holiness and worth. As the church makes itself present to God by the Spirit through its praise, the church also comes ready to listen, ready to be encountered and transformed by God. This foundation of the purpose of worship leads to the second important question, *how do we know what we are doing in worship is Christian?* Failing to address this assumed question leaves communal worship open to anything from wasted time to idolatry. In my experience, it is certainly not the case that liturgical leaders intentionally seek ways to form and plan idolatrous worship. Yet under the premise of "reaching the lost," "we have always done it that way," or "this would be cool," too many things find their way into a Sunday service that are very far from praising or listening to God. As mentioned above, all services have a liturgy, but is there any standard to what can be named Christian liturgy?

In light of this question it is important to point out two important philosophical fallacies that guide this conversation. One fallacy is the appeal to tradition. In this fallacy people affirm something good simply because people have been doing it a long time. The mirror fallacy is the appeal to novelty. In this fallacy something is deemed to be better or good, because it is new. Both of these fallacies must be safeguarded when answering the question what is and is not Christian worship. That being said, if I am going to lean in one direction, I think it is wise to lean toward tradition. This is not to say that things that are new and creative cannot be orthodox (which means right worship). However, tradition serves as an important anchor against the winds of relativity. When anything done in a sanctuary on Sunday morning can be called worship, in the end Christian worship comes to mean absolutely nothing.

In establishing some boundaries for what is and is not Christian worship I am going to begin by studying what the church has done in worship. The New Testament provides a window into the worship practices of the early church. In reading through the New Testament several practices and postures rise to the surface.

Communal Listening is Important

When listening to the New Testament, I first observe how important being gathered to communal worship was for the early church. Luke 4 describes Jesus coming home. "When he came to Nazareth, where he had been brought up, he went to the synagogue on the Sabbath day as was his custom" (Luke 4:16 NRSV). Jesus' own life modeled the importance of attending synagogue. This practice of gathering for worship is also found in the early church. "Every day they continued to meet together in the temple courts" (Acts 2:46 NIV). The early church found strength and encouragement in meeting together as often as possible. Yet eventually some early Christians found gathering together not to be important. The author of Hebrews offers this charge. "Let us not give up meeting together, as some are in the habit of doing, but let us encourage one another—and all the more as you see the Day approaching" (Heb 10:25 NIV). Meeting together was not simply fun, they believed it was a central practice that they were charged in joy to do as they waited for Christ's return. It seems today that the importance of communal worship needs greater emphasis and attention. Refusing the retreat into legalism, God provides communal worship to the church as a gift that is necessary for the continual growth and encouragement of believers. Yet today not all are convinced that communal worship is necessary.

My undergraduate *Introduction to Christian Theology* course covers several aspects of the Christian narrative. From class to class and year to year I always find it interesting what issues ignite students and which ones create little passion. However, there is one class session I teach every semester that I know will cause emotional angst for most of my students. It is a class on the church and worship. I offer to them three statements.

1. You cannot be a Christian if you do not worship communally with the body of believers.

2. You can go to church (communal worship) and not be a Christian.

3. Going to church (communal worship) does not make you a Christian.

The first point usually makes several of my students so angry they do not hear (or listen) to the second and third points. These points are a bit provocative, but I think they affirm something central to Christianity that speaks directly into what makes worship Christian or not. Christians have always gathered together to worship. While there have been pockets of Christ followers through the centuries that have not participated regularly in weekly communal worship, both Christian tradition and my own experience affirm the importance of coming together with other believers to worship, whenever and wherever possible. Points two and three clarify that going to communal worship is not some work that earns God's forgiveness and healing. Many hear legalism with this conversation. The central point is this: we do not fully or even mostly determine what it means to be Christian. Let me emphasize again that communal worship is a gift from God. Attending communal worship is God's invitation to be more fully human, by doing *the* primary thing God created you to do. For most of you, I imagine reading this is "preaching to the choir." All ministers and laity should not be ashamed to assert the importance of attending communal worship.

Many of my students do not like point 1, precisely because they do not go to church. They provide many reasons why they do not go. It is true that some have been hurt at church. It is true that some people who attend worship are hypocritical. It is true that some pastors do ungodly things. Yet as painful as all these experiences are, these are not reasons for persons to stop attending. For most of my students the real reason they do not attend is their laziness. It is simply not a priority. My goal is never to use guilt or manipulation, but to invite them again to the importance of worship, not as a work, but as an opportunity to encounter God and other broken people through listening, healing, and transformation.

Along with this emphasis on meeting together, what did the early church do?

> They devoted themselves to the apostles' teaching and to the fellowship, to the breaking of bread and to prayer. Everyone was filled with awe, and many wonders and miraculous signs were done by the apostles. All the believers were together and had everything in common. Selling their possessions and goods, they gave to anyone as he had need. Every day they continued to meet together in the temple courts. They broke bread in their homes and ate together with glad and sincere hearts, praising God and enjoying the favor of all the people. And the Lord added to their number daily those who were being saved. (Acts 2:42-47 NIV)

This passage speaks about their life beyond communal worship. They gathered together often for worship. The rhythm of my North American Christian friends is so frenetic that such a picture as illustrated here seems both impossible and for some irresponsible. Many are right to critique Christians when they turn into a closed off "clique" that is exclusive of others. Yet notice that in Acts, as often as they gathered, God was still adding to their number daily. Could it be that the life of these young believers was so radically different and appealing that when they came into contact with those who were not a part of the body, those persons wanted to become like these Christians? It seems this happens very rarely today. We must also remember that when these New Testament texts were being written Christians were facing heavy and intense persecution. These Christians were not socialites, looking for a nightly party. Their coming together often was under the threat of persecution.

What other liturgical practices are found, commanded, and encouraged in the New Testament? From the New Testament we find these liturgical practices: prayer, singing hymns and spiritual songs, the reading of Scripture, preaching and teaching, baptism, and the Lord's Supper.

Practices of Communal Worship

Prayer

Many texts refer to the importance of prayer in the life of Christians. The seminal text on prayer is recorded in the Sermon on the Mount (or the Plain). In Matthew 6 Jesus offers both practical instructions about prayer and offers a prayer we should pray. While Jesus' instructions celebrate the importance of prayer done in private, his instruction also pertains to prayer in communal settings. In many ways, I think we should expand what we think of as prayer, both in private and in communal gatherings. Prayer serves as a wonderful model and image of Christian communal worship in total. Prayer involves both listening and speaking. Prayer is not about data exchange, it is about people exchanging themselves with God and each other.

As a posture, we must see the importance of listening in prayer. Too often our practice of prayer involves rattling off a list of needs to God as if we are making an order at McDonald's or giving Santa our list. In our prayer life and specifically in communal worship how do we allow for space to listen to God? While we are called to listen to God in prayer, prayer is also a place for us to respond to God both individually and corporately. While Jesus harshly critiques prayer that is done for show, what should our prayers consist of? With the Lord's Prayer as a foundation I have found the ACTS model helpful, both in personal times of prayer and for Christian communal worship.

The first posture is *Adoration.* This posture focuses not necessarily on what God has done, but who God is. We come before the throne of grace to speak in praise of the glory and worth of the Alpha and Omega. Recall that this posture of adoration is desired by God, not simply because of God's need for a stronger self-esteem; rather, if we do not worship God we will end up trying to find ultimate worth in ourselves.

Confession is the second posture. Confession also needs expansion. Confession does include listing before God sins we have committed. Drawing upon the *Book of Common Prayer,* John Wesley gave to Thomas Coke and Francis Asbury this general confession for every Lord's Day.

> Almighty and most merciful Father, We have erred and strayed from thy ways like lost sheep. We have followed too much the devices and desires of our own heart. We have offended against thy holy laws. We have left undone those things which we ought to have done; and we have done those things which we ought not to have done; And there is no health in us. But thou, O Lord, have mercy upon us, miserable offenders. Spare thou them, O God, which confess their faults. Restore thou them that are penitent; According to thy promises declared unto [hu]mankind in Christ Jesus our Lord. And grant, O most merciful Father, for his sake, That we may hereafter live a godly, righteous, and sober life; To the glory of thy holy Name. Amen.[4]

Confessions like this form a great response to the God who has been listened to throughout the week and through the reading of Scripture and perhaps even through the singing of songs and hymns.[5] Confessions are not only postures for recounting moral failures; they can also be statements of faith. Many communal Christian worship services include a confession of the Nicene or Apostles' creed. The church's confession of faith is its response to the God who has been listened to and encountered.[6] Confessing creeds is much more than a *recitation* of beliefs. As a confession it is both a proclamation as well as a pledge to God to live into the implications of such beliefs. The sacrament of baptism embodies a powerful confession of the church. The baptismal confession not only presents one's failings to God in search of healing and forgiveness, but also confesses one's faith and trust in God and covenants to live into the healing and grace that has been and will continue to be extended as a member of the church.

Why is there so little confession in some Christian worship services? Fully exploring this would require more space than can be afforded here. Suffice to say, spiritual pride and past hurts cause some to be silent about what they have done or left undone. A spirit of confession will open a floodgate of vulnerability, honesty, and authenticity desperately needed for Christian communal worship.

Thanksgiving is the third posture that celebrates all that God has done. This posture of prayer remembers all that God has done, is doing, and will do. A spirit of thanksgiving reminds Christians all they have and all they can do comes as a gift from God. Too often those whom have been blessed with health, storehouses of food, and material possessions think they are responsible for the joy in their life. The receiving of tithes and offerings and the Lord's Supper are primary places in a communal Christian worship that celebrate all we have is from God and thus to truly receive it, we give it back to God in thanksgiving.[7]

Supplication is the fourth posture. This is what occurs most often in personal and communal prayers. Certainly God desires that we present our needs and the needs of the world to God. James notes powerfully that anyone who is lacking wisdom should ask God who gives generously.[8] Are any of you sick? "They should call for the elders of the church and have them pray over them, anointing them with oil in the name of the Lord" (Jas 5:14 NRSV). God longs and desires that we bring to God our needs and wishes by laying our burdens upon God.

These four postures are not meant to be exclusive or formulaic, but can serve as a guide both for personal and communal prayer. Many other important types of prayers are appropriate for communal and personal prayer. Unfortunately too often when persons are praying in worship, it seems as if they have absolutely no clue why they are praying. Prayers are often used as fillers or segue ways from one thing to another. Both clergy and laity need education both on the different types of prayer and training on how to pray. I would strongly encourage those who are not fully skilled at praying spontaneously (and few are) to write out their prayers ahead of time. While God can give inspiration in the communal moment, God can also inspire persons ahead of time as they prepare for liturgical leadership in the service.

There is one last posture of prayer that must be recovered in communal worship: lament. Many of the Psalms are songs of lament. Laments provide space in worship for persons to cry out to God, to formally give their complaint to God for the things that have not gone as they desired. Laments are places and spaces for people to offer to God their pain, hurt, and sorrow for things that others have done to them or others. Along with confessions, the church must provide more space for persons to cry out to God. Laments are not pious whining; they are acts of worship. Within the complaints offered, all laments end with the church placing its ultimate hope and trust in God.

Singing Psalms, Hymns and Spiritual Song

Singing is a central practice of Christian communal worship. The gospels record Jesus singing with his disciples following the Last Supper. One can only imagine the tone and tempo of their singing following this meal, which included Judas' betrayal and Jesus' ominous discourse about his future (Matt 26:30; Mark

14:26). Paul and Silas were praying and singing hymns to God in prison (Acts 16:25). Also in Ephesians 5:18-19, Paul offers a stern warning about their sobriety during their singing. Do not get drunk on wine; rather be filled with the Spirit as you sing psalms, hymns and spiritual songs. In an attitude of thanksgiving these spiritual songs make a melody to the Lord in their hearts. Colossians 3:16 celebrates that singing was not only an act of thanksgiving, but singing also served as a means of teaching and instruction. "Let the word of Christ dwell in you richly; teach and admonish one another in all wisdom; and with gratitude in your hearts sing psalms, hymns, and spiritual songs to God" (NRSV). Andrew Lincoln reflects on this verse by noting "hymns were meant to function as vehicles not only for worship but also for instruction. Much of what is hymnic in the Pauline corpus has a didactic and paraenetic function."[9] Hymns and choruses instruct and exhort. One of the best examples is the kenosis Christ hymn in Philippians 2:6-11.

Most Christians recognize the importance of music; however, it is curious that music now seems to dominate communal worship. This dominance occurs both in time given to it in worship and the anger and angst surrounding it. While people found many things in those "worship wars" to argue about, music and the instrumentation along with it (choirs or worship teams, drums or organ, hymnals or Power Point slides, etc.) were often at the forefront. Music and singing evoke great *pathos* (passion). Clergy and other worship leaders should not be afraid of this passion, but learn to embrace it in practices that are Christian. Unfortunately, with music's emotional power, music can be used, including in communal Christian worship, as a form of manipulation. This manipulation takes many forms. In fact as our young elder demonstrated earlier, often people will gauge their pleasure or displeasure to a service by the music used. In recent days, too often music in communal worship has been an occasion of idolatry. Music has become its own end marginalizing God. In regard to music in worship, Paul's warning needs to be heeded again. We must not be drunk on personal music preferences or emotional fixes; rather, we must be filled with the Spirit. Finally, we must not neglect Paul's reminder and exhortation that the songs we sing must also be on occasion of teaching and instruction. Songs not only serve as prayers of hope, joy, praise, and lament, they are also occasions of instruction and formation (either good or poor). Therefore, songs with lame or un-Christian theology should be deleted. One area specifically to be vigilant for concerns lyrics that are self centered, focusing on "me." Music must be an occasion for listening to the Spirit. With these reminders and cautions, we should sing with great energy and passion as an opportunity to pray to God and listen to God's speaking.

Reading Scripture

Scripture's declaration of its own importance is not "proof" of its significance. Yet the entire Old and New Testament serve as a testimony and witness to God's blessing, inspiration, and use of Scripture for divine-human listening-healing encounters. Jesus and the early church found Scripture to be central to their life and communal worship. As noted above, when Jesus visited his hometown synagogue he read the scroll from the prophet Isaiah. Another important passage celebrating the importance of Scripture is found in Paul's second letter to Timothy. "All scripture is inspired by God and is useful for teaching, for reproof, for correction, and for training in righteousness, so that everyone who belongs to God may be proficient, equipped for every good work" (2 Tim 3:16-17 NRSV). God desires to use Scripture for many things. Yet Scripture is not itself the focus of worship; rather Scripture is a tool and vehicle through which God speaks and the church is invited to *listen* and encounter God by the Spirit.

Emphasizing the importance of reading Scripture will hardly be shocking. Yet as I have grown up in church, I am alarmed at how many "Bible-believing" congregations fail to read scripture in worship. Even though one of the Protestant hallmarks has been *sola scriptura,* the pastor's sermon and what she thinks God is saying often leaves little or no time for Scriptures being read. As one looks at the history of the Scriptures and their use, the Bible is a gift from God primarily for communal worship. The Gutenberg press brought with it many blessing and perhaps a few curses as well. Certainly the Gospel's reach has been expanded as more persons have access to Scripture. However, using the Bible solely for private bible study misses the central purpose God gives the Bible to the Church. While God can speak any time and place, the importance of being gathered by the Spirit, to the Word (Jesus Christ) through Scripture in communal worship is unparalleled. In fact throughout the history of Christian communal worship the first part of worship has been called *The Service of the Word.* Of course this encounter is not simply with a book, but is most profoundly a sacramental means through which the Father speaks in the Incarnate Word through the Spirit.

Preaching/Teaching

Both proclamation and teaching are found in the early church's gatherings. In Acts 10, Peter recounts his preaching and encounter with Cornelius. As Peter affirms the Gentiles as proper recipients of the Gospel, Peter notes Jesus' commission for the apostles. "He commanded us to preach to the people and to testify that he is the one ordained by God as judge of the living and the dead" (Acts 10:42 NRSV). While Protestants have centered their worship around the sermon, which is intended to be a proclamation of the Word, some preaching has lost its focus. Preaching must remain centered around the exposition of who God is, what God is inviting us to, and a call for us to be and do what God is calling us to. Too often preaching has been reduced to self-help, self-esteem building noise. In my estimation, part of the problem is that preaching has moved too far from Scripture and thus from God. While many mediums and media can be used to illustrate a point, preaching should be a spirit-anointed proclamation of Jesus Christ. One of the gifts of Christian ordination is the gifting and empowerment to preach the Word. Centering on biblical proclamation in one's current context provides another key opportunity for God to speak and all to listen.

In conjunction with preaching is the ministry of teaching. The ministry of teaching should also occur in worship. In the Gospels, Jesus' activity in the synagogues is often described as teaching. "Jesus went throughout Galilee, teaching in their synagogues and proclaiming the good news of the kingdom and curing every disease and every sickness among the people" (Matt 4:23 NRSV).[10] This ministry of teaching was continued by those in the early church. Recall Acts 2: "they devoted themselves to the apostle's teaching." All things done in worship are instructive and thus formative. Yet the ministry of explicit teaching can also occur in the sermon or in other moments throughout the liturgy where the church can be instructed into greater understanding of the Christian faith. For example, many Christians are largely ignorant about a great deal of Christian worship. Many can tell you what physically occurs, but very few have a sound foundation as to why certain practices occur in worship as well as what makes worship orthodox. The goal of this education is not simply for cognitive mastery; rather, this teaching and preaching seeks to empower the church to be more present to God, oneself, and to each other. Being more present provides occasions for better listening and response to the God who speaks.

All of the above practices, while not exhaustive, reflect well the *Service of the Word*. Drawing upon the New Testament, Christian Communal Worship followed the *Service of the Word* with the *Service of the Table*.

Lord's Supper

Let us again reflect on Acts 2:42: "They devoted themselves to the apostles' teaching and to the fellowship, to the breaking of bread, and to prayer." The New Testament affirms that the early worship practices included singing, praying, reading Scripture, and breaking bread together. While not all scholars agree that what is being described in Acts 2 is a celebration of the Lord's Supper, it seems that the Lord's Supper played a central role in their worship.[11] Throughout the history of Christian worship the frequency and importance of the Lord's Supper has waxed and waned. John Wesley, an eighteenth century Anglican and founder of the Methodist movement, found the Lord's Supper to be a primary means of grace for those who are seeking God's healing and transforming grace. Many, including Wesley, take very seriously Christ's command to partake of the Lord's Supper.[12] A weekly celebration of the Lord's Supper is a fitting response to the God who has been encountered in the Service of the Word.

The Lord's Supper provides a climax of the communal worship listening-healing event. As the church has listened and encountered God's presence through psalms, hymns, prayers, Scripture preaching and teaching, the church responds most dramatically by offering its tithes and offerings. This act of worship symbolizes Christians offering themselves as a living sacrifice. In the Lord's Supper the church and Christ are renewed again as the body of Christ. Too many Christian ministers and laity have not been educated on the history and significance of the Lord's Supper. A failure of understanding does not eliminate what God can do in those moments, but teaching Christians the history and significance enables persons to be more fully present to God, oneself, and others at the Table.

As a primary healing encounter, four things should guide a Christian Eucharistic celebration. First, ministers should pay great attention to the liturgy and rubrics (the ritual actions) at the Table. I recommend that with teaching and instruction, ministers use some version of "The Great Thanksgiving." While there are many variations of this liturgy based on the days and seasons in the church year, there is a central core that provides both great instruction and listening. A tone and posture of thanksgiving pervades this prayer where the church remembers all that God has done, is doing, and will do. While this liturgy should not be thought of as a magical incantation, the Christian church has used this prayer for over a millennia and many use it today as a faithful Christian prayer. Using this liturgical prayer helps to articulate the three remaining emphases that are central for the Lord's Supper.

The second emphasis in the Lord's Supper celebrates in thanksgiving Christ's dynamic healing presence by the Spirit. Unfortunately too much time has been spent and too much division has resulted from trying to exhaust precisely how Christ is present. The Scholastic movement and the Protestant response focusing on accidents and species created division rather than unity. John and Charles Wesley's *Eucharistic Hymns* offer a helpful posture that centers the church's energy not in exhausting cognitively how Christ is present, but affirming that Christ is dynamically present.[13]

Third, the Lord's Supper is a sacrifice. In the spirit of Romans 12:1-2, the church offers itself with Christ who is present, as its living sacrificial offering. As a renewal of the vows made at Baptism, the church offers itself again with Christ by the Spirit to the Father as its profound response to listening and encountering Christ in the proclamation of Scripture and now at the Table.

Fourth, at the Lord's Supper God renews Christians with each other as the body of Christ. This renewal celebrates the unity Christians are to have with Christ and each other. This renewal celebrates that the Christian's true political party is membership in Christ's body with a vision and vocation to live into the present and coming kingdom of God. Also being renewed as the body of Christ, the church is sent out to be Christ's broken body and shed blood in the world. As the church has been gathered by the Spirit to listen and encounter God in Christ in communal worship, they are sent from the communal worship, literally blown out by and with the Holy Spirit, to continue Christ's ministry on earth.

The Service of Word and Table is a dynamic listening encounter with God and the church. This listening encounter is the primary healing and empowering event where Christians are renewed as the body of Christ. With the benediction the church is sent out in praise and thanksgiving for all God has done. As the church has listened and encountered God in communal worship the church is then provided the proper vision and empowerment that is only possible after this primary listening/healing encounter.

Conclusion

In the Service of Word and Table, God by the Spirit gathers the believers together to this divine-human listening and formational encounter. In Christian Communal Worship God is both the primary initiator, breathing in the church and the empowering force that sends (exhales) the church out to embody this ethical formation as the body of Christ.

In the Service of the Word, the church is encountered by God through embodied listening to the texts read, songs sung, and Word proclaimed. As the church listens it is moved to responses of adoration, confession, repentance, joy, praise, lamentation, and supplication. In the church's response, God listens to the praises and requests of God's people. In the church's listening and responding in the Service of the Word, the church is reminded again of God's faithfulness, its unfaithfulness, as well as God's gracious provision of further healing.

In the Service of the Table, the church in thanksgiving is invited to the Table. In the Great Thanksgiving the church celebrates in hope and praise the salvation history of God in the world and specifically the earthly ministry of Jesus Christ. As the church listens again to this Good News it responds by sacrificially offering itself with the doxological sacrifice of Christ. The church's offering of itself as a living sacrifice is united to Christ's joyful worship of offering himself to the Father. As the church is offered with Christ to God, God renews the church with Christ—Christ as the head and the church as the body of Christ. In light of this renewal, God sends the church out to be the body of Christ in the world. As the church is the broken body and shed blood of Christ in the world, it embodies the ethical formation that occurred in the Service of Word and Table. Furthermore, the church's ethics in the world are always doxological and centered in God's kingdom that is here and yet still to come on earth.

God gathers the church together that the church might listen again and be listened to by God and others. This dynamic listening event is a primary encounter where God continues to heal and renew the church as the body of Christ as a further coming of the Kingdom of God.

Notes

1. Brent Peterson, "Eucharist: The Church's Political Response to Suffering and Vocational Empowerment to Suffering Love," *Wesleyan Theological Journal* 43:146-164 (Spring 2008), 149.

2. Alexander Schmemann, *For the Life of the World* (Crestwood, NY: St Vladimir's Seminary Press, 1988), 25.

3. Peterson, "Eucharist: The Church's Political Response to Suffering and Vocational Empowerment to Suffering Love," 149.

4. John Wesley, *Sunday Service of the Methodists in North America* (London, 1784), A4.

5. Cf. Matt 3:6; Acts 19:8; Jas 5:16.

6. Cf. Rom 10:9; Heb 10:23; 1 John 4:15.

7. Cf. 1 Tim 4:4; Rev 7:12.

8. Jas 1:5.

9. Andrew T. Lincoln, *The Letter to the Colossians* (New Interpreter's Bible 11; Abingdon: Nashville, 2000), 649.

10. See also Matt 9:35; 21:23; Mark 6:2; Luke 4:15; 13:10; 19:47; 21:37; John 6:59; 7:28.

11. The early church celebrated Agape-Feasts that should also be included of celebrations of the "Lord's Supper" (Cf. Jude 12 and 1 Cor 11).

12. Cf. Matt 26:26-29; Mark 14:22-25; Luke 22:14-23.

13. Charles and John Wesley, *Hymns on the Lord's Supper*, #59, sts. 1-3, (Bristol: Farley, 1745), 49.

Chapter 4

Listening in Proclamation

Michael Pasquarello

Listening in Proclamation

This essay is a modest attempt to share with fellow preachers a way of thinking about the primary purpose of proclamation—listening to the Word of God. Many, if not most, contemporary books about preaching begin with the assumption that the primary task of preaching is "effective communication"–typically defined by the needs, desires, and expectations created by our consumerist and technological culture.[1] However, if preaching has primarily to do with the identity and activity of the Triune God who reveals himself by speaking his Word, then the nature and purpose of preaching cannot be determined by convictions that are less than theological. For example, Nicholas Lash suggests we consider the following important questions, "What does God's Word say?" and "What, in this utterance that finds flesh in Jesus, does God announce?" He writes,

> Christianity does not provide magical solutions or satisfying explanations; offer us tranquilizers or quick fixes, furnish us with short-cuts past the endless, bewildering and painful labor of making sense of things, of mending our confused and battered world. God's utterance announces nothing in particular: it announces—life! ... As performative utterance, what the Word says is what it does. And what it does is bring all things to life, in God.[2]

This essay follows such a God-centered approach which sees those who preach and those who listen as living in response to God speaking creation and salvation. Although a preacher is called to the ministry of speaking, he or she does so within and for a community of listeners who participate in a conversation which is initiated, sustained, and completed by the Father through the Son and in the Spirit. In my thinking about listening in proclamation, then, I am working with a fundamental theological conviction that has significant implications for preachers: as human beings we are those to whom God has spoken in the Word, and we are also those who are so made as to be able to hear and respond to the Word.

Nicholas Lash challenges the dualism of much modern preaching that separates knowledge of God's Word and human life by abstracting discrete bits and pieces of the Bible from the story of God's love for the world which finds its center in the person of Jesus Christ. Lash counters this kind of pragmatic and utilitarian abstraction by emphasizing the integral relation of the Word made flesh in Jesus and the vulnerability of our life and speech. He argues that our capacity for speaking is to be answerable and responsible to and for each other and to the mystery of God. In the midst of the abstracted, empty God-talk that characterizes our time there must be a community of prayerful listening to God since we are constituted "as 'hearers of the word' in every fiber of our being, turned towards, and attentive to, the voice that makes us and calls us home.... It is, after all, Jesus who is confessed to be God's Word made flesh; it is his life, and history, and destiny, that speak to us, inviting our response."[3] In other words, we do not speak to convince or persuade others; rather we speak because we have been called, invited, and authorized to speak what we have heard. It is God who is speaks in our response just as it is God who has spoken in his Word.[4]

As preachers we are therefore called to participate in the reality of the Word we hear. For this reason, our preaching will submit itself to be worked out within the history of weak and sinful people revealed in the biblical narratives of Israel, Jesus, and the church. As Lash notes, "in the Fourth Gospel the truth which shall make us free is truth en-fleshed, enacted, made finite and particular, arrested, tried, and crucified; but it is not truth sought elsewhere." The truth which authorizes us to speak and live is received in the appropriation of vulnerability, the form of God's self - giving in Christ by which the world is renewed in the Word.[5]

The integrity of preaching is defined by the church's primary calling—the joy of praising and knowing God whose Spirit leads us into a lifelong journey of transformation through union with Christ in his passion and resurrection, a way of following and imitating the Word in whom we re-turn ourselves and words to the One whose self-giving is the source of all that is. Through prayerful attentiveness to the Spirit's witness to Christ in Scripture we are formed in the life of holiness as glad respondents to God speaking. Eugene Peterson writes,

> The intent in reading Scripture—among people of faith—is to extend the range of our listening to the God who reveals himself in word, to become acquainted with the ways in which he has spoken in various times and places, along with the ways in which people respond when he speaks. The Christian conviction is that God speaks reality into being - creation into shape, salvation into action. It is also a Christian conviction that we are that which is spoken into a creation shape and a salvation action. We are what happens when the word is spoken. So we listen to find out what is going on....[6]

I would like to think of our listening in proclamation as having the shape of the conversation between Jesus and Nicodemus in the Gospel of John.[7]

John 3: Listening to Jesus in the Spirit's Witness

I remember when I first went to seminary and how overwhelming the experience was for me. It was truly like entering a whole new world. I was introduced to a new way of thinking, a new vocabulary, and a new way of speaking. In fact, I was introduced to things that were as odd and strange as anything I had ever heard. In the Sunday School and Vacation Bible School experience of the little church in which I was raised they did not tell me about such things as JEDP and the Hebrew Bible or the New Testament and the Synoptic problem. Nor did we cover the complexities of source, form, redaction, literary, rhetorical, canonical and narrative criticism. Neither did they lecture me on the Christological controversies of the early church or the Trinitarian affirmations of the ecumenical Councils. And they did not discuss the ways Protestants and Catholics in the sixteenth century argued over justification and sanctification, or how they fought to establish who had the right understanding of Baptism and Holy Communion. And then, we never had classes that helped us learn how to think through moral issues and stake out positions on matters such as war, abortion, sexuality, racism and discrimination, economic justice, poverty and homelessness.

Soon after arriving at seminary, I was forced to acknowledge just how much I did not yet know and still needed to learn. I began to wonder how in the world I had managed to survive as a Christian for so many years. It has now been thirty years since I showed up at seminary with my theological ignorance and I do hope I have learned a helpful thing or two since then.

However, there is one thing I can share with you and it is this: what I need, but don't always desire, is to know God. While I will acknowledge that I need more than anything to know and love as I am known and loved by the Father through the Son and in the Spirit, I must admit this scares me. After all, according to Scripture, knowing God in such intimacy comes only with a major shift in the center of gravity of our lives; that is, a shift from our selves to God. We are able to know God only by faith that comes by listening to God's Word as we are led in and by the Spirit's witness to him.

This is what is going in the third chapter of John's Gospel. Jesus invites Nicodemus to listen to the Word in the leading of the Spirit. Jesus is teaching and leading a prominent teacher and leader of the Jews, which is something highly unusual, since Nicodemus is an expert in the Law who has dedicated his life to studying and teaching the Scriptures of Israel. Can you blame him for seeking out Jesus at night under the cover of darkness? How embarrassing it must have been for him. Imagine, being seen consulting with a young unknown rabbi named Jesus of Nazareth. To his credit, Nicodemus approaches Jesus and greets him, "Rabbi, no one could do all the pointing to God and God revealing acts if God were not in on it." Jesus confirms this judgment. "You are right Nicodemus, my learned friend, unless a person is born from above, from God, it is not possible to see what I am all about—God's kingdom."

We know how the story goes. Nicodemus is baffled by this born from above, new birth, Spirit-blown talk of Jesus. He responds, "What do you mean by this? How does this happen?" "What?" replies Jesus. "You mean to tell me after all these years of study in Hebrew and Greek, courses in Old Testament and New Testament, classes in theology and biblical interpretation, in ethics, worship and preaching, and training in pastoral care, Christian education, and evangelism; you mean after all the exams and interviews, the papers and testing, and even after ordination, the title Reverend, and the many additional years of study and practice; you mean to tell me that after all this you still don't know the basics, the ABCs of faith?"

Poor Nicodemus—his whole reason for being, that is, his calling, is to study and teach Scripture. And yet Jesus has thoroughly confused him by challenging not only his professional authority and competence but also the purpose of his life: "I tell you these things, they are plain and right before you, and yet you don't believe; what use is there in telling you things you cannot see, the things of God?" Now, we might say that what Rev. Nicodemus needs is a good dose of humility. But Jesus says the matter is even more serious than this; Nicodemus is dead and needs a new life, a life that only God can give. And that is precisely what Jesus offers to Nicodemus. It is also what Jesus offers to us through our listening in proclamation. Listen to his words, for the One who is speaking is himself the Resurrection and Life.

Jesus says that he can speak such things, the things of God, because he himself is from God. Indeed, John has already borne witness to as much. The Word was first, as he proclaims in the prologue to the Gospel. The Word was present to God; God was present to the Word. The Word was God, in readiness for God from day one. Everything was created through him, all that exists came into being because of God's speech, and that speaking was Life, and the Life was Light to live by. And even more, says John, the Word God speaks became flesh and blood, he lived among us and in hearing him we were enabled to see the splendor of his love with our very own eyes, the truth and goodness of God with us in human form. Like Father, like Son, says John; filled to fullness and more with abundant, generous, and astonishingly amazing love. Yes, says John, God is now speaking his Life into being in the person of Jesus; and Jesus not only speaks the Word of God, he is the Word of God, so that the response of "I believe" which is intrinsic to conversing with Jesus draws us into a salvation story of which he is the Way, Truth, and Life.

What if John is showing us the salvation offered by Jesus is not a solution to our problems or an answer to our questions? What if he does not present a program filled with neatly organized principles that we can package in our sermons for our people to take home and apply to their lives? Most of all, what if Jesus does not offer a formula that can be reduced to fit on a bumper sticker, a website, or a banner at a football game? What if Jesus offers instead his own God given witness in the Spirit? Jesus says that just as Moses lifted up a serpent in the wilderness as a sign for disbelieving and disobedient Israel, so he, the Son of Man, is sent by God to judge the world in being lifted on a cross so that we will listen to God who is speaking all things to life.

As we listen to God speaking in Jesus and entrust ourselves and our destiny to him, we exhibit our truest and deepest answer to God's Word. In recognizing God as our loving Father who addresses us through the Word in Jesus, we are taken up by the witness of the Spirit into the life of God's children. And if you are like me and our clergy friend Nicodemus you are probably thinking to yourself, what is this all about? Why should people as professional as us, as educated as us, as morally upright as us, or as spiritually enlightened as us do such a thing with our lives? Give me a book to read, a course to take, a seminar to attend, a video to watch, a PowerPoint presentation to download, an iPhone application to use, a Tweeter to follow. But don't ask me to turn my life and destiny over to someone else.

Now, you may be wondering if I am suggesting that our education and training are for nothing and that we should give up reading, studying and thinking. This is not the case. According to the witness of John, unless our love of learning is an expression of desire for God, in loving attentiveness to the One whose Word is the source and goal of all things, then it is in vain. This is because our pride prevents us from discerning the witness of the Spirit who is calling us into loving communion with the Father.

But when we do listen in and with the witness of the Spirit, who is the original and best hearer of the Word, we are lovingly drawn away from our preoccupation with ourselves, from what we can know and understand on our own, from the constant self analysis that causes us to become fixated with our brokenness and sin, and most of all, from what we think we "need" to do to make things right with God and the world. In other words: "What must I do to inherit eternal life?" On the other hand, when we listen in and with the attentiveness of the Spirit we hear the Word who is the source and shape of our life in God.

According to the testimony of John, the Spirit's witness to the Word makes known just how much God loved the world: that he sent his Son, his one and only. This is why: so that no one need be destroyed, and so that we, and in fact, anyone, entrusting themselves to him can have a full, abundantly whole and lasting life. We must never forget that God did not go to all this trouble, sending his only Son, just to point an accusing finger at us, just to tell us and the world how bad we are and what we must do to fix things. He came to save us by turning our attention from ourselves to him; to free us from the self-absorption that prevents us from hearing him speak with such authority that the dead are raised to life. It is only because we refuse to enter into life that we are already under the dominion of death. And yet, even in our failure to listen, God continues to call us in the Spirit's witness of loving attentiveness to the Word.

This is the judgment, the crisis of listening evoked by Jesus. It is not a crisis of knowledge; that we need to know more. It is not a crisis of morality; that we need to do more. It is not a crisis of authority; that we need to be more. It is not a crisis of performance; that we need to prove ourselves more. It is not a crisis of psychology; that we need to experience more. What is revealed through the whole story of Christ's life, death, and resurrection is this: apart from the mystery of love which the Father and Son share in and with the Spirit, we are unable to hear the Word who is Life himself.

Martin Luther as Exemplary Listener to the Word

The preaching and ministry of Martin Luther provides an example of listening in the Spirit's witness to the Word of Christ who is revealed in Scripture. Luther's passionate desire for scriptural reform of the church included a high regard for the necessity of remembering the wisdom of the Christian past.[8] Scripture and tradition are two sides of the same process of hearing and speaking the Word of God; the story of the church through time is the practice of listening, interpreting, and speaking the word of Scripture through which the Spirit gives birth to the life of faith, hope, and love. Luther therefore asserts the Christian Church, as a visible assembly, "is the Mother that begets and bears every Christian through the Word of God…where Christ is not preached, there is no Holy Spirit to create, call, and gather the Christian Church, and outside it no one can come to the Lord Christ."[9]

Luther's vision may help us to understand better how listening affects the obedience of faith that forms the church as a people who in their witness are themselves an echo of God speaking.[10] Proclamation is the center of all the church does and the central point of its theology and mission. The oral address of the gospel, in its divine and human forms, communicates the Father's gracious promises in Christ for the salvation of the world. In this particular form of Christian speech, which is derived from Scripture and enlivened by the Spirit, Christ gives himself and his gifts, the "joyful exchange" of his righteousness for our sinfulness that opens the "gates of heaven" to all the continued gracious workings of God.[11]

According to Luther, the preaching of the gospel is the message of the cross and resurrection which is heard and received through faith that comes by hearing the Word of Christ. This is the message of Christ and what he has done which, by the work of the Spirit, snatches listeners away from themselves to participate in the gracious reign of the Lord who has acted on their behalf.[12] Bringing together the cross and life in the presence of God defines the distinctiveness for Luther of Christian praise and adoration. This is simply faith being freely itself before God, while the fellowship and life that flow from this are described as a way of living toward God with thanks and gratitude.[13]

> Faith is a living, daring confidence in God's grace, so sure and certain that a man would stake his life on it a thousand times. This confidence in God's grace and knowledge of it makes men glad and bold and happy in dealing with God and with all his creatures; and this is the work of the Holy Ghost in faith. Hence a man is ready and glad, without compulsion, to do good to everyone, to serve everyone, to suffer everything, in love and praise of God, who has shown him this grace.[14]

Luther's commitment to the oral nature of the Word was such that he devoted himself with single-minded purpose to breaking open the words of Scripture so that the gospel, the voice of God who speaks in the risen Christ through the power of the Spirit, might be a shout of praise in the church to reach the very heart and soul of its listeners—faith that comes by hearing the Word.[15]

This practice of listening, or prayerful attentiveness to God, is described beautifully by Luther in a sermon from John 14 in which he articulates this vision of the living presence of Christ in Christian worship affecting the union of himself and the church.

> When Christ commands His apostles to proclaim is Word and carry on His work, we hear and see Him Himself, and thus also God the Father; for they publish and proclaim no other Word than that which they heard from His lips, and they point solely to Him...the Word is handed down to us through the agency of true bishops, pastors, and preachers, who received it from the apostles. In this way all sermons delivered in Christendom must proceed from this one Christ.... For it is all from God, who condescends to enter the mouth of each Christian or preacher and says: "If you want to see Me or My work, look to Christ; if you want to hear Me; hear this Word"...there you may say without hesitation: "Today I beheld God's Word and work. Yes, I saw and heard God Himself preaching and baptizing." To be sure, the tongue, the voice, the hands, etc., are those of a human being; but the Word and the ministry are really the Divine Majesty Himself.[16]

Learning to Listen

Luther considered such confidence to speak of God as a gift of the Spirit which is received in and leads toward responding to the words of Scripture. Such listening is attentive to God's Word in Christ who, as judgment and mercy, restores us to our primary vocation of praise and adoration.[17] For this reason, the path that leads to truthful speech requires a willingness to be transformed and attentive to God's Word by allowing Scripture to interpret our lives rather than standing over Scripture as its judge. Luther's *Preface to the Wittenberg Edition of Luther's German Writings* invites students to cultivate the habit of prayerful, receptive study: "This is the way taught by holy king David (and doubtlessly used by all the patriarchs and prophets) in the one hundred-nineteenth Psalm. They are *Oratio* (Prayer), *Meditatio* (Meditation), *Tentatio* (Temptation)"[18]

Luther was convinced that every student of Scripture should meditate daily on Psalm 119, the Psalm sung daily in the monastic liturgy of the hours. The prayer of God's people, or the communion of saints, is the primary context in which our tongues are healed and we ourselves are changed by grace through faith to speak for the praise and glory of God.[19] "My lips will pour forth praise, for you teach me your statutes. My tongue will sing of your word, for all your commandments are right" (Ps 119:171-172 ESV).

Prayer: Students of Scripture pray humbly for the Holy Spirit to give understanding and strength in learning to wait on God who mediates his presence through Christ's promises to the church. This was exemplified by David who prayed "teach me Lord, instruct me, lead me, show me," to allow God as the true teacher of Scripture to speak the work of salvation in his life.[20]

Meditation: Students must also meditate prayerfully on Scripture, immersing themselves in the language of the Word through the practices of the church that make room for God's saving presence. Meditation requires repetition and careful attention to the pattern and wisdom of biblical speech. As we offer our loving attention to the Word the Spirit is uniting us with the Word.[21]

Temptation: Temptation is the touchstone that cultivates knowing and understanding the Word. This is an external experience, which when suffered, demonstrates the credibility and power of God's Word. Although public exposure to the Word provokes assaults and afflictions from the powers that struggle against Christ's reign, these are the conditions through which God shapes true hearers and teachers of Scripture.

True preachers and teachers posses a love of God's Word which is expressed in faithful listening. On the one hand, they are capable of speaking to young, imperfect Christians; on the other hand, they are also capable of addressing those who are wise and mature. Humbly listening to the Word cultivates the kind of practical wisdom required for discerning the proper way of speaking within the diverse conditions of life: to the young, old, sick, healthy, strong, energetic, lazy, simple and wise. Above all else, preachers must guard against the temptation of pride; against thinking too highly of their own wisdom and seeking the praise of others, since according to the book of Scripture only God is worthy of praise: "God opposes the proud, but gives grace to the humble."[22]

Luther's invitation to the study of Scripture was shaped by monastic spirituality and a deep knowledge of Christian doctrine. These habits infused his study with prayerful attentiveness to the Word who creates living faith and strengthens Christian identity.[23] This task, however, was not simply for the individual. Rather, its goal was the unity of God and God's people, a fellowship of faith and love which is constituted by the practices or "marks" created by careful listening to the Word.[24] The church, then, is an assembly whose worship is the essence of its life as a community which believes in Christ and has received the gift of the Spirit. The Spirit sanctifies the church daily through the forgiveness of sins and the putting off, purging, and putting to death of sins from which they are called, transformed, and made holy.[25]

Most important for Luther is that Christian people have the Word of God, the public proclamation of the gospel of Jesus Christ: "We are talking about the outward word, orally preached by human beings like you and me. Christ has left this behind as an outward sign by which one is to recognize his church or his Christian holy people in the world"[26] In addition to the external, orally proclaimed Word by which the church is formed and recognized in its activities of hearing, believing and confessing there are corresponding actions - Baptism, the Lord's Supper, the power of the keys or community discipline, the church offices and ordination, worship and instruction, and a life of discipleship in suffering and temptation.[27] David Yeago comments on the marks of the church,

> For Luther, these practices not only identify the church, they constitute it as church, as the holy Christian people. Luther speaks of these seven practices as..."holy things." Luther is saying, in effect, that these seven practices are true "miracle-working" holy things through which the Spirit fashions a holy people in the world. The church is sanctified by holy practices, which make up its common life through which the inward gifts of faith and the Holy Spirit are bestowed on the gathered people.[28]

The true character of the church consists of hearing the Word of God in the knowing act of faith that constitutes the communion of saints. As a creature of the Word, the church is holy, though not because it claims holiness as its own attribute. Holiness is instead attributed to the sanctifying work of the Spirit who confirms the church in its listening to the gospel, its responsive affirmation of the First Commandment, and its glad submission to the Rule of Christ by which it participates in God's life and work in the world.[29]

Proclaiming the Gospel

Luther's preface to *A Brief Instruction on What to Look for and Expect in the Gospels* provides a concise summary of the gospel narrative:

> Gospel is and should be nothing less than a discourse or story about Christ ... Thus the gospel is and should be nothing less than a chronicle, a story, a narrative about Christ, telling who he is, what he did and what he suffered ... For at its briefest, the Gospel is a discourse about Christ, that he is the Son of God and was made man for us, that he died and was raised, that he has been established as Lord, of all things.[30]

The gospel is a book of promise; when opened, read, and proclaimed, Christ himself comes to listeners just as listeners are brought to Christ. Robert Jenson comments on this conviction: "For the preaching of the gospel is nothing less than Christ coming to us, or we being brought to him...Christ speaks in preaching; and it is in rendering the person of Christ, the living Word, that God is his own Word, the 'good things' in God's Word are God himself; moreover, we are the 'good things' we hear in the gospel, by attending to them with faith we are shaped to what we hear."[31] For Luther, the most fitting response to the gift of Christ—as Savior and Lord—is the obedience of faith, which is expressed by loving neighbors in the manner God has dealt with humanity in calling the church into being.[32]

For Luther, preaching takes place within a context of listening, believing, and obeying. Preaching announces the good report that has been heard of the risen Lord who rules over and in the midst of a battle between God and the Devil for the life of the world. The focus of this hearing and speaking is the action of God in Christ who speaks through the scriptural witness to continue his work of creation and salvation which is interpreted in light of Christian doctrine and life.[33] Confident in the power of the gospel to soften even the most hardened hearts, Luther believed the witness of the Spirit effects the joy of listening in all those "who sing, thank and praise God, and are glad forever, if only they believe firmly and remain steadfast in faith."[34]

Nehemiah 8: The Joy of Listening

In the Gospel of John, our Lord offers a concise way of understanding the story of God and his people: "You search the scriptures, because you think that in them you have eternal life; and it is they that bear witness to me" (John 5:39 ESV). To help my students to understand more clearly the truth of these words, I have moved my preaching classes from an assigned seminar room to a seminary chapel. I have been pleased to see how this change of venue, which locates our work in a very different kind of home, has actually contributed to a change in students' outlook, attitude, and performance in their preaching. They realize that we are not simply looking at a text to find an idea or two that might be relevant, nor are we seeking to dig out some principles which can be applied to see if they "work." Rather, our intention is proclaiming the Word of God as an act of praise which is engendered by attentiveness to the words of Scripture for discerning the Spirit's witness to Christ.

The chapel where we meet has a large, prominent Baptismal font, a Communion Table, a Pulpit flanked by a tall wooden cross, Icons of Christ and the Apostles Peter and Paul, and a large, stained-glass window with the symbol of a Dove. Perhaps I can summarize in just a few words what I am trying to communicate in response to my students' attempts to make sense of Scripture and preaching: "We are listening to God." I am continually amazed at how these few words are often the most important I may speak during the course of an entire semester: I have begun to suspect that for some students my words function as permission to break with the conventional wisdom of our time by listening to God rather than talking about whatever may be on their minds. My hope is that God will equip men and women to be faithful hearers of the Word in the manner of Ezra, of whom the Book of Nehemiah states: "For Ezra had prepared his heart to seek the Law of the Lord and to do it" (Ezra 7:10 KJV).

The story of God's rebuilding of Jerusalem from ruin, of God's restoration of Israel after years in exile, is a major expression of evangelical faith in the biblical witness to the God of Israel and Jesus Christ. The story begins with Nehemiah, the cupbearer to the King and a devout man who grieved, wept and prayed over Israel's condition, calling upon God to remember his promises, to be steadfast in his covenant love, to be gracious and merciful towards his sinful people. With confidence in God that was grounded in the story of God's faithfulness in the past, Nehemiah reverently addressed the "great and awesome God" to intercede on behalf of his people:

> Remember the instruction you gave you servant Moses, saying: "If you are unfaithful, I will scatter you among the nations, but if you return to me and obey my commands, then even if your exiled people are at the farthest horizon, I will gather them from there and bring them to the place I have chosen as a dwelling for my Name." (Neh 1:8-10 NIV)

The first seven chapters of Nehemiah tell the story of returning and rebuilding in just fifty-two days during which Nehemiah brought organization, visibility, and security to a community of returning exiles. At the same time, the story makes it clear that Nehemiah is neither the source nor the center of this action but is only its servant and instrument. It is the living God whose mercy and power brought an end to exile, just as it is the living God who calls and welcomes home a displaced and disobedient people who have known more than their share of hardship, suffering, and disappointment.

I think there are many pastors, congregations, and Christian people who live in exile today. They have not been physically displaced to another country, nor have they been dislocated from their church buildings. For that matter, they may even be numerically, financially, and organizationally successful. However, in spite of such culturally approved outward signs many still feel lost and abandoned in a North American church that continues to forget the God whom we have been called to know, love, and serve; a church, in both liberal and conservative expressions, continues to distance itself from the identity which is given through the work of the Holy Spirit in the ministry of Word and Sacrament. A church, in both mainline and evangelical traditions, where many feel like strangers rather than friends who have been addressed by the Word and invited to the Lord's Table. A church where many feel more at home in the world which has set itself against the will of God revealed in a crucified Lord who rules heaven and earth through the power and wisdom of a Cross.

This contemporary accommodation of Christianity is directly related to amnesia, or a deep loss of shared memory and life. This forgetfulness has contributed to a widespread loss of prayerful, reverent attention to the Word of God which is our most precious resource for sustaining Christian identity in identity-denying times and places. And this loss of vital memory, language, and life as God's people has contributed to a pervasive sense of homelessness among Christian people who struggle to be faithful to their calling in an increasingly indifferent and even hostile world. But a church that has lost its memory of the past can only wander about aimlessly in the present and despair of the future. For only when we recover our identity from the past are we able to discern our vocation in the present while listening to the Word and Spirit who call us into the future.

It saddens me to see pastors and people just barely hanging on, overwhelmed by the chaos of our culture and discouraged to the point of despair by the decline of the church. Many folks seem to be grasping for anything or anyone who seems to have an answer, a solution, a new idea, the latest method or program that is guaranteed to work. And so we have 10 steps, 3 points, 6 proofs, and more principles of purpose than we know what to do with. And then there are requests such as, "Please find us a young pastor with children who will preach with charisma, has a great personality, and will attract new members with his or her charm!" I am sure you know what I mean.

Perhaps the greatest need our homelessness has created is a need to remember the scriptural witness to the story of God who creates and saves—in other words, a story of homecoming. The story of Nehemiah and Ezra brings to remembrance News that is good and which brings great joy. But this is also news of what God continues to do among our Sunday morning assemblies, weekly gatherings that are homecomings of sorts. In these gatherings God renews our life in the covenant made through the calling of Israel, the sending of Jesus, and the outpouring of the Spirit who builds up the church to be a living Temple in which the living Word dwells.

These weekly gatherings are sacred, as are all assemblies in which the Word is heard and a Holy Meal consumed in communion with the Risen Lord who speaks with such power that his voice can raise the dead. And these gatherings are invitations to come home, assemblies in which we are blessed by the living Word whose work is to establish God's rule of love, joy, peace, and goodness in the Holy Spirit.

But the rebuilding of the wall was only a prelude to the restoration and re-construction of a people which is the work of the Word and Spirit. Ezra opened the book in the sight of the people and when he did so the people stood listening attentively with reverence and love. Perhaps this means the Torah was held up at this point, just as it is in the synagogue today; just as Scripture is held up in many congregations when it is read, "The Word of God for the people of God," and the people respond, "Thanks be to God." This is not a meaningless ritual. This is a liturgical activity, not as in either high or low church, but as in the work of the people for the praise of God: "Ezra praised the Lord, the great God; and all the people lifted their hands and responded, "Amen, Amen!" Then they bowed their heads and worshipped the LORD with their faces to the ground" (Neh 8:6 NIV). But this is not merely a matter of preaching style or technique, but rather has everything to do with the identity of God and our identity as God's people, chosen and beloved in Christ, our life ordered by the Word of the Father who speaks all things in the Spirit's power.

This is why Ezra, the faithful scribe, did not simply talk about the Bible. His preaching was not the transmission of information followed with a time for mo-tivation. Nor did Ezra give a list of things to know and things to do for "practical application" which, in the end, still leaves us in control but with little room for God. Ezra's reading and speaking were acts of worship, listening to God and speaking of God, so that by hearing and believing the congregation was moved as one in offering thanks and praise to God. What we see in this story is the con-gregation of God's people hearing and receiving the Word with joy. They were "all ears" as they listened to God calling them out of the past into a future which the Spirit was unfolding in their midst. As Jesus announced in his first sermon at Nazareth after reading from the prophet Isaiah, "Today this is fulfilled in your hearing." The power of this story is the Spirit's witness to the Word who creates and redeems all things. And this story is still read, proclaimed, and heard as a primary means of grace by which God welcomes his people home.

What a great story about a great God. In a situation that gives every indica-tion of God's abandonment the Word is opened, read, and spoken in a manner that satisfies the deepest longings of all who listen. The lively, life-giving Word recalls the story of God and his people that unfolds from creation to the Exodus from Egypt. This is a story which tells of great love lavished upon a poor, little community; a story which is capable of softening the hardest of hearts and turn-ing sadness to joy; a story which inspires wonder and amazement in the pres-ence of such astonishing goodness and mercy. To hear this story evokes great joy in response to God's extravagant love that overflows in sharing generously with the poor and needy among our neighbors. And the practice of assembling for the particular purpose of listening to the Word continues into the present. God is still with us through the ministry of the Word, filling us with his joy as we participate in his mission to the world.

What a strong word of encouragement for us! Despite our loss of memory, identity, and vitality, God continues to be with us through the faith that comes by hearing the Word. Because God has spoken in the past, we may be confident that God is speaking in the present, while the hope of final redemption calls us into a future God will continue to speak in the Spirit's power. And the Word we hear in our proclamation recalls the story in which we live, move and have our being; God speaks *us* in the Spirit's witness "today." This is us, the church, at our best when we are listening to God.

> Lord, open our hearts and minds by the power of your Holy Spirit, that, as the Scriptures are read and your Word proclaimed, we may hear with joy what you say to us today.[35]

Notes

1. Here is important to mention the following helpful works on preaching with respect to listening: Thomas G. Long, *The Witness of Preaching* (Louisville: Westminster/John Knox Press, 1989); Eugene H. Peterson, *Working the Angles: The Shape of Pastoral Integrity* (Grand Rapids: Eerdmans, 1987); Roger Van Harn, *Preacher, Can you Hear Us Listening?* (Grand Rapids: Eerdmans, 2005)

2. Nicholas Lash, *Believing Three Ways in God: A Reading of the Apostles' Creed* (Notre Dame: University of Notre Dame Press, 1993), 72-73.

3. Nicholas Lash, *Holiness, Speech, and Silence: Reflections on the Question of God* (Aldershot: Ashgate, 2004), 92, 69-90.

4. Rowan Williams, *On Christian Theology* (Oxford: Blackwell Publishers, 2000), 146-147.

5. Nicholas Lash, *The Beginning and the End of 'Religion'* (Cambridge: Cambridge University Press, 1996), 247-8.

6. Eugene H. Peterson, *Working the Angles: The Shape of Pastoral Integrity* (Grand Rapids: Eerdmans, 1987), 62-63.

7. For depicting the conversation between Jesus and Nicodemus in John 3, I have relied upon Eugene H. Peterson, *The Message: The Bible in Contemporary Language* (Colorado Springs: NavPress, 2002). While *The Message* is a helpful paraphrase, I would not recommend it as a source for use in serious exegetical work.

8. Cited in Heiko A. Oberman, *The Dawn of the Reformation: Essays in Late Medieval and Early Reformation Thought* (Grand Rapids: Eerdmans, 1992), 285; see the discussion in Paul Hinlicky "The Lutheran Dilemma," *Pro Ecclesia* 8:4 (Fall, 1999), 394-8; part of this section is revised material from my *Sacred Rhetoric: Preaching as a Theological and Pastoral Practice* (Grand Rapids: Eerdmans, 2005).

9. Cited in Hinlicky, "The Lutheran Dilemma," 400.

10. Ola Tjorhom, "The Church as the Place of Salvation: On the Interrelation between Justification and Ecclesiology," *Pro Ecclesia* 9:3 (Summer, 2000), 294-6.

11. See the discussion in Fred W. Meuser, "Luther as preacher of the Word of God" in ed. Donald K. McKim, *The Cambridge Companion to Martin Luther* (Cambridge: Cambridge University Press, 2003; 136-48; Richard Lischer, "Preface," *Faith and Freedom: An Invitation to the Writings of Martin Luther* (eds. John F. Thornton and Susan B. Varenne; New York: Vintage Books, 2002) xiii-xxvii; Dennis Ngien, "Theology of Preaching in Martin Luther," *Themelios* 28:2 (Spring, 2003): 28-48.

12. Gerhard Sauter, *Gateways to Dogmatics: Reasoning Theologically for the Life of the Church* (Grand Rapids: Eerdmans, 2003), 124.

13. Hardy and Ford, *Praising and Knowing God*, 64.

14. Cited in Hardy and Ford, *Praising and Knowing God*, 64.

15.David C. Steinmetz, "Luther and Formation in Faith," *Educating People of Faith: Exploring the History of Jewish and Christian Communities* (ed. John Van Engen; Grand Rapids: Eerdmans, 2004), 252-62; Heiko Oberman, "Preaching and the Word in the Reformation" *Theology Today*, 18:1 (April, 1961): 16-29; John W. O'Malley, S.J., "Luther the Preacher," *The Martin Luther Quincentennial* (ed. Gerhard Dunnhaupt; Detroit: Wayne State University Press, 1985), 3-16; Stephen H. Webb, *The Divine Voice: Christian Proclamation and the Theology of Sound* (Grand Rapids: Brazos Press, 2004), 141-6.

16. Martin Luther, *Martin Luther's Basic Theological Writings* (ed. Timothy Lull; Minneapolis: Fortress Press, 1989), 66-67.

17. Hutter, *Bound to Be Free*, 179-80.

18. Luther, *Luther's Writings*, 283-8. Here I am indebted to the discussion in Reinhard Hutter, *Suffering Divine Things: Theology as Church Practice* (Grand Rapids: Eerdmans, 2000) 72-5, and David C. Steinmetz, *Memory and Mission*, 164-73.

19. Hutter, *Bound to Be Free*, 180.

20. Luther, *Luther's Wrtings*, 66.

21. Luther, *Luther's Wrtings*, 66.

22. Luther, *Luther's Wrtings*, 67-68.

23. Oberman, *Martin Luther*, 172; see also Heiko A. Oberman, *The Two Reformations: The Journey from the Last Days to the New World*, (ed. Donald Weinstein; New Haven and London: Yale University Press, 2003), 40-43; Hagen, *Luther's Approach to Scripture*, x-xi.

24. Hutter, *Suffering Divine Things*, 75-76.

25. Luther, *Luther's Wrtings*, 540-1.

26. Luther, *Luther's Wrtings*, 545.

27. Luther, *Luther's Wrtings*, 545-63.

28. David S. Yeago, "A Christian Holy People: Martin Luther on Salvation and the Church," *Modern Theology* 13:1 (January, 1997), 110.

29. Christoph Schwobel, "The Creature of the Word: Recovering the Ecclesiology of the Reformers," *On Being the Church: Essays on the Christian Community* (eds. Colin E. Gunton and Daniel W. Hardy Edinburgh: T&T Clark, 1989), 118-21; Yeago, "A Christian Holy People: Martin Luther on Salvation and the Church," 118; David S. Yeago "Ecclesia Sancta, Ecclesia Peccatrix: The Holiness of the Church in Martin Luther's Theology," *Pro Ecclesia* 9:3 (Summer, 2000), 352-4.

30. Luther, *Luther's Writings,* 117-24.

31. Jenson, "Luther's contemporary theological significance," 283.

32. Luther, *Luther's Writings,* 108.

33. Hinlicky, "The Lutheran Dilemma," 383-4.

34. Luther, *Luther's Wrtings*, 27.

35. *The United Methodist Hymnal* (Nashville: The United Methodist Publishing House, 1989), 6.

Chapter 5

The Listening Leader

David Drury

The line stretches around the block. The leader has to listen to every single person in the line today, one after the other. Some have a major crisis to deal with, the kind of problems that will take a great amount of empathy and compassion. Others have an argument to settle with their neighbor or co-worker. One guy claims his business partner bilked him. Another says her husband cheated on her. One couple can't seem to control their young son anymore. For every draining, authentic crisis that requires a major emotional involvement there are ten petty complaints that irritate the leader and require way too much time. The leader doesn't know which is worse. These are the demands on the lives of most leaders. It's why leaders love to hear the story of Moses and Jethro in Exodus 18 which recounts this kind of scene and offers a solution.

A Visit from the Consultant

Moses sits in his chair all day long as the grievances are brought to him. His schedule is packed from dawn to dusk, and he is understandably weary. That's when Jethro the Consultant[1] gets to work (okay, it's his father-in-law, but he sure could have charged a good consultant fee for this one). Jethro gives Moses some priceless wisdom. Many have called the advice of this consultant "The Jethro Principle," including John Maxwell.[2] The wise words melt like chocolate on the tongues of overworked leaders.

The basic message Jethro brings is this: "You need to develop other leaders to listen to the complaints beneath you, so that only the most important issues reach your chair, Moses!" Or at least that's the message that has been told us.

It's true, in part. But it misses half the message of the passage. The Jethro Principle as told by so many only reveals part of the point. The other half has to do with everyone else but Jethro and Moses.

Leaders know what Moses' shoes feel like. We too have been overworked and underpaid, over-demanded and under-appreciated, stretched too thin with a schedule packed too full. We've run out of shoulders to offer other people to cry on, and we're not sure if our "I feel your pain" expression seems as authentic as it did when we started out. Not only this, but we're tired of hearing the whining of the leaders under us. If they are volunteers, we think: "Just do what I trained you to do." If they are staff, we think: "Just do the job you're paid for." We don't like to admit we think such things, but we do. As did Moses, and even God. A common description used by scripture for those complaining people following Moses around in the wilderness is "stiff-necked" (e.g., Exod 32:9 NIV). So when we bump into a few people on our teams with stiff necks of their own, Moses feels our pain.

So we take the advice we're told Jethro gave and apply it. Jethro's advice to Moses led him to divide up the entire people of Israel into sub-groupings: tens, fifties, hundreds, and thousands. Those with "simple cases" brought those to the judges of the smaller groups above them but those with "difficult cases" might bring them all the way to Moses, if the judge over them couldn't figure out what to do. Our court systems today roughly reflect this system, although in Jethro's plan, Moses, who functioned like a one-man supreme court, would bring the ones he couldn't figure out right to God. This may sound a bit like God's pyramid scheme but it worked. Cases were heard and Moses didn't burn out.

So, what are we missing? How have we missed part of the point of the Jethro story? The reason is that we leaders automatically put ourselves into Moses' shoes and think about all the advantages for us. We are eager to free up more time, and to limit the amount of trivial matters that come to our attention. But a closer look at what Jethro really said shows so much more than that motivation.

"What are you doing?" Jethro was astonished to see the scene of scores and scores of people waiting to get a hearing with Moses. Each morning, he discovers, this happens. Before dawn they line up like extreme Christmas shoppers, and Moses listens to cases all day long, and if he doesn't reach everyone then they go home to sleep, coming back the next day. Those that are most committed might hold their place in line all night.

Jethro not only points out the toll this is taking on Moses, but stresses how this isn't right for the people. "Why do you sit alone as judge, while all these people stand around you from morning till evening?" (Exod 18:14b NIV). Put yourself in the shoes of those people standing around and your perspective of the Jethro Principle shifts. Jethro confronts like any good consultant would—because needs are being unmet. He implies that the people are going home unsatisfied in the current system. They aren't even being heard. We often hear the point as "Moses, you will not last in this system," but what Jethro said was "You *and these people*...will only wear yourselves out" (Exod 18:18 NIV, emphasis mine).

And this is the point we miss. Yes, we leaders are over-worked, but our goal in life is not to have a good working environment for ourselves. Our comfort is not the mission. That's why we need to invert the Jethro Principle. It's not a system of delegation; it's a system to ensure people are heard. It ensured people had someone that would listen to their concerns and if they were over their head, entrust it to the leader over them.

Seth Godin's basic question is, "What does it take to create a movement?" This is a question true leaders ask. We don't want just to lead an organization; we don't merely want the position, the power, the parking space. We want to see a movement unleashed that is truly bigger than us. Godin answers his question by saying, "Great leaders create movements by empowering the tribe to communicate. They establish the foundation for people to make connections, as opposed to commanding people to follow them."[3] The famous consultant Seth Godin didn't invent this idea of empowering tribes to communicate, of course. Jethro the Consultant did. And when Moses followed the advice and learned to listen strategically, all twelve tribes that were empowered to communicate.

My Door is Always Open

I have a pad of extremely small sticky notes someone gave me, perhaps an inch square. In tiny 6-point font they read: "If you have a complaint to submit please write it in full on this paper." Even the most fine print couldn't fit more than five or so words on the notes. This is how we come across as leaders. We send mixed messages. We say we want input and feedback, but we make it difficult. And when input is actually given we often respond with general defensiveness or a passive aggressive attack on the complaint itself.

When I have worked formal processes for feedback with my staff and leaders, I am always struck by a handful of people who note that they don't feel I'm accessible enough or that are worried I push back on criticism. I consider myself to be very accessible and approachable, and I've even been praised by many for it, but there are always some who feel a barrier. It is my constant struggle to remain open and use such anonymous feedback to help build open relationships on the team. However, when I read such feedback I do get defensive at first. Like you, I think, "My door is always open." Someone could come to me with anything. But if I'm not inviting feedback, if I'm not creating space and conversations that invite critique, then the door to my office may be open, but the door to my heart and mind is not.

Two different friends of mine, one man and one woman, both wanted to become better preachers. They were early in their ministries and didn't have many opportunities to preach. However, I did hear both preach and in each instance I made a list of things I thought could help them in their content and delivery, and some general tips for preparation. In each case, I put the list into a file in my office with their name on it. I wasn't going to schedule a meeting to give them a truck-load of critique out of the blue. It needed to be invited.

In the case of the man, I kept the feedback sheet for more than a year, then stumbled upon it, and threw it away—realizing that though he had many times told me he felt called to preach, he had never once asked me for specific feed-back. I'm not sure he's much better at preaching now than then.

In the case of the woman, I kept the feedback sheet for many months, and began to worry that it would also go unused. Eventually when she made a re-mark to me about wanting to preach more and improve, I confronted her, saying: "You know, you say that but I'm not sure you mean it. If you did, you would really be asking people for feedback and critique." So later on she did just that, setting up meetings with me and dozens of others over many months to learn more about the process and become better at preaching...which she did. Much better.

You can't just say your door is open. Critical conversation and formal processes must be developed so that we as leaders show that our hearts and minds open, not just our office doors.

Openness and the Red Cross

It was hard to think of an organization more universally recognized for benevo-lent work than the Red Cross. Since it was founded in 1881 by Clara Barton, it has been recognized as a trusted and neutral organization in areas of strife and crisis worldwide. But during the crisis following Hurricane Katrina the Red Cross faced something new: a wave of criticism for their purportedly failing response. After the waves and rainfall hit the Gulf Coast and, in particular, New Orleans, a groundswell of detractors on blogs, discussion boards and social net-working sites also hit the reputation of the much-respected organization.

So the Red Cross hired Wendy Harmon as their first social media manager. In her book *Open Leadership*, Charlene Li recounts Harmon's simple explana-tion: "I was hired in part because the leaders knew that people were saying real-ly bad things about the Red Cross's response to Katrina...and they wanted someone to make it stop."[4]

This is often the response of organizations to the new, open world the inter-net has fostered. Leaders want to protect the name and reputation of their organ-izations—deleting anything negative and limiting access. In fact, the Red Cross had even blocked employee access to sites like MySpace and Facebook so they couldn't even see the criticism, much less interact with it.

As Harmon investigated things, however, her approach was more nuanced. Instead of merely managing the negative she sought to release the positive to overwhelm the negative. Thousands of people had great things to say about the Red Cross, and only a few were critical. She addressed each negative post pa-tiently and extensively, but didn't make that the focus. She began, rather, on a campaign to get local Red Cross chapters more engaged online and more vocal in their support and mobilization to help. By amplifying the need of readiness and response online, the Red Cross went from an organization with many de-tractors online, to one where most posts in reaction to a crisis need would sound more like "My bags are packed and I'm ready to go."

Harmon knew she was on to something when the fundraising started to shift. When retailer Target was empowered to run a Facebook-based fundraising campaign, the Red Cross was able to use their social media leverage to raise $793,000 from that effort—all on Facebook alone.

Another mega-crisis arrived with the Haiti Earthquake. But the Red Cross was now a new organization in terms of empowering openness and online participation. Instead of worry about detractors, they were mobilizing involvement. In January 2010, they activated mobile giving and raised $10 million in just three days, driven by an easy donation on Facebook and Twitter. Charlene Li summarizes this transformation: "By letting go and embracing social technologies, the Red Cross was better able to complete its mission."

Letting go in order to listen is so hard, however. Leaders often go through much to get control of something. Many of us inherited a situation so out of control that a strong hand is needed to get things running again. Others of us built something from the ground up—and letting go might mean others will destroy what we worked so hard to build. Ralph Moore notes this tension throughout scripture and calls it letting go of the ring (like the challenge of Frodo in *The Lord of the Rings*).

> As you move on through scripture, you come upon Moses forsaking the riches of Egypt to serve God. You find Daniel, abandoning potential success in the king's house, by eating the way God commanded in the Law. You discover young Jeremiah leaving his occupation, and Amos selling his fig farm to go serve the Lord. Shadrach, Meshach and Abednego not only let go of the ring of power and position in Babylon, they laid their lives on the line when they refused to worship the statue of the king.... Letting go is hard. But it's the only way to success.[5]

There are many factors to letting go by listening, but without letting go the movement is never unleashed. If you only do what you can do then all that will be done is within your own reach and power. We leaders intuitively know that we need to empower others to do much more—to extend much farther than our own reach alone. There are many moments where a challenge to listen more is needed, but perhaps none are more palpable than three we should investigate now. Good leaders listen while deciding, before communicating, and in helping others change spiritually.

Leaders Listen Before Deciding

Decision-making is one of the most difficult facets of leadership to keep open. Leaders are hired or appointed for roles of decision-making. Groups and boards are elected to make decisions. Granting authority is merely giving someone the gift and responsibility to decide for you. This is true for leaders above you or those you delegate decision-making authority to under you. Napoleon once said: "Nothing is more difficult, and therefore more precious, than to be able to decide."

Why would we open up the decision making process to those that do not have the authority nor necessarily the wisdom and experience to make decisions? Leaders know the answers are ownership and innovation.

John Maxwell has many times reminded us of the leadership proverb: "If you think you're leading and no one is following you, then you're only taking a walk."[6] You can make all the decisions you want but if no one follows you down a decision's path, then the decision, no matter how wise, is ineffective. Making decisions is not just a matter of executing; it's a matter of involvement. Many leaders pride themselves on their decisiveness, scoffing at what they see as waffling weakness in other leaders. While there is truth to that, decisiveness should come at the moment of *final* decisions. Decisiveness reflects unwavering commitment once the decision is made, but it doesn't imply that you don't involve many in giving input before the decision is made. Think of it this way: Leadership is facilitating the process of decision-making and then decisively pursuing the decision's path.

Increasing participation in making decisions also improves the innovation, not just involvement. Followers can see through a leader whose mind is made up but who is merely conducting an elaborate ownership process whereby they are or coerced into agreeing. Good leaders know that if they really open up their process, some of the best ideas come out. There are some decisions that should be centralized, but that doesn't mean that they cannot be marked by input prior to the decision. If the decision is sensitive, input may be more informal or confidential, but input should still be sought. Otherwise the leader is no longer being effective—they are merely being narcissistic: "Only I could make such a decision."

Leaders Listen Before Communicating

As a pastor, I am fond of saying, "You can't write a sermon by committee." This is a defense against those that would seek to make the preacher a puppet of the corporate strategy, or to force "preaching the announcements", that is, using the sermon to advertise for the ministries. That concern is valid. However, some experiences have led me to open up the preaching preparation process more than I ever thought I should before.

My friend and colleague Steve DeNeff, Senior Pastor of College Wesleyan Church in Marion, Indiana, is the consummate preacher of my denomination. Many lead pastors at churches consider themselves primarily visionaries, or people developers, or staff-managers. One well-known pastor calls himself the "Lead Architect" of his church and another I've met calls himself the "Spiritual Gardener" of his congregation. Well, if Steve had his druthers he would just be the "Preacher." Preaching is what he does first, last, and in-between everything else. In a somewhat old-school fashion, he hides away in a room with musty commentaries begging for a Word from the Lord in prayer.

However, this process is not closed to others. Little acts open up the communication process. He asks college students what they have going on in their lives in order to influence his selection of upcoming series. He gathers select groups of people to listen to their hunch on what the church needs to hear and what in the culture needs to be addressed. In the end, of course, only Steve writes the sermon, but before it's written, Steve is a listening leader.

This is the process of "Staying Editable." Have you ever noticed when you send a document as an e-mail attachment, it sometimes says: "Read Only"? This means that you cannot edit the document. It's coming to you done: you're only to read it, not change it. Listening leaders don't do this in what they communicate—they stay open and editable. They invite others to suggest improvements or co-opt what they've said and add to it themselves. They ask others to "reply with changes."[7]

In Li's *Open Leadership*, six kinds of openness in information sharing are outlined which would help us to examine our thinking about opening up communication processes. Li's examples and applications have to do with corporate leadership, but here I want us to translate them into the spiritual leadership context, where listening in leadership and remaining open carry even greater moral weight.[8]

Explaining: This is the process of creating buy-in for those for whom ownership is important. Much can be solved by simply explaining why things are done. More important than *what* is said is *who* it is said to and *when*. For any leader, the stages of communicating something are important. Key contributors should know the explanation far before peripheral fans or attendees. The speed with which we cycle through these circles is truncated greatly in our information age. Once upon a time you could announce something at staff meeting, make phone calls to the board the next day, send a letter to members that would arrive a few days later and then finally post it to your website a few weeks after that. Those days are gone. Timelines for communication for true ownership are compressed down into hours, perhaps minutes in some cases. Someone may be Tweeting the news from the first place it's told.

Updating: What information has been created and what actions are being taken? Many things go on in each organization that are continuations of previous decisions. Leaders must update key players along the way about shifts in the tenor of the decision. Adaptation is crucial, so while not everything must be concretized along the way. Problems develop if people don't know "how it's going now" and cannot communicate what they think of such developments.

Conversing: This involves conversations which improve the operations of an organization. By creating safe environments to share best practices and possible improvement strategies the best leaders find that they don't need to invent all solutions themselves, they merely find people to implement the best ideas that rise to the top.

Open Mic: This is a matter of encouraging participation and getting more random and heart-felt input and feedback. Watermark Church, a recent church plant in Grand Haven, Michigan, embedded a practice that encouraged random participation by opening up staff meeting each week. Anyone could show up and speak what they thought and influence the key leaders of the church and help shape its DNA. Solomon's Porch Church in Minneapolis, Minnesota has a Bible study related to the messages that will be preached in their worship gatherings. They also literally set out open microphones in their worship space so that people can engage and interact with the message.[9]

Crowdsourcing: This means solving a specific problem by empowering a larger group to tackle it together. This is just the logical technological extension of "two minds are better than one." Well, if that's true, then fifty minds are better than five and 5,000,000 are better than 500. A great example of crowdsourcing came when a 7th grade class found something on Mars that all the astronomers in the world had missed.[10] The students in Dennis Mitchell's 7th grade class at Evergreen Middleschool were looking for studying lava tubes on Mars. They did this by using the Mars Student Imaging Program, an education program designed to introduce students to the study of the universe. The students in this program actually got to command a Mars-orbiting camera to take images and then try to answer questions they had about the red planet. In this process Mr. Mitchell's class found something NASA had missed, since they directed the camera to take a photograph of a volcano on Mars that had yet to be mapped. In the process these 7th graders discovered a large cave that had yet to be seen.[11] Why did this discovery happen? Because of a type of crowdsourcing. When those with control of information release it to get more eyes on the information, then more is spotted—even with this cave where kids spotted it before scientists. It's just a matter of getting more eyes on the ball, in this case the ball is just the size of an entire planet.

Platforms: This final component of open communication involves setting standards and sharing data. When you create a space for dialogue and openness some wonderful things can happen. Many leaders are reticent to do this as they worry that can, and will, say anything. However, people are going to say anything they want whether you like it or not. The blog and social-network age enables every person on the planet with an internet connection to become their own publisher—disseminating their opinions for as many friends or readers or viewers as would enjoy knowing their opinions.

I participated in one such project for my own denomination. The Wesleyan Church has a quadrennial meeting simply called "General Conference." Before General Conference 2004, a website discussion board (back when such things were fairly novel) was started. People posted the upcoming proposals and resolutions, their opinions on upcoming votes (for elections or policies), and provided help in attending the conference, such as posting local maps that were missing on the official site. Some considered this underground effort as a threat to the leadership of the denomination because there was discussion as to which leaders should be voted in or out. However, after some debate the website was allowed to function without much direct interference, and something interesting happened. Many denominational watchers came to the site and posted their thinking, too. The discussion ended up balancing out in a quite healthy way. Even when offenses were made, there were apologies and retractions. I posted on the site all the while with my real name, and, when I attended the conference, was amazed at how many people had been tracking with the discussion. It gave an energy and excitement to that conference. The denomination has its own Facebook page where a vibrant dialogue is always taking place—given a home and even promoted by the denomination.[12]

Leaders Listen for Shifts in the Soul

Leadership in the church world is more than decision-making and communication, however. Church leaders don't deal with things, but with people—and not just people, but the *souls* of those people. Why? Because in our economy the bottom line is the eternal soul. Nicholas Berdyaev said, "In a certain sense, every single human soul has more meaning and value than the whole of history with its empires, its wars and revolutions, its blossoming and fading civilizations."[13]

At my church we are rediscovering what Eugene Peterson calls "the Pastoral work of the cure of souls." He claims that many are on this same journey. "One by one, pastors are rejecting the job description that has been handed to them and are taking on this new one, or, as it turns out, the old one that has been in use for most of the Christian centuries."[14] Listening to the soul is a growing part of what we are engaging in as we do our work. This has started with our Elders and Pastors, whom C.S. Lewis called, "[t]hose particular people within the whole church who have been set aside to look after what concerns us as creatures who are going to live forever."[15] Indeed, we are set aside for that task, to listen to what shifts are already happening in the soul—and even more to listen to what shifts the Spirit would lead people to make—what we might recall as "conviction."

However the task of listening to shifts in the soul is one given to all Christians, not just professional ministers. And of course, pastors themselves need those who would listen to their souls. Eugene Peterson sums it up this way: "The doctor who is his own doctor has a fool for a doctor.... If those entrusted with the care of the body cannot be trusted to look after their own bodies, far less can those entrusted with the care of souls look after their own souls, which are even more complex than bodies and have a correspondingly greater capacity for self-deceit."[16] In the end, listening leaders also need to be listened to—in an authentic relationship of trust. Being listened to helps us learn better how to listen.

Starfish and Spider Leaders

What can we do if we long to become better listening leaders? How can we become leaders with ears to hear those whom we lead? We can start by being a catalyst for participation, communication and involvement in the culture of our organizations.

A listening leader serves the function of "Catalyst." Ori Brafman and Rod Beckstrom, authors of *The Starfish and the Spider*, point to the many advantages a starfish-like organization has over a spider-like organization. Spiders, they explain, are limited by their centralized systems, so that if you cut off a leg, the leg is gone, perhaps the whole spider. Certainly this is true if you cut off the head of the spider!

However, the starfish has no head to cut off, and if you cut off an arm it will grow right back. In fact, some species of starfish are such that if you cut them in half both halves will regrow an entire starfish. Organizations have similar structures that impede their multiplication and resiliency with either distributed or centralized structures. The authors unabashedly favor the starfish type, giving many examples of how they work better in our new economy so influenced by Web 2.0 values[17] of participation and editability. Let's examine seven of the qualities Brafman and Beckstrom say are needed in the catalyst role which will help us listen better as leaders.

We must begin as catalysts that (1) have genuine interest in others. As Brafman and Beckstrom say, "to a catalyst, people are like walking novels."[18] When you are fascinated by people, they are energized beyond any other motivation. Likewise, (2) develop loose connections with many, many contacts, not just a handful of people. Catalysts know how to listen to every person that comes across them, and whether it's a five-minute conversation or a five-year relationship, they retain that connection, beginning to (3) map a relational network of people. Brafman and Beckstrom say, "Catalysts think of who they know, who those people know, and how they all related to one another, and how they fit into a huge mental map."[19] Just as helpful is to (4) display the passion you have for your mission. We often think that vision is shared in speeches in front of crowds, or in slick communication pieces and videos. But most vision is caught in conversation, and catalyzes the involvement of the other person, because you (5) meet people where they are. "There's a difference between being passionate and being pushy."[20] So while you share your passion in conversation, the point is to have an actual conversation—where your hearts and mind overlap, instead of a forced infomercial on your passion. Finally, catalysts learn to (6) tolerate ambiguity as listening leaders. "Ambiguity creates a platform for creativity and innovation."[21] This is a struggle for most leaders that want clarity and control. But as we hinted at earlier, the grey area of relationships and communication allow the brightest spots to shine. In the end it's the role of the catalyst to (7) recede from the empowered people they catalyzed, instead of remaining there to control it over time. Brafman and Beckstrom write, "[A]fter catalysts map a network, make connections, build trust, and inspire people to act, what do they do? They leave."[22]

Conclusion

We began by examining the Jethro Principle inverted, sitting in the seats of the followers, so to speak, and realizing that such distribution of authority is actually a distribution of listeners. This is invaluable in an organization. Along the way we noted that having an "open door" is useless unless we're truly open to input and feedback, and then, in turn, looked at three dynamics of listening for leaders: decision making, communication, and the work of the soul. Finally, we've considered how to become more effective listening catalysts so that we can truly see a movement start from our work—something that outlives us as leaders. If we lead this way, listening our way through leadership challenges, the many that follow us will drown out our own voices. Can you hear it already? It's there. You just have to listen.

Notes

1. Robert Greenleaf calls Jethro the "first consultant of record on leadership" in *The Servant-leader Within* (New Jersey: Paulist Press, 2003), 42.

2. John Maxwell, *Developing the Leaders Around You* (Nashville: Thomas Nelson, 1995), 13-15. For other comparable treatments of the "Jethro Principle," see Carl George and Robert Logan, *Leading and Managing Your Church* (Old Tappan, N.J.,: F.H. Revell, 1987), 115; C. Gene Wilkes, *Jesus on Leadership* (Carol Stream, IL: Tyndale, 1998), 234. For contrasting position, similar to my own, see Steven P. Eason, *Making Disciples, Making Leaders: A Manual for Developing Church Officers* (Louisville: Westminster John Knox Press, 2004), 8. However, the authors stop short of a focus on the needs of the people being met through effective listening as their analysis is focused on distribution of the weight of leadership into the hands of multiple leaders in the church.

3. Seth Godin, *Tribes: We Need You to Lead Us* (New York: Penguin Group, 2008), 23.

4. Charlene Li, *Open Leadership* (San Francisco: Jossey-Bass, 2010), ix-xi.

5. Ralph Moore, *Let Go of the Ring* (Kaneohe, Hawaii: Straight Street Publications, 1993), 13-14.

6. John Maxwell, *Success 101* (Nashville: Thomas Nelson, 2008), 61

7. See Joe Myers, *Organic Community* (Grand Rapids: Baker Publishing Group, 2007).

8. A hefty portion of consultant Charlene Li's case studies are drawn from the information technology sector. I would have liked to hear more examples from traditional leadership scenarios and in particular the non-profit sector. This might lead one to believe that the tech industry is the best place for application of open leadership practices she advocates. However, I believe the principles are immediately transferable. In reality, churches, which are without a product and where any lines of "employee and customer" are forced and fabricated, I find the principles to be even more critical and applicable. A pastor that doesn't lead with even a modicum of openness will find themselves without a flock to lead in short order.

9. This is what their pastor Doug Pagitt calls Progressional-Dialogue Preaching. See Doug Pagitt, *Reimagining Spiritual Formation: A Week in the Life of an Experimental Church* (Grand Rapids, MI: Zondervan, 2004) and Doug Pagitt, *Preaching Reimagined: The Role of the Sermon in Communities of Faith* (Grand Rapids, MI: Zondervan, 2005).

10. "Seventh Graders Find a Cave on Mars," June 17, 2010. Available online at http://www.physorg.com/news196003436.html

11. I think they should let the kids in this class name the cave whatever such 7th graders think would be a cool name for a Mars geographical feature, but no news on that yet.

12. Here is an example of how quickly things can change: Facebook wasn't even started until 2004.

13. Nicholas Berdyaev, *The Fate of Man in the Modern World* (Ann Arbor: University of Michigan Press, 1969), 12.

14. Eugene Peterson, *The Contemplative Pastor* (Grand Rapids: Eerdmans, 1989), 56.

15. C.S. Lewis, *Mere Christianity* (New York: Macmillan, 1976), 97.

16. Eugene Peterson, *Working the Angles* (Grand Rapids: Eerdmans, 1987), 165.

17. "Web 2.0" has become a shorthand way to reference a second phase of internet use where multi-dimensional participation, two-way communication and user collaboration are valued over the initial internet build-up, which tended toward an older *broadcasting* model of one-way information dissemination.

18. Ori Brafman and Rod Beckstrom, *The Starfish and the Spider* (New York: Penguin, 2006), 120.

19. Brafman and Beckstrom, *The Starfish and the Spider*, 122.

20. Brafman and Beckstrom, *The Starfish and the Spider*, 124.

21. Brafman and Beckstrom, *The Starfish and the Spider*, 128.

22. Brafman and Beckstrom, *The Starfish and the Spider*, 128.

Chapter 6

Listening with the Spirit:
A Model for Listening in
Pastoral Care & Counseling

Anne Gatobu

Much has been written over the past decade about listening. In the counseling and pastoral care realms, listening is considered the foundation for all forms of care and counseling. It is the bedrock for communication: one cannot effectively communicate with another without first having the ability to listen. Various authors including Michael Nichols[1] and Howard Stone[2] have argued that listening as part of effective communication is one of the most important skills for establishing relationship, affirming and validating another in a care-giving or counseling encounter. It is also a major indicator of successful marriages, business relations, customer service, and uplifting encounters.

Considered from a Pastoral Care perspective, listening is a scriptural mandate for servants of God to be attuned not only to God's call and direction in their lives but also to one another. The writer of James underscores the importance of listening as a Christian calling when he states that we should be "quick to listen and slow to speak" (Jas 1:19 NIV). In similar consideration, the grace of prayer, highly valued within the three Abrahamic religions that trace their roots to the Old Testament, suppose that there is a living, listening God who hears and answers the prayers of people. Many times God answers the prayers of people through other people in community—which makes those who are attuned to listen, well positioned to be used by God in answering prayers.

Listening has also been nuanced to go beyond verbal listening to active listening. Listening is an art that one must take time to learn, practice and understand its tenets.[3] Yet, research has shown that most mental anguish problems, relational problems and familial conflicts are direct results of a culture in which we listen less and react more to situations.[4] Even the very professionals who have been trained in the art of listening and know how to pay attention to people's verbal and non-verbal communications, will tell us that it is not easy to listen. More often than not, they miss cues and other forms of communication from people with whom they are working.

This chapter will explore the uniqueness of listening in pastoral care and counseling, highlighting the unobvious ways that parishioners and other potential care receivers may be "speaking" in ways to which we are not accustomed, and calling for a model of listening in pastoral care that enlists reliance on the Holy Spirit. It will therefore call to alert the need for caregivers to listen not only to what people express verbally, but also, through attentiveness, to listen to truths that can only be revealed by God; attention to subtle yet powerful forms of cries for help that may be expressed in non traditional ways; attention to social-cultural nuances that may not be so obvious to the non attentive listener; and spiritually grounded awareness to the religious and social-political climate that may surround such cries for help. It also calls for listening with an openness of God, a willingness to be responsive and the risk of expecting whatever the outcome from God. You may call it, "Listening *with* the Spirit!"

Once the case has been made for Listening with the Spirit, I will offer a model of *how* to engage the Holy Spirit in listening to those we care for: Listening that can be honed through the fruit of the Spirit.

Listening with the Spirit

As the expression points out, *listening with the Spirit* is simply relying on the Spirit to be sensitively aware of those seeking to be heard; to discern discrepancies that could short-circuit effective listening; and to rely on the Spirit to be the interpreter of that which we hear and perceive. The apostle Paul states that the Holy Spirit intercedes for us in those times when we cannot verbalize our experiences, in sighs too deep to fathom (Rom 8:26-27). Listening with the Spirit is partnering with the Holy Spirit in this kind of deep discernment with people with whom we are pastorally involved. Note the use of the preposition *with* as opposed to *through* or *to*. It presupposes a partnership with the Spirit. It insinuates that we as the care-givers are bringing something to the listening table in terms of our experiences, understandings, reasoning and traditions. This is an express acknowledgement of the Wesleyan quadrilateral emphasis to honor our subjective and objective interpretation of the scriptures, engage in our mental capacities (reasoning), our experiences of the Spirit and the dynamic context of our tradition, even as we rely on the Spirit for guidance and direction.

Before submitting propositions of how to listen with the Spirit, it is important that we first be clear about what we mean by "the Spirit": *which spirit*; and more important *why the Spirit*.

The Spirit in this chapter refers to the Holy Spirit. This is an important characterization of the Spirit in the ensuing conversation of Listening with the Spirit. The Holy Spirit is the Spirit of Christ and of God the Father. In the Christian tradition the Holy Spirit is the third person of the Triune God. When discussing listening with the Spirit then, we are speaking through the Christian tradition, that the Holy Spirit is imparted to us through baptism, dedication of our lives to Christ and invitation of Christ into our lives, and invoked to active duty through ongoing engagement in Christian graces of scriptural immersion, prayer, communion, and worship.

Listening with the Holy Spirit is essential because he is the counselor, the mediator, and the empowering agent for Christians. Jesus sets the example for us to follow in ministry by waiting for empowerment from the Holy Spirit before he begins his ministry. At baptism we read that the heavens opened up and the Spirit of God in the form of a dove descended and rested on Jesus' (Matt 3:16; Mark 1:10). In this public moment, Jesus is *filled* with the Holy Spirit![5] Later in ministry when the Pharisees ask in whose authority Jesus is healing and performing miracles, there is no question that it is God the Father, through Holy Spirit, who is at work in Jesus. This is the same Holy Spirit whom Jesus spoke about before he ascended into heaven. Jesus promised his disciples that he would continue to be with them by sending a counselor, the Holy Spirit, who would continue to minister *to* and *through* them. Through this counselor, Christ would continue to be with them to the ends of the earth (John 14:16-18).

Role of the Holy Spirit in Listening

The role of the Holy Spirit for effectiveness in pastoral care and counseling is indispensable in four major ways: First, in Galatians we read that the Holy Spirit produces in us the fruit of the Spirit. The nine-fold fruit of the Spirit is "love, joy, peace, patience, kindness, goodness, faithfulness, gentleness and self control" (Gal 5:22-23 NIV). In a way, presenting these nine as *a* fruit implies that one characteristic is not sufficient manifestation of the Holy Spirit without the others. In essence then to be patient one must also be kind and gentle. One cannot genuinely show kindness if one is not loving, gentle, at peace with oneself and the other, and so on. Goodness or kindness without joy is empty. As the Holy Spirit produces fruit with the nine characteristics, our listening skills deepen and grow: We listen with *patience* and *self-control* of our emotions; it is the *goodness* and *kindness* of the Spirit in us that prompts us to listen; we *love* those we listen to unconditionally; we respond with *gentleness* even to the harsh things we hear; we follow up on that which we have agreed in our listening with *faithfulness* and *joy*. We find ourselves in unbelievable *peace* as we listen to stories and experiences that may otherwise irk our spirits. It takes having the fruit of the spirit to become good listeners. Indeed the fruit of the spirit manifested in these nine characteristics is the foundation of effective listening.

The use of the word *fruit* connotes that these characteristics are a result of certain inputs. They are not just gifts of grace, but, rather, the end product of some sowing, pruning, fertilizing, watering, and intentional care. Note the distinction made of fruit from the passage in 1 Corinthians 12, which speaks of varieties of gifts for varieties of people but the same Spirit. The gifts listed in this passage are gifts of grace that manifest in people, whereas the fruit requires our input to grow.

What then would be equivalent to fertilization and care in order to produce fruit of the Spirit? The Spirit's presence is nurtured through regular attention to things such as reading and meditating on the scriptures, formal training in ways of the Spirit (for instance in listening courses), fellowshipping with other believers, worship, prayer, and so on. Hence, one can be a Christian who has accepted Christ in his or her life and yet not bear the fruit of the Spirit if he or she neglects nurturing the production of fruit of the Spirit. If it takes the fruit to become a good listener, then nurturing the fruit is an important part of honing the art of listening.

The second way in which listening with the Spirit is essential is that, distinct from other helping professions, pastoral care and counseling happens in the context of informal ministry. David Benner states that unlike professional counseling in which the hurting person must initiate a structured care process, pastoral care and counseling may be initiated by the caregiver and will generally happen in very unstructured contexts.[6] Simple encounters that may be unstructured and unplanned may, in the wider context of ministry, call for pastoral caregivers to be tuned to having an ear for listening at all times and in a variety of ways. These pastoral care situations often lead to a time of unplanned prayer; a time of exploration of ways that a community of faith can support physically or spiritually; a time of engagement in existential and theological discussion on how another is experiencing or not experiencing the presence of God in their situation; a time when caregivers explore ways that the person can feel empowered and supported. Aside from the Spirit, these opportunities can go unheeded.

I have had occasions where I am focused on getting to the office to attend to some administrative business, only to stop by to say hello to a parishioner who is just getting in their car to go see their loved one in the hospital. Other times people stop by the office just to say hello. The reception of some of these casual stops has brought up issues in the life of a parishioner who may have been struggling to figure out how they can talk with someone and just did not have a direct way to broach the subject. In many cases a casual office stop to say hello turns out to be an assessment by the parishioner to see if the pastoral counselor is worthy of hearing their story. Other times a pastoral care moment has been initiated by simply asking someone, "How are you?" in the hallways or in a department store or even on an evening walk. The indication to stop and listen becomes an invitation to the person to tell of a burden she may be carrying at the moment and an answered prayer. Such instances become embodiments of God's caring, loving and powerful presence at all times in all places. On the other hand, when we miss these subtle but necessary opportunities to listen, we are communicating that God is not yet ready to listen or that God is only available in a church or that God does not believe the other is worth listening to. Hopefully, realization of meanings sent to people by not taking time to listen will prompt us to be more conscious and attentive the next time we say to anyone, "How are you?"

The unstructured nature of pastoral care calls to attention that many care-receivers may be seeking audience in ways that are not traditionally associated with listening. One of the most clandestine cries to be heard that I ever experienced was a series of poems I continually received from a parishioner who had just been diagnosed with cancer. About once a week during her fight against cancer I would receive a neatly stacked folder with a poem or several under my office door. I would comment on what a lovely poet she was and that she should get the poems published. Throughout this period I totally missed the point of the anguish, fear, guilt, joy and faith that she was trying to communicate to me through the poems. Did I care for her during her period of need? Yes, I did. Could God have used me more effectively in my care had I consciously invoked the Spirit in my listening to her? By far, *yes*! I would have heard of her fear to go through chemotherapy. I would have heard the intensity of anxiety about her worried family. I would have heard her need to continue to be valued instead of her new inscription as "cancer patient," and therefore contribute to her faith in herself as the still useful parishioner I had always known. These fears and anxieties were never voiced in our conversations. Instead I only saw a strong woman and often wondered with admiration how strong she was in the face of the diagnosis and what lay ahead of her. It was not until after the critical period of needing pastoral care that I went back to the poems, just hoping to enjoy them, and realized the messages that this woman had been trying to communicate to me. She was looking for an opening that would engage some theological reflection on her experiences. She was hoping for someone to see that she was not strong and was ridden with anxiety. She was hoping for someone who would listen to her "Why, God?" questions without judging her. But I had missed it all and cared for her in technical and physical ways that were not as effective as could have been had I been attuned to listen with the Spirit.

Third, the Holy Spirit will give us as pastoral caregivers and counselors direction and guidance in how to respond to that which we listen. It may be said in subtle but powerful ways that the Holy Spirit is the internal Diagnostic and Statistical Manual of Mental Disorders for pastoral counselor and caregivers. This can be a scary thought because most people would rather have a manual that states, "When you observe this and that, the diagnosis is this and the problem should be fixed in this certain way." Unfortunately, most issues of care that come to pastoral caregivers are not packaged as a formal problem with diagnostic clarity. There are no magic words that will take away the pain of one who has lost a loved one. Neither is there prescription medicine that can quickly fix one who is struggling with existential questions because of a critical life experience or issue. It is this very lack of clear prescriptive instructions for pastoral counseling situations that scare most pastoral persons from engaging in a very integral part of ministry. Yet as we acknowledge the unsettledness of such ambiguity in pastoral care prescriptions, we must be reminded of Christ's words in his great commission to the disciples, "All authority in heaven and on earth has been given to me. Therefore go and make disciples of all nations.... And surely I am with you always, to the very end of age" (Matt 28:18-20 NIV).

The scriptures are replete with assurances of God working through people to accomplish his ministry of care for people: Moses, very scared and uncertain of the task God is calling him to do of demanding the Pharaoh's release of the Israelites, says to God, "O Lord, I have never been eloquent, neither in the past nor since you have spoken to your servant. I am of slow speech and slow of tongue" (Exod 4:10 NIV) Yet God promises Moses, "I will help you speak and will teach you what to say" (Exod 4:11 NIV). As Jeremiah is called to be a prophet of God, he responds "Ah, Sovereign LORD...I do not know how to speak; I am only a child." But God replies, "Do not say 'I am only a child.' You must go to everyone I send you to and say whatever I command you. Do not be afraid of them for I am with you and will rescue you" (Jer 1:6-8 NIV). As we listen with the Spirit, we rely on the Spirit to guide us in what to say, when to say it and how to say it. We rely on the Holy Spirit to be the real comforter to those that are hurting; to be the guide to those that are lost or needing direction; to be the prompter to those being called to forgiveness, reconciliation, repentance, change of heart and desires. Indeed, Paul reminds us that it is only through the Spirit that we can exercise our gifts of wisdom, knowledge, healing, prophecy, working of miracles, and others (1 Cor 12:7-11).

Fourth, listening with the Spirit must be marked by a genuine non-judgmental acceptance of all whom God brings our way for care and counsel. Humanly this is an impossible task because our very nature calls us to make judgments in ways of attribution and making meaning as we encounter the world and others. With the help of the Holy Spirit, however, we can genuinely receive people with love, joy and faith that God is able to change any situation.

A Model for Listening with the Spirit

Having established a place for the Holy Spirit in our lives, I now offer a simple model of how to listen with the Spirit. The model may be presented by the acronym ADORE, which describes how listening with the Spirit is essentially trusting and demonstrating faith in what God can accomplish through us for his creation. Essentially we are showing faithful adoration of the Triune God. In brief, the way to listen with the Spirit entails five levels of listening and attending with the Spirit: Awareness, Discernment, Openness, Responsiveness, Expectation.

1. Awareness: Some people walk around the world totally unaware of their surroundings. Others live striving to be aware and informed of happenings around them. To be an effective listener, one cannot afford to live a life of unawareness. Listening entails honing sensitivity. Sensitivity is nurtured by seeking to be aware of that which may be unfamiliar and seemingly removed from our world. It calls us to rise above social political convictions on issues around us.

Let me offer an example: What awareness do you, as pastor, have of domestic violence? Often it is easy to overlook that there is no particular profile of a domestic violence perpetrator. Seemingly nice church members can perpetrate spousal violence; seemingly nice church families can be experiencing domestic violence. Without such awareness, empathy, understanding, and informal listening may be lacking. Such unawareness can create an uncomfortable situation of being either for or against, thereby moving away from pastoral care-giving.

Similar awareness is necessary regarding all sorts of issues including divorce, rape and sexual molestation, spiritual crisis, marital problems, and drug abuse. As pastoral caregivers, to be effective we must be grounded on as much knowledge about these issues as possible. We must be aware of the psychological, socio-political and cultural dynamics affecting the issues. We must be aware of empirical and statistical data informing these issues that plague our communities. We cannot afford to be in shock with those that we help. We must be a step ahead of them in being aware that these issues can be or are present within our communities and be prepared on how to respond or connect people with necessary resources. As we make ourselves aware of current issues, the spirit will be faithful to reveal even beyond research, the psycho-social dynamics that inhibit healing.

2. Discernment: This is one of the Spirit's most crucial roles in listening. There are always two sides to every storied experience. We only need to speak with a couple in marital conflict to underline why listening to both sides of the conflict is important. Yet people naturally side with what they identify or understand. Even though the need for objectivity is great in counseling training, we must never overlook that there is always a considerable level of transference that happens in any given session. Nichols defines transference as "all the ways in which a person's experience of a relationship becomes organized according to the configurations of self-image and expectations of others that unconsciously structure his or her subjective universe."[7] In other words, it is the loss of objectivity by therapist in any counseling relationship whose issues have aspects that mirror the counselor's own experiences. Being aware of high probability of considerable levels of transference despite our knowledge and effort to seek objectivity is an important aspect that helps us value the role of the Spirit to help discern two sides of a conflict. If we can remove ourselves from succumbing to the challenges of transference, then there is a possibility that we will truly let the Spirit speak truth to the situation on hand. It is only then that we will rise above the influence of connivers, persuasive speaking, lies, and justifications that we have to deal with as we care for people in counseling. The Spirit will reveal to us the spirits of the persons before us. As we listen to people, let us learn to pray and ask the Holy Spirit to help us discern truths, unclean spirits and how to stand firm against such spirits.

3. Openness: People with closed minds and hearts generally do not make good listeners. Closed minds and hearts imply, "I know it all; I am grounded in this and there is nothing anyone can say or do to make me think otherwise." Of course, there is a difference between being closed and being grounded. The apostle Paul identifies being grounded in faith as a maturity when he writes, "Then we will no longer be infants, tossed back and forth by the waves, and blown here and there by every wind of teaching and by the cunning and craftiness of men in their deceitful scheming" (Eph 4:14 NIV).

How can we distinguish between being closed and being grounded? Faith in God the Father and Jesus, and the belief that the Holy Scriptures hold the truthful guide to our lives are appropriate groundings. In the Wesleyan quadrilateral, John Wesley realized that openness to our reason, tradition and experience are virtues that supplement our grounded faith in God and the scriptures. In a profound way he was calling to an openness of mind and heart. Being of open mind and heart is not equivalent to agreeing with every new teaching or being all things to all people.

The level of openness that I propose in listening to the Spirit is one that honors our grounded faith in God and the guidance of the Holy Scriptures, but also relies on the Holy Spirit to interpret and reveal God's truth, which may or may not be aligned to human wisdom. It is the kind of openness that acknowledges that our ways (reasoning, interpretation, knowledge, experience) are not always God's ways and that the Holy Spirit can only reveal God's truth to us. It is the kind of openness in listening that Nichols calls "self transcendence."[8] It is the kind of empathy that "can be achieved only by suspending our pre-occupation with ourselves and entering into the experience of the other person."[9] Self transcendence involves consciously setting aside our daily covert pre-occupations like worries, anxieties, hopes, dreams, grudges, assumptions and knowledge, in order to open ourselves to receive and confirm the experience of the other.

It is one thing to want and think that we are open and objective as caregivers and another to live a life that is truly open in embracing those we receive in our care. A simple test of this disparity is observing with honesty our inner reaction to certain people. For instance how do we react at gut level when a disheveled beggar or an unkempt bearded youth smelling of alcohol appears in our office? What exactly goes on in our mind when a single mother walks into our church (not on Sunday!) for the first time with several kids? How about when a parishioner seeks our counseling because he has been diagnosed with HIV/AIDS? What is our inner sense when a parishioner comes to speak about struggles that suggest he or she is gay? What is our gut reaction when a teenager approaches us because she is pregnant, scared to death and contemplating abortion? The list of issues we have strong opinions and beliefs about is endless.

The inflexibility of closed minds and hearts can take the form of desiring to change the person before us. In the long run, serious forms of being closed cause the caregiver to lose objectivity as a listeners and work to reshape them in the caregiver's image. Unwittingly, we become judgmental and begin to detest the very people we are caring for.

To reach the level of openness we are being called to achieve as pastoral caregivers, we must deep down in our hearts be at *peace* (another characteristic of the fruit of the Spirit) with our beliefs, our convictions and ourselves. We must be at peace that God's Spirit is at work in us, but also at work in those we minister to. We must be at peace and truly believe in the main objective of pastoral care which is to reconnect people with God[10] and be at peace that once reconnected, God will do the real work of healing though his Spirit in them. We must believe that everything is possible with God (Luke 1:37) in spite of our experiences, observations and prior knowledge that has worked to form the strong opinions we have about people and people groups.

To reach this level of openness in listening we must also hold in faith what the scriptures tell us that God's grace is sufficient even for the most depraved person. The Apostle Paul had come to this conviction because when he wrote that he was given a thorn in his flesh to torment him, he also wrote that he firmly believed that God's grace is sufficient (2 Cor 12:7-9).

4. Responsiveness: The fourth level of our listening in this model is responsiveness. As I discuss this level I call to attention its opposite, *reaction*, which connotes speaking to something out of our emotions and feelings and without reflection and without the Holy Spirit. In crisis intervention literature, this distinction is pertinently made because the objective of the crisis intervener is to calm a situation of disequilibrium by being the non-anxious presence, and aiding or influencing individuals to return to pre- crisis levels of functioning.[11] Most people in conflict or in a crisis will engage the issues in fight or flight mode. The anxiety level is high. Fear, confusion, obscurity of thought, disorganization, can be normal. Others who come our way with issues that are not categorized as crisis, may have similar characteristics, with the additions of fear of being judged, uncertain of their trust in the caregiver, and anxiety concerning letting another into their secret chambers of life. Reaction to whatever we hear will send such people spiraling right down into the abyss of situations already fraught with turmoil. *Reaction* communicates that the crisis is untouchable and too complicated even for us to deal with. What is most scary about communicating this kind of message, however unaware we may be, is that it also communicates at a very profound level that God, whom we represent as pastoral caregivers cannot also handle this issue.

Responsiveness has the exact opposite effect. It communicates, "I hear you, and I acknowledge your pain. I may not understand exactly what you feel and are going through but God is willing to hear your experience from your perspective. I am willing to get into those dark places that you may be living in right now by yourself." This message is empathic and empowering!

Responsiveness involves active listening, which is the art of knowing how to give attention, appreciation and affirmation.[12] The actual art involves knowing when to paraphrase, interject, encourage, empathize, and use silences to say, "I hear you." Responsiveness can only be right if we are open to hear. I find it interesting that when I teach listening skills, most students want a sort of manual that states, "Say *this* when a person says *that*." If there was such a manual, there would be no reason to listen. As a matter of fact we could automate pastoral care so we have pre-recorded responses that one could call in and be responded, to whatever one says.

Beyond active listening skills, responsive listening must involve the Holy Spirit in us. It is only the Holy Spirit that can help us empathize with the person's situation because in truth we would never understand exactly how they feel. It is only the Holy Spirit that can interpret for us the cry for reconciliation in an otherwise voiced reaction of another. It is only the Holy Spirit who can prompt us to hear a sigh signifying denial and attempt to hide behind, "I am okay." It is the Holy Spirit that will guide us to the proper responses and wisdom in any given situation.

Hence, we can wonder what we are going to say to people we are caring for and thereby preoccupy our minds with searching for eloquent speech and human wisdom and in the process not really listen to the person before us and consequently react or say something totally out of context. This is what counselors refer to as shadow listening. Or, we can rely on the Holy Spirit to be our *core-listener* and just open ourselves to the moment, trusting that our core listener in us will guide us in how to be responsive to the person we listen to.

5. Expectation: Expectation is the final element of listening in the Spirit. As we listen we must have faith that something will happen; that there will be positive impact. Think about it, how much would we invest ourselves in a futile activity? I bet very little. Almost anything we do, we do it because we *expect* some change, advancement, enjoyment, and other positive experiences. There is an expectation that when I sleep I will wake up rested, when I take medicine I will get well, when I visit with someone that we will enjoy one another's company, that when I eat my body will be nourished, that when I teach my students will learn something, that when I preach the message will make a difference..

In similar ways, pastoral caregivers *expect* and hope for something to happen in the lives of those they care for. If this is so obvious then why does expectation feature in this model as a level in listening? Because the contention is not if we have expectations as we listen in pastoral care, but that our expectations are aligned with our opinions and beliefs, and are not necessarily aligned with God. In most pastoral care encounters, our expectations are not aligned to an openness that communicates our trust in the Holy Spirit to bring the healing, the comfort, the reconciliation in his own time. Instead we look out for certain changes and milestones in our expectations.

This kind of expectation is so linked to lack of openness that it is inseparable. When we do not see that specific change which we are looking for, we give up and feel like failures in our pastoral care. Other times we link our expectations to our skillfulness and eloquence. In the end we beat ourselves up when we come short and do not see the desired change. When we think about how we *expect* in our pastoral care encounters, it is really all about ourselves and less about the person for whom we care and least about Christ's glorification. True expectation as we listen with the Spirit must also be open to the impact that God desires in that person as opposed to our set gauges and expectations. Sometimes, God will choose to impact the life of the person in ways that are far from our hopes and expectations. We must trust the process and believe that just as the Holy Spirit guides us in what to say, the Holy Spirit also continues to work in the life of the person we care for. We must trust in the work of Him "who is able to do immeasurably more than all we ask or imagine, according to his power that is within us" (Eph 3:20 NIV). Indeed we should be prepared to be surprised by what God can do in the lives of people we work with.

Conclusion

Good listening skills are essential to pastoral care and counseling. Of course, others have argued that for decades. However, in approaching listening skills and a listening character through the person of the Holy Spirit, I have then made a case for Listening *with* the Spirit as an appropriate approach for effectiveness in pastoral care. In describing this relationship of listening as *with* the Spirit, we see that the caregiver must be cognizant of what they bring to the pastoral relationship, and how they influence what they hear by either invoking or neglecting the promptings of the Holy Spirit. This approach is summarized in a model (ADORE) that facilitates Listening with the Spirit in pastoral care and counseling.

The strength of this model, I believe, is its attention that listening is an art that can be trained in and practiced, and in which the Holy Spirit can play an active role in the lives of the people we care for. The Holy Spirit can also bring peace to pastoral caregivers in whatever direction God chooses to take the caregiving and its outcome. In listening, God has entrusted you the role of being his ears, yet he has left the Comforter who will open your ears and give you ears to hear.

Notes

1. Michael P. Nichols, *The Lost Art of Listening: How Learning to Listen Can Improve Relationships* (New York: The Guilford Press, 1995), 13.

2. Howard W. Stone, *Crisis Counseling* (Minneapolis: Fortress Press, 2009), 32.

3. Nichols, *The Lost Art of Listening,* 62.

4. Nichols, *The Lost Art of Listening,* 3.

5. William Barclay, *The Gospel of Mark.* (Philadelphia: Westminster Press, 1956), 11.

6. David Benner, *Strategic Pastoral Counseling: A Short Term Structured Model* (Grand Rapids: Baker Academic, 2003), 20.

7. Nichols, *The Lost Art of Listening,* 41.

8. Nichols, *The Lost Art of Listening,* 129.

9. Nichols, *The Lost Art of Listening,* 10.

10. Benner, *Strategic Pastoral Counseling,* 27.

11. See Kristi Kanel, *A Guide To Crisis Intervention* (Belmont, CA: Thomson Brooks/Cole, 2007), 2; Stone, *Crisis Counseling,* 4.

12. Nichols, *The Lost Art of Listening,* 109-19.

Chapter 7

Listening as they Choose their Way: Discipleship, Listening, and Young Adults

David A. Higle

Listening in Discipleship of College Students

Every September, our college holds a three-day series of special services for the purpose of uniting our campus around the person of Christ as we begin a new academic year. Services often conclude with an invitation for students to respond to the Word as they sense the Spirit prompting them. The altars are usually full of praying, seeking students. At its best, it is a time of deep personal examination for those students who bravely make their way down the aisle to kneel and pray humbly. Many students point to these times as moments of personal transformation when God challenges them to consider who they are becoming in relation to Christ and the world.

I always look for a student with whom I can pray, considering it a privilege to be part of the deep mystery that occurs in the human heart during these sensitive times. On one such occasion, I noticed a young woman in her second year (we'll call her Susan), quietly praying alone off to one side. I did not know her well. I knelt beside her and asked the two questions I always ask in such moments: "Would you like me to pray with you, or would you rather pray privately?" She wanted me to pray with her. Then my second question: "Do you know why you are here?" I have found that students do not always consciously know why they respond to such invitations. The question helps to clarify their thoughts and intents. She was quiet for a moment and I sensed either embarrassment or reluctance to answer my question. One must be prepared to hear anything in such times! Eventually, Susan responded with her head down, as if ashamed to tell me what she was really thinking. But she did. "I have doubts," she confessed. "I have doubts about whether God exists or if any of this is true at all." By "this," Susan meant the entire Christian story. Was *any* of it true? How can I know? How can I be *sure?* We spoke quietly for a few moments and prayed together. I then invited her to meet with me the next day to talk further if she so desired. She seemed glad to accept my invitation. And so we met.

Susan's experience is fairly typical for college-aged students. They are just beginning to cross the threshold into young adulthood. For the first time, they are leaving the safe confines of home, family, church, and friends. Ready or not, they are leaving adolescence and striking out toward a more independent future. The faith journey of college-aged students, typically considered to be 18-22 years, is often a rapid one. The potential for positive spiritual change is enormous during what Sharon Parks has termed "the four critical years."[1] However, whether not this potential is realized depends on a variety of factors.

This chapter explores this emerging capacity of college-aged students to reflect more deeply about their faith and the positive role that compassionate listening can play in helping to foster spiritual growth. First, certain developmental characteristics of college-aged students and young adults are explained that relate to their increasing capacity for personal reflection. Second, certain factors that can help to prompt students to move deeper in their faith journey will be explained. Pastors who "listen" for these hallmarks will be in a better position to assist their discipleship. Third, the role of the Church as a compassionate, listening community is presented as indispensible to authentic discipleship. Pastors and key lay leaders should adopt a posture of listening for the movement of the Spirit in the lives of these young adults.

Characteristics of Young Adults: Emerging Capacity for Self-Reflection

Psychologists talk about "stages" of personal growth and development, but this is too simplistic. The concept of stages implies that we grow steadily in incremental and compartmentalized steps or leaps, totally leaving the last phase of our lives to enter a fresh a new stage. But human growth is not so tidy. Rather than stages, we might think about growth as spiraling upward, but often cycling back around again to where we were before continuing to move up again.[2] We do not jettison our history, but incorporate and recast it in new ways into who we are becoming. This is a truer reflection of what really happens when we grow. It is also true with regard to spiritual growth. We gradually discover a path into new ways of thinking and being in the world as we understand ourselves, experience God, and relate to others. It is important to keep this in mind as we describe some of the common developmental characteristics of college-aged students and young adults. There are three characteristics that we will consider and that we "listen" for in working with students.

One of the most important characteristics is the emerging capacity of young adults to reflect critically and self-consciously about their identity and their place in the world. Similar to Moses' questions about his own identity and God's nature,3 these questions often come during pivotal transition periods in life, such as the college years. Entering college (or the workplace) after high school, these young people are straddling the border between late adolescence and young adulthood. Like Moses, young adults often feel like they are entering an unnerving wilderness of shifting landscapes as peer groups change, pressures mount to make life choices among a bewildering set of options, and the demands of competing voices of authority clamor to be heard. For many, it is not an easy time as they become more consciously aware of the need to decide who they are becoming. This includes issues of faith and discipleship. Pastors do well to listen for certain hallmarks that characterize emerging young adulthood and the implications for ongoing spiritual development, discipleship, and connection to the church.

Choosing One's Own Identity

One note of young adulthood to listen for is the continuing (from adolescence) questions and statements about identity as they compose the narrative of their lives. The questions being asked about their own narrative are: Who do I choose *to be*? Who do I choose to *be with*? Where will I choose *my place* in the world? Some developmentalists believe that while younger teens may feel like they have chosen their own beliefs and values, it is more accurate to say their values and beliefs have largely chosen them through the various groups and significant others in their lives.[4] Adolescents typically view themselves through the mirrored image of those they admire. However, as young adults, they have an increased capacity to reflect and consciously choose who they are becoming: what groups they will be part of, what beliefs to hold, and what causes to be committed to. Pastors should pay attention to this increased independence. The following two examples illustrate the contrast between adolescence and young adulthood and the capacity to choose who one is becoming.

Several years ago I was driving with my 15 year old daughter when she told me about a conversation she had with some friends at school. They had been talking about their various church experiences. One of her friends attended a Pentecostal church and told them about speaking in tongues. Unfamiliar with this experience, my daughter asked me, "Dad, what do *we* believe?" Listening carefully, I understood the deeper issues underlying her question. She was really saying, "Dad, I really don't know much about speaking in tongues, but I do know it is different from what we believe about our faith. I need some reassurance about this. If I know what our family believes, that can help me right now. So, what does our family believe? What do *we* believe?" In adolescence, the group—what Sharon Parks calls "the tyranny of the they"[5]— speaks with shaping power in adolescent lives. In my daughter's case, she was experiencing the pressure of the beliefs of her peer group and weighing them against the pressure of her family group—both groups vying for authority in her life, shaping her identity, helping her to know who she is. In this instance, she identified with our family.

However, as young people transition out of adolescence and into the college years, questions begin to stir deep down with greater force about personal individual identity, values, and place in the world. And so the college years are often considered a time to test, consciously, various perspectives for determining who one is choosing to be. College students and other young adults are gradually becoming more independent and self-aware. This is illustrated in a personal reflection paper written by one of my students, a 19 year-old female freshman:

> First of all, growing up in a Christian home, I never felt the need to really explore my faith until recently. My attitude had always been that if my parents believed it, then I would too. I thought that the prayers that we prayed before meals, before bedtime and on Sunday morning would be enough, and that my parents would take care of the rest. Over the past two years or so, *I have really been trying to explore what I believe and to make my beliefs my own,* meaning that my prayer life itself has only been developing over the past little while. Also, last year I experienced some hard times that affected a huge chunk of my life. While I may not have realized it at the time, my faith was affected as well. It seems as though my prayer life took a hit during this time....[6]

For this student (we'll call her Gail), there is a greater capacity for self-awareness and critical reflection, something not as evident only a year or two prior. Up until this point, Gail's personal faith commitments have not been challenged or tested to any significant degree. But it is evident that she is now encountering ideas in college that are challenging her tidy view of the world. Fowler states that such challenges to one's beliefs are necessary for young adults like Gail to grow deeper in their faith commitments—to "make my beliefs my own," as she says, rather than "borrowing" from the faith of her family or church.[7]

Exploring options is typical for young adults and must be respected by pastors. This is a sensitive time. For many students, particularly those from Christian homes who now attend Christian colleges, this can be a relatively pain-free and even joyful time of coming to embrace personally the beliefs from within their own faith traditions. But for many others, the young adult years can be confusing and even painful. Cherished beliefs are challenged. Students may become unsure of the validity of their faith. The meaning they found within the group experience of church and family may diminish as they bump up against new opinions and options from the world around them. It may also be painful for parents, pastors, and significant others as they watch. Compassionate pastors will listen for the signals of changing meaning structures in the hearts of their young adults. Young adults may question the cherished beliefs they once held, the beliefs of the church and family, as illustrated in the earlier story of Susan. But it does not mean they have *abandoned* their faith—in many cases, they are simply *asking for guidance from those whom they believe still care about them.* This is crucial. It indicates a type of paradox from what one might expect.

The Need for Supportive Community

Erik Erikson is helpful in this regard.[8] Erickson states that young adults find themselves living in tension between two poles: on the one hand, they are self-consciously seeking independence, to choose their own identify apart from what their parents and others think; on the other hand, they fear being isolated from others, not finding their place in life, and may find it difficult to commit themselves to others. They are seeking both independence and intimacy, the capacity to be "their own person" while seeking to give themselves away to others and causes larger than themselves. These are crucial issues for all Christians to consider, especially spiritual leaders. The ability of young adults to navigate these waters successfully, neither being pushed around by the opinions of others (thereby losing their sense of who they are) nor wandering through life without a meaningful sense of connection to others, depends on the continued support of key people and communities in their lives. Young adults still look for the valued support of mentors to affirm who they are becoming even while they strike out on their own. For Christian leaders, the implications of how to relate to young adults should be clear—to adopt a steady presence, a listening posture of support, encouragement, and compassionate guidance as they wrestle with God and themselves to solidify their faith.

Characteristics of Spiritual Mentors

In relation to all that has been said, it is just as important *who* the pastor is as the knowledge she or he imparts. Young adults who express sincere doubts or honest questions about cherished beliefs and practices will grow silent or leave church altogether if they perceive they are being judged.[9] Maintaining a compassionate and listening presence in the lives of young adults is vital as they encounter contrary ideas and experiences that test the durability of their faith. It is important for pastors to listen carefully and compassionately for what groups and ideas with which they now associate. Listening with authenticity is essential as they talk about their favorite professors, new extra-curricular activities, budding work relationships, musings about vocational possibilities, and encounters with new ideas. All are significant for understanding who they are becoming and where they are heading in the world. These young adults are carving out their place in life, and doing so with a greater sense of independence apart from the group. However, in doing so, they still look for guidance from key people, but will be very selective in who they choose.

In the local church community, pastors in particular, along with other key adults, are potentially important sources for guiding the spiritual growth of students and young adults. In essence, they may function as mentors or guides for students as they encounter the various experiences that push and pull their faith into further maturity. Mentors are typically thought of as older, wiser individuals who enter into personal relationship with a (usually) younger and less experienced individual for the purpose of guiding and sponsoring that person into more mature understanding and growth. They serve as teachers, guides, advisors, models, counselors, friends, and encouragers. In doing so, they may effectively enhance one's sense of personal competence and identity.

Indications are that mentoring appears to create a fundamental transformation in the way protégés perceive themselves.[10] This has implications for creating a "safe" environment that is conducive for adolescents and young adults to encounter potentially life-changing experiences. Peter Wilson quotes psychologist Daniel Levinson as saying that mentoring is not so much defined in terms of formal roles played, but "in terms of the character of the relationship and functions it serves."[11] As such, mentoring can be one of the most developmentally important relationships of early adulthood.

Pastors as compassionate mentors can enhance certain aspects of the faith and spiritual growth process by being consciously aware of their potential influence. Wilson advocates that mentors ask themselves key questions in order to raise their personal awareness of how they can fulfill this role. Such questions might include how one can be of encouragement to a student who questions his/her faith, or in ways one can facilitate the student's reflection of a traumatic event, to see more deeply into its ultimate dimensions. Wilson notes that mentors should not ask the question of "What shall I do?" in relation to a protégé, but rather, "Who shall I be?"[12] Pastors who will have the most impact have certain characteristics such as a meaningful relationship with God, a sense of humor, and emotional transparency.[13] Such characteristics are vital in affecting certain types of change. Overall, however, Wilson cites the core mentoring virtues as integrity, courage, and care, which he states are roughly synonymous with the Apostle Paul's Christian virtues, faith, hope, and love.[14] Integrity provides an undergirding sense of trust which helps establish relationships. Courage will enable a pastor to assist a student to take heart and not submit to fears. In doing so, students will often "borrow" courage from their mentors as they face anxiety from crisis situations.[15] As collegians and young adults grow through the various crises they face, they often lean upon their mentors. The goal is to assist them in solidifying their faith as they strive toward independence even while they seek connection. Wilson cites research that indicates other effective qualities of spiritual leaders may also include, among others, honesty, sincerity, humility, godliness, prayerfulness, wisdom, patience, and service.[16] But he emphasizes the significance of the three core virtues of integrity, courage, and care.

Discipleship Occurs Only within Community

A Christian disciple is one who has decided to follow in the way of Jesus.[17] Dallas Willard uses the metaphor of "apprentice" to characterize the relationship between a disciple and Jesus.[18] An apprentice is one who spends time with the master in order to learn the skills and virtues necessary to become skilled. To be a disciple one has to spend time with Jesus.

Eugene Peterson argues that authentic discipleship cannot truly occur simply through mass programs and classes as if the meaning of Christian faith and discipleship can somehow be adequately transmitted through workbooks and DVDs.[19] Such approaches to discipleship belie the very meaning of what it means to follow Jesus: to be growing in intimate union and communion with God and others through Christ by means of the dynamic indwelling presence of God's Spirit. The very nature of discipleship—indeed, the very nature of what it means to be a human being—calls for interaction at close range. Human beings in close proximity, living in community, is the primary means by which God has chosen to reveal himself: first and foremost, through the incarnated presence of

God in Jesus the Christ, and now, by the Spirit, through the Church in and to the world. Technology, books, and classes have their place, but God's primary way of revealing himself is through incarnate means.

Jesus and Paul both teach in this vein. Matthew 18 is an important narrative for understanding the significance of interpersonal relationships within God's kingdom. In Matthew 18:5-6, Jesus states whoever "welcomes a little child," whom he defines as "little ones who believe in me," is tantamount to welcoming Jesus himself. In Matthew 18:15-19, Jesus teaches the importance of relational accountability and the necessity of confronting those who injure others through their sin. If necessary, it may require that at least two people go together to confront the offender. If that still does not engender the desired response, then the church is to get involved. It is within this context of interpersonal and communal discipline, however, that Jesus makes a startling declaration regarding his presence: "For where two or three come together in my name, there am I with them." It is Jesus' active presence among, in, and through the Christian community—incarnated in their lives and actions—that creates the binding authority for confronting sin within the church. Paul also states explicitly that the Church continues to manifest the presence of God, being "a dwelling in which God lives by his Spirit" (Col. 1:22) and "through us [God] spreads everywhere the fragrance of the knowledge of him."

Discipleship in the local church, therefore, must be mediated through relationships with others. It cannot be done at a distance. And, it is a two-way street of listening: Disciples need to listen to their mentors and mentors must also listen to their protégés.

This heightens the significance of the church as a community of believers that provides not only compassionate care for her members, but influential shaping power over the course of a lifetime. The notion of community implies responsibility for one another (*koinonia*), not just a gathering of people with similar spiritual experiences and moral values. Christian community, the Church, is the flesh-and-blood context within which individuals are situated and grow. At its best, the community of believers provides an accountable, but nurturing matrix of compassionate love for individuals such that they *find themselves growing* over time.[20] At times individuals will find themselves challenged, prodded, questioned and even rebuked (see again, Matthew 18). At other times individuals will need to be encouraged, healed, and provided for.[21] Whether encouraging or disciplining, the Church is always motivated by the compassionate and fierce love of God. And so, the community of believers, the local church, also adopts a posture of attending and listening to her young adults. The apostle Paul is clear that the Church consists of all those who have been reconciled by God through faith in the life, death, and resurrection of Christ, and who are now *united together* by his Spirit and empowered to minister *corporately* as the body of Christ in the world.

The notion of community runs against the dominant North American culture of individualism. Individualism, articulated in what has virtually become a classic in sociological literature through Robert Bellah, is the notion of being interested primarily in one's own immediate affairs to the neglect of the wider, common good of others.[22] It is in community, Bellah argued, where people come to know who they are, and where their sense of place is in society: "We never get to the bottom of ourselves on our own. We discover who we are face to face and side by side with others in work, love, and learning.... We find ourselves through the various voluntary institutions we are a part of."[23]

Nowhere should this be more the case than the "voluntary institution" of the church. Empowered by the Spirit of Christ, the local church community can posture itself to listen attentively to young adults as they continue to search for a valid faith and their place in the world.

The Power of Community in Shaping Faith

In an age with a multiplicity of narratives vying for allegiance, it is no wonder college students have difficulty committing themselves to any particular narrative, let alone a meta-narrative like Christianity.[24] However, the community of believers can make a significant difference in the continuing embrace and deepening of the faith of collegians and young adults. The community can also drive them to abandon their faith. An extensive study of evangelical college students suggests that environments that blend challenge with communal support provide the necessary climate conducive to positive faith change and spiritual growth.[25] Just like a greenhouse, the conditions are important: harsh conditions such as cold temperatures, lack of nutrients, and little water will result in stunted growth or killing the plants. Likewise, in communities, a lack of loving support in the form of judgmental criticism, shunning, and other forms of insensitivity may cause students to leave or develop false forms of guilt and shame. Conversely, greenhouses that are too warm, have excess amounts of fertilizer and water will also fail to grow healthy plants. It is possible for congregations to lend too much support, smothering students so they are never allowed to encounter complex ideas or to give expression to honest questions and doubts. The community may feel threatened or fear that students may forsake cherished beliefs. In such cases, the community may tighten its grip in other ways or shut down communication altogether. Students may feel ostracized, confused, or abandoned.

Even while the young adults are attempting to create a vision or story for their own lives, the community may be narrating something completely different. In this case, when young adults eventually do encounter life experiences that challenge their cherished beliefs, and they recollect that their honest questions and doubts were met with stony silence or treated with irrelevance, they may prematurely conclude that the church's narrative is not capable of interpreting life in meaningful ways. Without a nurturing, caring community that listens with patience and compassion, these young adults may abandon their faith and leave their communities of faith. As Chan states, "What is right can be expressed wrongly, and what is truthful loses its appeal because of the unworthy manner in which is it presented."[26] Chan states this in relation to evangelizing a postmodern generation, but it also applies to students and young adults who already attend our churches. They need to be heard first if they are going to listen to what the church has to say:

> Reaching our postmodern generation entails investing time and effort to listen to their stories and share our stories. It is in the context and process of the sharing of stories that we introduce God's story, a story of the divine love and search for lost humanity. It is only befitting that God's love story should be communicated in a loving manner. And learning to speak the truth in love is crucial in commending Christ to the postmodern.[27]

In short, congregations can provide conditions that support and challenge at the same time; too much challenge or support can stunt spiritual growth.[28]

Positively, local bodies of believers can serve as mentoring communities to address the faith and spiritual vitality of young adults. Sharon Parks defines a mentoring community as "a context in which a new, more adequate imagination of life and work can be composed, anchored in a sense of *we*."[29] If students are to be engaged in the larger meta-narrative of the Christian faith that transcends personal self-interest and seeks to transform the world with the Gospel, then it is important they be a part of a mentoring community, not just with a single mentor.

Young adulthood is a natural time of recomposing meaning of self, world, others and God. As such, young adults need such a network of belonging that assists and confirms them in a strong, personally owned faith, but one that is shaped and strengthened within community. Parks advocates a number of factors that make up a mentoring community, such as a trustworthy "network of belonging"[30] that allows for a "spacious home for the potential and vulnerability of the young adult imagination in practical, tangible terms."[31] For Parks, the community serves as the community of confirmation and contradiction. It encourages and holds accountability at the same time. It also extends "hospitality to big questions." This means that the community allows questions of ultimacy—questions of meaning, purpose, and faith; questions of oneself, the world, and oneself in relation to the world.[32] Questions work both ways, however, as a mentoring community will ask these same big questions of students.

While it may be unnerving for pastors, parents, and congregations to witness young adults and collegians testing the boundaries and cohesion of their faith, it is inevitable that they will do so. To grow deeper in faith, *self-consciously choosing* to remain in the faith, they must encounter ideas, people, and experiences that challenge the *status quo* of their current beliefs. This carries inevitable risk that they will reject the beliefs of their upbringing. However, a mature faith community can play a vital role in minimizing such risk.

Conclusion

It is truly astonishing to see the rapid personal and spiritual growth among college students and young adults. The individual pastors, adult mentors, and Christian communities that speak into their lives are invaluable for helping them to hold on tight as they make their faith their own. It is how God has intended the Church to work.

This was powerfully illustrated to me in a recent conversation with a 23 year-old senior, just getting ready to graduate. I asked her to tell me the difference between her walk with Jesus when she arrived here over four years ago, and now, on the brink of embarking on the next chapter of her life. She stated that she entered college with a fearful faith, afraid to ask questions, afraid to probe her faith, even though her heart was taking her there anyway. She stated that in her home church, "To question things was not explicitly forbidden or anything but it did not seem to be encouraged.... I could not ask so I did not learn. I grew but I did not flourish." But upon entering our college she found a faith community that supported her and encouraged her to keep asking questions, to keep the wheels turning:

> I was challenged to ask the 'why' questions.... I had professors and mentors who came along side of me and encouraged my curiosity for knowledge. They answered my questions, guided my understanding, and even challenged me to think in a new and deeper way. I was loved and accepted every step along the way even if I was questioning something that I should have known. When the people around you encourage and allow you to ask the deep questions without judgment or a rebuke faith flourishes. I flourished![33]

Gradually, she found her footing. She smiled broadly as she talked about her walk with Jesus now. "Do you feel that you follow Jesus with more joy and freedom than you did four years ago," I asked? "Oh, yes!" she said, her face beaming. "Being here has made all the difference." "Here" is a place. "Here" is a community of believers that provides the positive tension of nurturing care and personal challenge so necessary for authentic disciples to grow. "Here" is a place you can help create by listening.

Notes

1. Sharon Parks, *The Critical Years: Young Adults and the Search for Meaning, Faith, and Commitment* (New York: Harper Collins, 1986).

2. For a fascinating understanding of this spiraling dynamic, and the changing complexity of how people create meaning at different stages in life, see Robert Kegan, *In Over Our Heads: The Mental Demands of Modern Life* (Harvard University Press, 1998).

3. Exod 3:11-14.

4. James Fowler, *Stages of Faith* (New York: Harper Collins, 1981), 154, 161-2.

5. Quoted by Fowler, *Stages of Faith*, 154.

6. This quotation is published with permission from the student. The paper is her own account of how she perceived her spiritual growth during her first year of college. The italics are mine for emphasis.

7. Fowler, *Stages of Faith*, 153-60.

8. See Erik H. Erikson, *Childhood and Society*, second edition (New York: W.W. Norton & Co., 1963), 263-266; also helpful is Fowler, *Stages of Faith*, 75-77.

9. See the several studies conducted by Lifeway regarding why young adults are leaving the church: "LifeWay Research Uncovers Reasons 18 to 22 Year Olds Drop Out of Church," available online at http://www.lifeway.com/article/165949/; Mark Kelly, "LifeWay Research: Parents, Churches Can Help Teens Stay in Church," available online at http://www.lifeway.com/article/165950/

10. Peter F. Wilson, "Core Virtues for the Practice of Mentoring," *Journal of Psychology and Theology* 29, 2, (2001): 121-30.

11. Wilson, "Core Virtues," 122.

12. Wilson, "Core Virtues," 128.

13. Wilson, "Core Virtues," 124.

14. Wilson, "Core Virtues," 126-7.

15. Wilson, "Core Virtues," 127.

16. Wilson, "Core Virtues," 125.

17. There are various understandings of discipleship. For a general overview of options and models, see Michael J. Wilkens, *Following the Master* (Grand Rapids, MI: Zondervan, 1992), 24-47, 339-47; Eugene Peterson presents biblical discipleship in contradistinction from hostile cultural forms of discipleship in *The Jesus Way* (Grand Rapids, MI: Eerdmans, 2007).

18. Dallas Willard, *The Divine Conspiracy* (Grand Rapids, MI: Zondervan, 1998), 271-310.

19. Eugene Peterson, *The Jesus Way* (Grand Rapids, MI: Eerdmans, 2007).

20. Eph 4:11-16 speaks to this process of growth within the context of Christian community.

21. There are countless Scripture passages that speak to these obvious truths. For example, Acts 2:42-47; 4:32; 6:1-7; Rom 12:13, 15; Eph 4:29-5:2; Col 3:12-14; Jas 1:27; 1 Pet 4:8-11; 1 John 3:14-20

22. Robert Bellah, et al., *Habits of the Heart: Individualism and Commitment in American Life* (Berkeley, Calif.: University of California Press, 1996).

23. Bellah, *Habits of the Heart*, 84.

24. Mark L. Y. Chan, "Following Jesus as the Truth: Postmodernity and Challenges of Relativism," *Evangelical Review of Theology* 31:4 (2007): 306-19.

25. G.L. Holcomb & A.J. Nonneman, "Faithful Change: Exploring and Assessing Faith Development in Christian Liberal Arts Undergraduates," *New Directions for Institutional Research* 122 (2004): 93-103.

26. Chan, "Following Jesus as the Truth," 315.

27. Chan, "Following Jesus as the Truth," 315.

28. Holcomb & Nonneman, "Faithful Change," 93-103.

29. Sharon Parks, *Big Questions, Worthy Dreams: Mentoring Young Adults in Their Search for Meaning, Purpose, and Faith* (San Francisco: Jossey-Bass, 2000), 134.

30. Parks, *Big Questions*, 134.

31. Parks, *Big Questions*, 135.

32. Parks, *Big Questions*, 137-8.

33. This quote was taken from a transcript written by the student in her own words after I conducted an "exit" interview with her, as I do all the graduates. It depicts the exact sentiment of our conversation.

Chapter 8

On Improving as a Listener[1]

Frederica Mathewes-Green

Listening Involves the Whole Body

Don't listen with your ears alone; use your eyes, as well, to gather clues from the person's expression, stance, and overall demeanor. The body can reveal the soul. In writing about Eastern Orthodox spirituality, Metropolitan Anthony Bloom (1914-2003) said that the body is like a Geiger counter;[2] it can disclose what is going on in the soul. He was making the point that it is not necessary for a monk to continually plumb the psyche, because his own body will disclose his inner spiritual and emotional processes. We can use that insight as well. By paying attention to what the other person's body communicates as we listen to them, we can discern what is going on inside the heart, soul, and understanding.

The main thing is to pay attention; consciously pay more attention than you usually do. Take note of what the other person is saying nonverbally. Sometimes you gain more insight when you think about it later; you don't get it all at the time of conversation, but the elements come together later.

While you're listening, and any time afterward that you ponder the conversation, pray and ask the Lord to give you insight. He understands everyone completely, and knows us better than we know ourselves. I get comfort from St. Paul's line in the 13th chapter of 1 Corinthians, that one day we will be able to understand as completely as God understands us now: "Now I know in part; then I shall understand fully, even as I have been fully understood" (1 Cor 13:12 RSV).We have been fully understood, we who hardly understand ourselves. The Lord understands the person you want to listen to, so ask his help.

Also, be sure that you are bearing love toward the person you're listening to. Make a conscious decision to be hospitable toward them. Your presence is like a living room, and you are inviting them to come in and be comfortable. If you keep this in mind it will feel natural to hold your arms open toward them and signal welcome with your own body language. It is necessary to love the person you are listening to, if you want to hear them accurately. If you are short of love for this particular person, ask God to help you stand within his love for them.

Here's an exercise you can do to hone your ability to notice and feel what another person is feeling—a simple and very literal exercise, focused on what they are feeling *physically*. You might notice, for example, that the other person's foot is pressed up against the chair leg; imagine feeling that as well, and sense what same pressure would feel like at the same place on your foot. Or be aware that, as she stirs her tea, the spoon must be getting hot; try to replicate that same sense of heat in your fingertips. This was a game I made up as a child, but over the years I think it helped me to develop the ability to pay attention to another person, to take them in with steady attention and empathize. I try to feel what the other person is feeling, in many senses of those words. It helps me listen accurately, and that is the foundation of any help we can give.

Mirroring

As you grasp what the other person is feeling, you can use your body, face, and voice to reflect it back. This will draw them out and strengthen the bond between you. It is as if you are becoming a concave mirror that receives and then reflects back their presence.

Sometimes this even happens naturally, when we are listening to someone and empathizing with them. You might find that you naturally begin to mirror the expression, gestures, and posture of a person you are listening to, in order to help them have a sense of being in synch. If you are not sure what you're hearing, try doing that mirroring deliberately (though of course in a subtle and natural way, so as not to distract the person you're listening to). For example, imagine you're standing, facing someone you are listening to. If the other person is resting their weight on their left foot and their left hand is on their hip, you might begin to rest your weight on your right foot and put your right hand on your hip. In terms of posture, you provide a mirror image, and it is inviting; the other person opens up. One body is "listening" to the other.

In another case, the person may be physically and emotionally closed up, keeping you at a distance. They are likely to show this by folding arms across the chest, or not facing you directly but turning toward the side. These gestures can have limiting effects on you, if they impact you without your noticing it. When you notice these distancing efforts on behalf of the other person, the right thing to do may be to respect it, and leave them alone. But there may be times when you want to at least lay the foundation for more open conversations in the future. In that case, be aware of your own body language. Resist an impulse to mirror their closed gestures. Keep your arms down, or hold them open to the other person (if it is possible to do that in a natural way, for example, if you can lay your arms along the arms of a chair). You may have to keep deliberately reminding yourself to do this, because otherwise you may mirror their closedness automatically.

Using mirroring in order to listen can take place even after a conversation has finished. For example, once you get home you may keep thinking about the conversation, but have the feeling that there was something you missed. You feel that something more was hinted at, but what it could be lies just beyond your grasp. The reason you feel this way may well be that something in the person's facial expression (or gestures, or posture) didn't match the words they were saying.

In a case like that you can attempt to replicate what they were presenting physically. You can think, "Now the mouth was like this"—forming your mouth that way—"and the shoulders were like that"—hunching or drooping your shoulders. If you can do this, sometimes insight flashes in immediately: "So that's what it was—that was fear" (or anger, or sadness).

At this point, you don't necessarily know why the fear or other emotion was there, so you haven't completed understanding them. But you have a clue. You are left with the question, "Why would she be feeling that?" Keep thinking things over, and praying for the person. Keep going back over the mental notes you took during the conversation.

Discontinuity

Pay attention to the times when elements of the person's presentation don't harmonize. For example, consider the tone of voice. You can begin to notice, not only which words are used, but whether they are spoken in a distinctive way. Whenever he comes back to this topic, does he talk very fast, as if trying to get past it quickly? Does he end each sentence with a lift, as if it were a question? Does he grow very somber at this point? Does he say he is happy, but look worried? As you listen, keep aware of whether there is unity between the content of the words and the way that they are expressed. A point at which they diverge is worth thinking about further.

The kind of facial expression called "microexpressions" can also give you clues about what is going on below the surface. Microexpressions are facial expressions that flash across the face in an instant, in as little as a fifteenth of a second. They are involuntary, and disclose an aspect of what the person is actually thinking, no matter what they might be trying to convey. Microexpressions have been studied, in particular, to train policemen to discern when someone is lying. A project to locate people who have an eagle-eye for truth tested 20,000 people for this gift, and found fifty.

Some people appear to have a natural gift for catching microexpressions. Those not born with this talent can improve their ability just by being aware that these flashes exist. As you keep looking at the face of the person talking to you, continue scanning for harmony within the face. If they are having an inner conflict over what they are saying, discontinuities will appear.

An example of discontinuity is the smile: a real smile involves the muscles that surround the eyes, and those are muscles a person can't control voluntarily.

A person can shape the mouth into a smile, but cannot force the corresponding muscles around the eyes. As a result, you can tell a real smile from a fake smile pretty easily, and probably have always been able to tell, unconsciously. You just didn't know before why it was that some people's smiles made you feel uneasy.

We see this often in photos of celebrities. As a result of having to interact constantly with strangers, many celebrities get into the habit of exhibiting false smiles—the mouth is curved but the eyes are flat. (Another reason for them to cultivate this false smile is to keep the forehead smooth and avoid wrinkles.) In some cases, the expression is almost hostile, like a dog showing its teeth. I don't condemn celebrities for giving false smiles; who could begrudge any strategy used, given the stress of a constantly-exposed life. But when you see these smiles on the cover of magazines in the check-out line, look more carefully, and discern whether you see hostility, coldness, or simple weariness.

Sometimes the discontinuity between facial expression and content is more of a constant state, rather than fleeting microexpressions. I used to go to a doctor who made a lot of jokes. Eventually it dawned on me that, for all his joking, he never smiled. While at first I was only registering the joking content of his words, I eventually became aware that I felt sort of uneasy when I saw him. I felt some stress because of the disconnect between what he was saying and what his face communicated. Perhaps someone had told him, "It's a good idea to joke around to make your patients comfortable," but there wasn't any joy in it. Because the surface content was distracting, I didn't register the disconnect immediately. Yet, in a case like this, I could listen to the unsettled feeling in my own body, and eventually locate the cause in the difference between the way he looked and what he said. Once I became aware of this was able to understand the situation more accurately, and to show him kindness rather than only amusement.

The Role of the Listener

The signals we send while listening can make it easier for the person speaking to relax and open up. As we nod, smile, offer open body language and a gentle tone of voice, the listener communicates an active interest in the other person's story. The dynamics of your voice are in themselves very influential. A lift in the voice signals interest, and conveys liveliness and alertness. Imagine for yourself how relaxing it is when you're telling a story, and your hearer responds with bright eyes, and nods in rhythm with the narrative. It helps you open up.

In the same way, you can enable someone to speak more freely through the signals you send in body language and tone of voice—perhaps echoing the other's tone of voice, and then leading it to a different place. For example, you might notice that, although the person you're listening to is talking about superficial things, they seem sad or worried underneath. You can try to match their tone of voice, speaking at the same pitch and speed—then bring it down a little, speaking more lowly and slowly. You can say something, pause briefly, then say, "You know, you just seem worried today."

✳   The role of the listener is like that of a midwife, because the only way people can solve their problems is from the inside. You can't force someone to have an insight. But you can provide an opportunity. Of course, these techniques must never be used aggressively, in order to dominate or expose the other. But skilled listening, practiced with love, gentleness, and sincere care for the other, meets them where they are.

This sort of unfolding conversation can only proceed one step at a time. You can't be in a hurry to shove the conversation to deeper waters. Just take it down one step: talk more slowly, allowing more space in the conversation; add more "ums" and "ahs." Then take it down another step and then another, as the conversation rolls on from there. This type of skilled, reflective, and loving listening will allow some people to open up more than they expected, becoming aware of underlying issues that would otherwise have remained hidden.

A bit of advice I heard long ago, which has remained very useful, is "Don't ask questions." For example, if a man is talking about a dangerous moment, if you ask, "Did you feel frightened?", he will be tempted to respond "No!" He might not want to see himself as fearful, even though he truly was. With that one question, you just ended the conversation!

Instead, you could say, "You felt frightened," and, hopefully, they will just keep on rolling: "Yeah, and then..." Or you could say "How frightening!" Anything that identifies the emotion, phrased as a statement rather than a question. If it might be a sensitive topic, you could make it a statement about yourself: "If that was me, I would have been so scared right then." The listener can pick this up and keep going: "Yeah, I was!"

Making a statement, rather than asking a question, facilitates communication in a way similar to jiu-jitsu: you use the momentum of the conversation to take it to the next place. But if you ask a question, the person speaking has to stop and stand outside themselves, and try to see themselves objectively; if they don't like what they see, they may begin resisting it. The conversation begins to become less honest.

It's useful to roll the conversation forward with simple, murmured responses like "Uh-huh" and "Yes," which don't interrupt the flow. But if you use them too much, they can also sound like boredom or, worse, like you're using a listening technique. Intersperse these quiet responses with statements that reflect what the person has said. Use language that the speaker would recognize as accurate, and avoid slipping in a personal opinion, if it is something they would resist. At this point you're still taking in the situation, and want to help them go on talking with freedom.

In your responses, pick up and re-use any words that seem to carry particular importance to the speaker. Or you can offer a new word, and see whether they employ it as they go forward. Sometimes people are very grateful for your supplying a term that fits; they may be having trouble coming up with just the right word, and if you can supply it, it's a big help.

When you offer something and they take it up and repeat it, you and the other have communicated. This propels the conversation forward in a direction faithful to the speaker's original trajectory.

You may have a hunch about something to say, but feel like holding it back in case you're wrong. But, actually, it doesn't matter if your guess is wrong. If you say, "You must have been frustrated," and they respond, "No, I wouldn't say frustrated, it was more like...," the other will fill in the blank with their own term. Guessing wrong can still be helpful, because in considering in the speaker can rule out a possibility, and that helps them focus more accurately on what the right term would be. The speaker continues to remain the one setting the pace for the conversation.

So take care about asking questions. You might inadvertently take over the direction of the conversation, by supplying a new direction that it should go. Though questions are the most obvious and literal way to invite a person to open up, they often disrupt the flow of conversation, by forcing the other to step out of their thought stream and instead turn toward self examination. Statements, however, facilitate the flow of conversation. If you slide your observation into the stream as a statement, the other will not have to externalize and lose their train of thought, and instead can continue embodying their thoughts and feelings. Using words and phrases can lay more tracks for the conversation, and thereby allow the other to remain in control, while facilitating the direction the listener is discerning.

Facilitating Groups

When listening in a group context there are more factors to keep in mind. One task for the person who is trying to facilitate group decision-making is to prevent any one group member from usurping leadership and imposing his or her decision. If one member of the group is overconfident and overly certain of what should happen, she might—intentionally or not—steamroll other people, and their own good ideas will go unheard. This may be a person who has a dominating personality to start with, while others in the group are more flexible, or simply less invested in the outcome. Group dynamics can be fluid and volatile. Just the presence of a person with a strong opinion can be enough to make other members of the group think, "Well, our work is done. I'll just agree with her and everything will be fine." Keeping the topic open, and postponing arrival at a decision until the group feels the right solution has been found, is essential.

Group facilitators must also concretize verbalizations in such a way that strength of voice or opinion does not increase the weight of an idea. A whiteboard or chalkboard can be helpful to keep track of different recommendations and ideas, equalizing them. Any idea on the board is the equal of any other, regardless of who originated it, whether a soft-spoken person or a verbal steamroller. When the list of solutions is written down for all to read and reread, everyone in the group can keep sifting them, and nothing will be forgotten because it was expressed less forcefully.

Group facilitation and listening also require continually inviting the silent members to put forth their ideas. It is best, therefore, if group facilitators are not invested in any particular solution and if they are not commissioned to bring about a particular point of view. The group facilitator, as listener, provides an audience for anyone who may see drawbacks or potential problems in what a strong personality has recommended. Group facilitators as listeners can continue to draw attention to the fact that there could be other solutions, and embody an invitation for members to suggest these alternatives.

When I was assisting with the Common Ground Network, trying to help pro-choice and pro-life people learn to dialogue with one another, we learned that instead of getting people to talk about their opinions, we should get them to talk about their experiences. The group would be gathered in a circle, and the pro-life person might go first and say, "This is what happened to me, this is the experience I had that brought me to my position," rather than "This is what I think about what is right and wrong, and this is my reasoning." Then the person on the other side would reflect it back, saying, "You had this experience and you drew these conclusions." The idea was for them to mirror the other respectfully, so that they could say, "Yes, that is accurate; you understood me." It is very liberating to be understood. Thus, the group did not seek *agreement*. Our basic assumption was that we were not going to come to agreement, and so trying to persuade the other was against the ground rules. Our goal was not to agree, but to clear up misunderstandings and false assumptions. Perhaps you could say the goal was sincere *disagreement*.

On Offering Suggestions

Do listeners offer suggestions? Remember that a listener is not (usually) called on to meddle. Yet if you become a good listener you can be used for healing and clarifying in people's lives. The key is to know how you are called to do such work in any given conversation.

In my case, I can hardly help but offer suggestions; I do it all the time, usually after a period of listening, and this might be a flaw. After listening and getting a sense of what is going on, if I see a way forward, I always tell it to the person I'm listening to. Of course, that can be a place where I can begin to lose the connection with the other: he might not be ready to listen to any solutions yet, and may still need time to ventilate. The premature offer of resolutions and recommendations can risk losing connection with the other.

When thinking about whether to give advice, the listener must also take into consideration whether there are real or perceived inequalities between the listener and the other. This can include conversations between men and women, bosses and employees, professionals and laborers, young and old, and other relationships in which inequality may be felt. If such is the case, be careful to leave your advice as a suggestion that they may consider, rather than an order. (Unless, of course, your authority in the situation is appropriate, and you do intend to direct them to take this course.)

In general, I think it is good to state, after a time of listening, "Well, it seems to me the best thing to do is this," or "Have you tried that?" The other may respond to your suggestion a number of ways. Some will immediately reject it and point out its flaws. Some people, in fact, cling insistently to "That won't work," no matter what you say, and conversation hits a deadlock; go back to active listening to see if there is an open spot at any point in the person's thinking. On the other hand, some people quickly accept the suggestion and say something like, "Wow, I never thought of that; that would probably work." This is very gratifying, of course. And sometimes the other may even seem to ignore the suggestion and gloss over it. You can give your advice, but have no control over how others receive it. Listeners must simply be at peace with this.

The key in offering suggestions and advice is to regard them as a new step in the conversation, rather than its conclusion. Don't listen with the aim of figuring out what the solution is, so you can fix it and end the conversation. Your advice must not be an "equal but opposite reaction" to the other's concerns, designed to put an end to the conversation, but rather a catalyst that moves it forward.

Sometimes the listener himself is blocked, and you notice that he is repeating himself. It seems like they are riding around a circular verbal train track: a series of four or five points in their mind simply loop together, without resolution, and keep going round and round. This may be evidence of ambivalence about a situation. They may not see clearly which path to choose. Rather than offering suggestions in such a case, focus on helping the other think it through. Possibly what needs to emerge is something they don't yet recognize, and so they go on repeating what they do know. They may be stymied by the impression that all the factors in a situation bear equal weight. You may be able to help them by pointing out that some factors are not as important as others, or that among outcomes some are more likely than others. This can loosen a log jam.

Some cases involve a *persistent* impediment, to the point of immobilizing conversation. Perhaps the other is afraid; perhaps they were hurt. In these cases, quietly waiting is not enough. The listener must help the other dig a little deeper into the block and bring it to the surface. Focus on the emotion that is lurking below the surface. Then the other can talk about their emotion, which perhaps is something they *can* verbalize fully, thereby gaining momentum.

Christian traditions involving guidance in one's prayer life and advice in decisions from spiritual fathers reveal the benefit of such proactive listening. Sometimes a false idea—a *logismos* in the Orthodox faith—can control and dictate the other's actions without their knowing it. An insightful elder or spiritual father may be able to expose it to the light, and break its power with a single statement. A single sentence can break some ancient bonds. The other can suddenly see, "Oh—I never needed to worry about that." Sometimes it takes another person to break through a tangle of confusion. Listening is not a passive or noncommittal; you must always be actively engaged with the other, in love. And there are times when the listener must step forward and say bluntly, "I'm going to tell you honestly what it looks like to me." Pray and discern so you do the right thing at the right time.

Overcoming Roadblocks in Listening

(1) Be patient. Listening doesn't happen all at once. Sometimes more than one conversation is needed to listen well. It might take weeks or months of listening to get things all cleared out. There is a process of helping people work through

ideas, potential blocks, and (potentially distracting) excitements. I know that, when I perceive that there's a problem, I want to get the problem solved, but I have to keep that impulse in check. It's hard work not to rush the other person. That would be like trying to rush a hardboiled egg: while you may (in your opinion) know what the hardboiled egg ought to look like, you can't do the boiling for it, or rush it. It may take month after month for the other to work towards a solution. Thus, you need to have as your goal not fixing the problem, but enabling the process that emerges with time. It is like enabling a rose to bloom. You can't rush that; you have to let it do that on its own schedule. Patience is hard work, but it is necessary in listening.

②Develop a listening character. It's hard to do listen effectively if you don't, to some extent, love the other person. Patience with the other is the fruit of love. It's more than just a technique. You have to see the complexity and beauty of another human being, and respect that, without trying to force it in one area or another. I sometimes think that, as fascinating as the best novels can be, every person you meet is a novel God is writing, the best novels of all. So the most important thing about listening is love for the other, because God is love, and the presence of God is love. This means that the listener's presence can communicate the presence of God. This is not a technique; this is the love God has for the other, and it can empower you to love with his own love. God's love for the other gives you patience, and the gift of listening in the midst of struggle. The listener is free to dwell in this loving presence of God, rather than solving a problem, or offering correct thoughts, opinions, and advice. Listening means allowing the Lord to be present, loving the other person as he knows best.

③Allow the other to solve the problem. Someone has said that no one hears anything except what comes out of their own mouth. To listen means to help someone come to the point that the solution comes rising up out of their own heart and mind. Even if the solution is something that you could have told them at the first session, listening helps the other get to the point where they can enunciate it themselves. Then the truth of that outcome will be apparent to them because it will have grown organically, out of their own experience and from within their own history.

④Keep the other in focus. A common pitfall for well-intentioned listeners is turning the spotlight toward themselves. The temptation is to usurp the conversation by telling one's own story. Say someone is worried about their mother's illness. The listener might be tempted to show sympathy by saying, "Oh, my mother was sick, too, and how I felt was this."

It seems like that should work, in theory, because you're being sincere and showing that you understand. But in reality, it has the opposite effect: instead of listening, you have dragged the spotlight over to yourself. The other has to stop talking about her burden, and stop following the track of her own thoughts, and instead focus on you. So keep in mind that, no matter what has happened in your past, it is never *exactly* the same as what's happening to the other now. The other has a different personality, a different history, and different spiritual experience. They will draw on different resources. Each situation truly is unique, so let people be truly unique, especially if in the midst of suffering or sadness. Let the other, for the space of this conversation, be the only person in the world who knows what their own circumstance is like.

In conclusion, I'd like to stress what a gift good listening can be. Most people don't get enough listening; they go around hungry for understanding. And I think people today are lonelier than ever. All our freedom from other people's meddling or opinion also means that we don't have the close, supportive relationships we used to have. If you can be a good listener you can bless others a great deal. It's a way to serve God by loving his people.

Notes

1. When Frederica was invited to contribute an essay to this book, she had just been interviewed on the subject of honing our listening skills. The reflections of this essay are based on a transcript of that interview. The podcast can be found here: http://ancientfaith.com/podcasts/frederica/ listening_skills.

2. Right Rev Anthony Bloom, *Asceticism: Somatopsychic Techniques in Greek Orthodox Christianity*, Guild Lecture 95 (London: The Guild of Pastoral Psychology, 1957).

SECTION 3

LISTENING AND THE SPIRITUAL LIFE

Chapter 9

Listening to God, Shaped by the Word[1]

Edith M. Humphrey

Had Mary had been up all night, or was her sleep troubled in the wee hours of the morning by dreams that matched the emotional turmoil of the past few days? The day before had been the first Sabbath that she had spent without the presence of Jesus for a very long time—no doubt it seemed like no Sabbath at all. Her master and healer had released her from the torment of the demonic: perhaps the agony, the void, and the darkness now made her question whether her sanity was impermanent, or whether it even really mattered. There was no rest for Mary and her devastated friends without the one who came to gave them rest. Whether completely or only partly sleep deprived, Mary went to the tomb while it was still dark. No doubt the whole thing seemed surreal, the happenings of the past week like a dream from whom she wished she could awake. And, indeed, this *was* the pre-dawn not only of Mary's awakening, but the awakening of the whole world. It was dark, but the evangelist tells us it was the first day of the week—that day that would soon become the day of the Lord.

It was dark, but there was the hint of light on the horizon. It was dark, but before soon she would be face to face with the One who had the power to pronounce, "Let there be light." She arrives at the inexplicably opened tomb –had she, in her grief, mistaken where they had laid him? No, this *is* it: what on earth has happened? In disbelief, she is compelled to enter, and there, in the darker shadows of the cave, she glimpses a vision of two angels. They ask her "Woman, why are you weeping?" What a bizarre question—why wouldn't she be cry-ing? Then she turns away from the inner darkness, and looks outside towards the world. She sees a figure *standing,* in silhouette against the early morning light: yet she does not know him. Why would she expect to see a slain man standing? Why would she expect to see the dawn after an eternal night? Again comes the question, this time from *him,* "Woman, why are you weeping?" And yet another question: "Who are you looking for?"

Our Lord is the consummate teacher. He instructs by startling Mary with his presence, by speaking to her, even in the darkness, by asking us questions. At a moment when we think that all is over, that there is nothing left to hear, he silences us with astonishment, and teaches us to listen again. Though what he speaks is of cosmic proportions, God speaks his words, addresses his questions, to us. It was this way at the beginning of our dying world: "Adam, where are you?" "Woman, what have you done?" (But God asks *no* question of the serpent, since there is nothing left to do but render judgment where that character is concerned.)

Here again on the resurrection morning, at the dawn of a new world, a new creation, the living One engages the one he loves, one of his own, with questions, inviting Mary into his council: "Who are you looking for?" Mary, however, is intent upon her own program, and continues in the train of thought that he has sought to interrupt—where is the body? Mary is looking for a body; the risen One invites her to look for a *person.* Her grief prevents her from hearing Jesus' question, and so he calls her *by name.* And as he names her, she knows him—*whom* she is bound up with, and *who he is.* She was looking for a dead man, and is surprised by joy. Here is something for which she was *not* consciously looking: here is the presence of the One who makes all things, including herself, new.

Peter also was there that morning. There is a kind of dance that takes place in those early hours, a dance recorded a little differently in every gospel, as Mary, Peter and the other disciples enter into knowledge concerning the most astonishing chapter of human history, the resurrection of their Lord, and the beginning of the new creation. Isn't it interesting that Peter does not himself see Jesus in that early morning hour, but must (for a time) content himself with the wildly joyful words of Mary Magdalene, the one whom the church calls "apostle to the apostles"? This is a bit of a surprise, since Peter had been privileged, several months before the ordeal of the crucifixion, to behold Jesus in glory. At that time, the time of the shining Transfiguration, only three— Peter, James and John—had seen the sight, and heard the divine words about Jesus, which they passed on to the others in God's good time. Then, the rest of Jesus' followers had been dependent upon Peter and the inner circle; but on Easter morning, even Peter and the beloved disciple (John?) are dependent on the words of a woman, whom they have difficulty believing.

It is to the women, who stayed at the cross until the end, to those who saw where the body had been laid, that the news of the resurrection is first given. And it is most particularly to Mary that Jesus appears in care and in love. Even the leading disciples must listen to what they, and she, have discovered. These astonishing lines of communication indicate the way of the new creation, the mode of living in the new body of believers that is being forged around Jesus. His followers are interdependent in every way, bound up in an intricate symbiosis, as they come to know the One who gives them life, as they grow into what they are meant to be. The disciples' inter-dependency in "seeing the Lord" recalls Paul's words regarding the mutuality of the members of the body of Christ, whether head, foot, fingers or lungs, whether male or female: "In the Lord, neither is woman independent of man, nor is man independent of woman" (1 Cor 11:11 NASB).

 ## Our Light and Word

It seems as though Peter –or perhaps it is one of his pupils, but let's call him "Peter"—were meditating upon this interdependence, this common vision of the members of Christ as he recalled the events on Mount Tabor, and all that followed, in the second epistle of Peter. Here he gives his commentary upon the Transfiguration, and emphasizes how it is that we come to understand *together* God's wisdom, God's being and God's life. *Together* we grown in grace, together our faith is strengthened, our common love formed, and our hope nurtured:

> His divine power has given *us* everything *we* need for our life and godliness through *our* knowledge of him who called *us* by his own glory and goodness.... So [all of you—the "you" is plural!], make every effort to add to your faith goodness, and to goodness, knowledge, and to knowledge, self control; and to self-control, perseverance, and to perseverance, godliness, and to godliness, brotherly [and sisterly!] kindness, and to sibling kindness, love. For if you [together] possess these in increasing measure, they will keep you from being ineffective and unproductive in your knowledge of our Lord Jesus Christ." (1 Pet 1:5-8)

It is as we come to know Christ together, as the light from him shines upon us together, that we learn who we are in the church! Notice how the apostle speaks about the gifts of God, and about our growth in Christ, always using "we" and *plural* "you" language. The letter emphatically addresses its readers as a group, and depicts their growth towards the character of Christ as something that happens to them *together*. (Though it is interesting to note that when the writer issues a warning in verse nine, he gives it to the individual, and thus calls the one who may have "forgotten" to repent, himself or herself!) But the growth in grace is to happen to the whole group together, to the "we" who are in Christ: Peter addresses his "brothers" and his "sisters."

At the same time, the epistle claims a kind of authority for the apostle. Peter is a brother and servant, but also an apostle, upon whose witness the community is dependent. He, along with the other apostles, had seen the majesty of the Lord, and depicts this vision of Jesus as something of utmost importance for the community to recognize. The word of the Lord, the sight of the Lord Jesus, is pictured as a singular light piercing our darkness, enabling us to see: "We have the prophetic *word* made more sure...as a *lamp* shining in a dark place" (2 Pet 1:19). *The community of Jesus has a sure word, a lamp that shines.* We are dependent upon each other: but more than that, we are dependent upon those who see better than we do by the light of that lamp.

Our focus for this conference is "listening to God, shaped by the Word." We all know that good "words" go far in the formation of a person. The recent film, "V is for Vendetta," begins with the lament of Guy Fawkes's sweetheart, who cries out, as she watches him executed, "you cannot hold or touch an idea;" the movie ends as the main character, V, triumphantly proclaims as he comes to his own death, "Ideas never die!" The film actually is quite subtle in enclosing its action in this debate between the hero and a hero's sweetheart, a debate concerning the endurance of ideas or words. For Christians the debate is, it would seem, unnecessary, for the written and human Word of God are conjoined. Sometimes we forget this, and speak only of the Scriptures as God's word, concentrating upon "Christianity" as simply a set of good ideas. But when Christians speak of God's eternal Word, they are talking about more than good words or an undying idea. They are celebrating the One who is the Word, and who died in love for them, and who rose to live eternally. To be shaped by this Word is not just to listen to a message from God and allow it to change our mentality: it is to be given life by the One who is the Word, from whom all life and every true word comes. True words, the words of Scripture, the words of Christian proclamation and witness, are important in God's family, because they point to the One who is Himself the Word. The fullest Word that we have is One who can be seen, touched and heard. Indeed, he touches us.

Our Light and Word is Christ

The early disciples knew this, and tended not so much to talk about "Christianity" as about being "in Christ." Peter tells us that the word of the prophets has been *confirmed* by the "power" and the "coming" of Christ who is himself the "prophetic Word," God's word in the flesh to us. Listen again to his meditation upon the sight at Mount Tabor, and who Jesus is:

> For we did not follow cleverly devised myths when we made known to you the power and coming of our Lord Jesus Christ, but we were eyewitnesses of his majesty. For when he received honor and glory from God the Father and the voice was borne to him by the Majestic Glory, "This is my beloved Son, with whom I am well pleased," we heard this voice borne from heaven, for we were with him on the holy mountain. And we have the prophetic word made more sure. You will do well to pay attention to this as to a lamp shining in a dark place, until the day dawns and the morning star arises in your hearts. (2 Pet 1:16-19)

The prophets spoke truly; and the eyewitnesses of Jesus, the apostles, spoke even more truly, for they not only heard God's word, they *saw* the One who was the Word, they lived with Him, they were shaped by Him, and they worshipped Him. They came, in the presence of Jesus, to learn that God's Word is a Person, someone who calls us to be *with* him: "we were *with him*." Our walk in Christ is a fascinating thing, for we are dependent one upon the other, but we also are called, particularly, and together as the Church, to be intimate with Christ. For us there are many witnesses, many intercessors, many older brothers and sisters;

for us there is also a calling to be directly in communion with the Lord, by the Holy Spirit. When we speak about the apostolic witness, upon which we are dependent, we are not speaking simply about a body of teaching that has been handed down—wonderful though this is! We are not speaking simply about a holy and true history that has won for humanity freedom from sin and death—wonderful though this is! No, the apostles bear witness to the living Word, to the transforming Life, to the intimate Way into the very heart of God: they bear witness to the Lord Jesus, whose delight is to cleanse from sin, but to call us into life, true life with him.

Peter describes in this letter how it is that he and the others began to be changed, and how it is that we are changed, too. We discover from his words that the transformation occurs when we recognize that Jesus is in the center. On the mountain, God visited them through sight as well as sound: they were eye-witnesses of Jesus' majesty and excellence, and they *listened* to what God said concerning Jesus. God's word particularly marks out Jesus, and honors Jesus, who was shining before them. The words of the Father are the divine counterpart to our words of worship: indeed they are the catalyst for our worship. Peter says that the Father gave honor and glory to Jesus, who has majesty and glory in himself, and said, "This is my Son; I love him; with him I am well pleased." In echo, our best worship says, "this is my Lord; this is my brother, my friend, my teacher; I adore him." The Father's words teach us how we are to worship!

Peter tells us that the eyewitnesses of Jesus' transformation paid attention to God's words about the Son, the Beloved One, and allowed these words to confirm what they were seeing. They were attentive to this revelation that they had together, for what their eyes had seen was confirmed by the very word of God. The apostles saw, listened, and believed; Peter calls upon those of us who are reading his letter to do the same. There may be many cleverly and artfully designed human stories that would seek to capture our take our attention, but here God's own word, God's very own revelation, God's very own light in the darkness. Be attentive, listen and heed this, Peter says.

But there is more, it seems. The New Testament doesn't simply speak about attentive listening, followed by submission to the word. (That would be wonderful, in itself, if we were to obey well; but obeisance is not the full dynamic of Christianity, but rather the central idea of Islam, whose very name means "submission.") No, Peter says that we have the prophetic Word more fully confirmed, because Jesus the Lord and Christ has been seen and known, and has been honored by God. Jesus himself is the "lamp shining in a dark place,"—a light who is himself God's promise, whose delight it is to enlighten us at the very centre of our beings, "in our hearts." Peter knew what it was to be "shaped by the Word." For him the formation began with listening to the Word, but it had to do with coming to know Jesus by means all of the faculties God has given—with the ears, as well as the eyes, the whole body, and the heart.

The Light and Word Transforms Us

The tenor of the letter of Peter gives to us the sense of a document written at the end of a believer's life, as a testimony to Jesus, and as a kind of "last will and testament," passing on to others what has been learned from Christ. If we were to read into chapter two, we would see that there is some concern for the pernicious effect of greedy and false teachers, and for carelessness among those Christians who are tired of being attentive for the word and work of God. Some, the letter tells us, have even distorted the careful and wise teaching of the Scriptures and of the letters of Paul (2 Pet 3:16), and there is danger that Christians will be carried away by these distortions, or by the brilliant and compelling stories that others are telling about the world. But the letter is not in "panic mode," because the writer has become assured that the Christian community already has been given "everything needed for life and godliness"—after all, God has given no mere idea, no remote word, not even a shining vision, but His very self to us! So the apostle knows, at the end of his life's journey, that there may be (perhaps soon for him!) a road out, an *exodus* (2 Pet 1:14-15) from this world, but there is equally a way *into* God's presence, an "entrance into" (2 Pet 1:11) all that God has called him (and us!) to be. He speaks in wonder concerning the way that God shapes us, how God uses us to minister to each other, and how God calls us *together* to "participate" in the divine nature!

None of this happens by accident, nor automatically, but it is a living process, a growth that comes to us out of the very life of Christ. Coming to know Christ may seem, from one perspective, like a choice that *we* make. Becoming more like Christ might seem, from one perspective, like a whole string of choices against evil and for the truth. But it is, indeed, all of God, who has given us, through his Son, what we need to "enter." The letter begins with the prayer that "grace and peace *be multiplied to you* in the knowledge of God and Jesus" (2 Pet 1:2). Peter then launches into the description of how we should grow in Christian character, adding virtue to virtue. But, at the end of this progressive list, even where it seems that human effort has been stressed, he concludes by saying, "The entrance, or 'way into' the eternal rule of our Lord and Savior Jesus Christ will be *abundantly supplied to you*" (2 Pet 1:11). This abundant supply, this road into the rule of God, has been made available, of course, through Jesus' very own "exodus" (Luke 9:31) which he accomplished for us on the cross.

Despite the darkness around, despite the need for vigilance and effort, this letter is full of celebration and thanksgiving— without being "Pollyana-ish." The apostle is happy that his readers have been established in the truth, but wants also to stir them up, to encourage them to continue to pay attention to the true light, to the majesty of Christ, to the Word of God. He is under no illusion that he himself is *needed*, for he is not himself the light or the way. Yet he knows that God comes to us, speaks to us, is worshipped by us, as we are together, in communion. He had seen God's glory in the presence of other disciples, and knows that Christians more easily see the majesty and power of God as they do it with each other. So, he tells us of the "we" who saw the majesty of Jesus, and the glory that was given to Jesus by the Father, a homage heard by the "we." Indeed, so important is the "we" factor that the apostle takes his time to correct those who think that they may individually understand God's will. At 2 Peter 1:20, he insists that one of the basic lessons we must learn is that "no prophecy of Scripture is self-interpreting," nor does prophecy come about through a single human will. Rather, it is when the Holy Spirit moves within inspired *human beings* (plural) that, God speaks by them, and it is by the Holy Spirit that *together* we discern what God has said. Just as the vision of Jesus was not vouchsafed only to one person, so the word of God is not delivered only to one, for God's life is communion. God intends to make us "communers," "sharers," "participants"—with himself, and so with each other; with each other, and so with himself.

Frequently we stop short, not recognizing the full scope of the salvation, the wholeness, into which we have been called. We think most of cleansing from sin, and sometimes about healing from disease. But this letter reminds us that these reparations are not all God has in store for us. First Peter declares, astonishingly, that the Father has acted in the son Christ so that, by the Spirit, we might be "called to his own glory" and become "partakers of the divine nature." The same Father, who gave glory to the Son, and who by the Holy Spirit, enabled the apostles to understand who Jesus was, wants for his human children to have that very character of mutuality that he exhibits with Son and Spirit. Father, Son and Spirit are, The Triune God is, where "love" finds its beginning, its fullness, and its end—to enjoy each other is what life is all about! This is the mystery of eternity and concerning this mystery *the community of Jesus has a sure word, a lamp that shines.* It is my prayer that as we search the Scriptures, and particularly meditate upon the Transfiguration of Jesus, we will come to understand more and more nuances of this "sure word" and the many facets of this "shining light," by which—by *Whom!*—we are together being transformed.

Casting Away the Ancestral Curse

Let's return to Mary, alone in the garden with Jesus. We have seen the importance of the "we" factor in God's Word—that may be true for Peter's letter, but what do we do with the fact that Jesus' word was for Mary herself, alone on that first Easter morning? Surely, if there is anywhere in Scripture that speaks of individual intimacy, it is *here*. (Perhaps some of you, like me, hear an echo of the old gospel song "I come to the garden *alone*...."). Isn't this story a sign that God's word can be heard and understood by a sole brave woman who would just be tenacious enough not to give up, to continue to look for the truth? No; Mary is one of those exceptions that prove the rule. (There are others, too, like Jacob who wrestled with an unknown stranger until daybreak, and Elijah who in the wilderness complained that he alone was faithful to the Lord God). Indeed, we know from the other gospel accounts that Mary was *not* alone, but in the company of other women; John's account doesn't mention this, but does speak of her making a second trip to the tomb *with* Simon and the other disciple. Still, John's gospel emphasizes the personal word that Jesus had for this "Woman," this "Mary" and tells us how Jesus conversed with Mary alone after the disciples had gone back to their homes. Mary, willing to stay there, daring to be outside her comfort zone, is arrested first by the word of angels, then—joy!—met by the one who is the Word. His word for her is personal, and particular—he calls her name—yet what he says is not couched in terms of "individual" or privileged revelation. Jesus calls her attention to his communion with the Father: "I have not yet ascended to the Father." (Yes, I know that the full importance of this mysterious statement is difficult to understand, but let's leave the theology of resurrection and ascension aside for now, and simply notice that at the very least he is calling attention to the communion of the Triune God).

How sad that, in trying to rehabilitate Mary, many contemporary scholars focus on what they perceive to be a "power play" in the New Testament, so that the battle between male and female is perpetuated in the early Church! I suspect that many of you have been asked questions concerning the role of Mary in, for example, the *Da Vinci Code*, or that some of you have been queried regarding the role of Magdalene and authority of female goddesses in the Gnostic gospels. Most recently, Elaine Pagels and others have appealed to the Gnostic gospels as examples of "Christian" texts that give women a natural place in ministry. It is true that in some Gnostic texts, female names are dominant—but Gnosticism is a varied phenomenon, and some of these texts actually depreciate women and the body, as with the *Gospel of Thomas*. In any case, the genius of Gnosticism is to appeal to human pride, flattering the one who is "in the know" about spiritual reality, and giving in to the seductions of specialized and esoteric knowledge. All these speculative mysteries are far removed from the emphasis of our faith, and of the Scriptures, upon the winsomeness of Jesus and his personal gift of himself to us, to the point of death. Recently, I reviewed an impassioned and sophisticated book by Ann Graham Brock, called *Mary Magdalene, The First Apostle: The Struggle for Authority*. Her thesis is that there are "many patriarchal tendencies within certain branches of early Christianity and [an attempt] to suppress the significance of women's leadership roles, especially that of Mary Magdalene."[2] She argues, as she compares the gospels of Luke and John, that Peter is exalted in Luke's gospel at the expense of Mary, who is silenced. Unfortunately, Brock does not notice the many ways in which women take a key role in Luke's work, for she is looking at only one feature. At any rate, the purpose of the gospels is to focus upon what God has done and is doing through Jesus, not to dwell specifically upon the priority of any group—whether apostles or patron-women. Brock misses the beauty, the collegiality, the mutuality of the disciples' fellowship, with all its blemishes, because she is reading the New Testament against its grain, interrogating it in a manner not natural to it. After all, the gospel is not about power-plays, or about who is in ascendancy. Paul's embarrassment about these questions of power is an indication to us regarding the true nature of Christ: Remember his humiliation in 2 Corinthians, as he has to plead with his congregation to accept him as their apostle, over against false apostles who are questioning his competency and leading them astray?

So it is that on the resurrection morning, Jesus does not give to Mary, in the first place, a creed, or a position. No, Jesus calls Mary by name, and blesses her as a member of her spiritual family, and as a follower of himself, the one who has died the humiliating death on the cross. As the morning dawns, he commits Mary to her family: "Go to my brothers and say to them, 'I am ascending to my Father and to your Father, to my God and to your God." Jesus, the Word, speaks to Mary, and tells her something about his own personhood, bound up with the Father, and about her true life, bound up with the others who love Jesus. She might have thought to "cling" to Jesus for herself, but this is the way of love—what she has seen and tasted must be given to others.

Mary's personal moment with Jesus, then, confirms what we have heard and seen of God's Word—*together, the community of Jesus has a sure word, a lamp that shines in the darkness.* That light and word is the witness to Jesus, but also God's very gift of himself, by whom we are transformed—and it is he who undoes darkness, who breaks down divisions in this fallen world. It is as though Mary, in the garden, is a New Eve, freed by the risen Jesus to speak a "good word" to her brothers, a word that is linked with the undoing of the "ancestral curse" that was enacted at Eden. An ancient hymn of the resurrection speaks of this great joy:

> When the women disciples of the Lord
> learned from the angel the joyous message of the resurrection;
> they cast away the ancestral curse
> and elatedly told the apostles:
> "Death is overthrown.
> Christ God is risen,
> granting the world great mercy."[3]

That first garden had been the site of deceiving words, stolen fruit, distorted relationships, death, and broken communion. On Easter morning, the sight, voice and touch of the risen Jesus was the beginning of a new creation, expressed in the speaking of truth, the offer of the bread of life, the mending of relationships, and our growth into an astonishing intimacy with God and with each other. *The community of Jesus has a sure word, a lamp that shines.* He has granted to the world—and to us—great mercy! The mercy of God is Jesus' presence with us, and the life of the Holy Spirit among us.

Notes

1. This essay was originally published as "Listening to God, Shaped by the Word," *Anvil* 24:1 (2007): 11-19. Most Scripture references are left without translation, as it appears in the original essay.

2. Anne Graham Brock, *Mary Magdalene, First Apostle: The Struggle for Authority* (Cambridge, MA: Harvard Divinity School, 2003), 13.

3. This hymn is the fourth Troparian of the *Great Vespers*. Available online at http://www.athanasius.com/data/troparia.htm

Chapter 10

Developing Ears to Hear:
Listening and Meditative Prayer

Daryl M^{ac}Pherson

The Holy Longing

There Must be Something More

The human heart longs for meaningful connectedness to God. We were created for intimate communion with the divine supernatural. Such communion is our privilege through simple meditative prayer. For most pastoral leaders, among the many hopes and aspirations we bring to ministry, we assume and expect to continue growing in a joyful, intimacy with our Lord. Not in our wildest dreams could we anticipate that ministry life could sabotage this intimate connection with God. This is, however, the unfortunate irony for many.

Take a look at your typical day, week, or month. How would you characterize the pace of your ministry? Do sermon deadlines, strategy meetings, and denominational commitments consume enormous amounts of time and creative energy? Expectations (personal, local, and denominational) for ministry effectiveness impose huge pressures on us. Throw into the mix constant interruptions, urgent and not-so urgent pastoral care needs (often unmet), inevitable misunderstandings and church conflicts. Add in time demands for family, personal health and fitness and the elusive "miscellaneous." Images of a desperate juggler in twisted contortions come to mind. There's just never enough week or enough pastor for all that's supposed to be done. Emotional reserves run close to the empty line. Prayerful meditation fostering intimate, nurturing communion gets short-shrift. Perfunctory performance of "doing devotions" or exegeting a Bible text for the next sermon pose as meager substitutes for prayerful meditation. Spiritual formation for one's self and one's parishioners is reduced to 30 minutes per week (the Sunday sermon). And yet, still that holy longing for the something more persists.

Jesus extends an invitation to abide in him—to make our home in him, to be at home with him (John 15.4-9). The image invites a deep soul intimacy of being known and loved in reciprocating relationship between ourselves and God. Just imagine! God created us for fellowship; he seeks us out. Awareness of *his* desire for *our* fellowship comes to us through this unquenchable longing for spiritual communion. Brennan Manning voices this universal longing: "The deepest desire of our hearts is for union with God. From the moment of our existence our most powerful yearning is to fulfill the original purpose of our lives—'to see Him more clearly, love Him more dearly, follow Him more nearly.' ...We are made for God, and nothing else will satisfy."[1]

Moreover, the Apostle Paul testifies to the interior divine dynamic of Christian life and ministry: "To this end I labor, struggling with all his energy, which so powerfully works in me" (Col 1:29 NIV). Contra performance-based evangelical ambition, one's life lived "in Christ" provides the inspiration for holiness, ethical behavior, and love. An abiding passion to know Christ in his resurrection power (Phil 3:10) sustains ministry focus. Paul's prayer for believers to know in experiential fashion the fullness of Christ's love in one's inner being evokes a deep longing in the heart of his readers:

> For this reason I kneel before the Father, from whom his whole family in heaven and on earth derives its name. I pray that out of his glorious riches he may strengthen you with power through his Spirit in your inner being, so that Christ may dwell in your hearts through faith. And I pray that you, being rooted and established in love, may have power, together with all the saints, to grasp how wide and long and high and deep is the love of Christ, and to know this love that surpasses knowledge—that you may be filled to the measure of all the fullness of God. (Eph 3:14-19 NIV)

Ministry leaders' hearts resonate with this passionate vision of faith communities of Spirit-filled believers experiencing individually and corporately Christ's exhaustless, expansive love. Most of us only dream of lives of wholeness and holiness internally rooted in this eternal love empowered for mission to a disoriented human family.

This is no less the transformational vision of meditative or contemplative[2] prayer: dwelling in union with God's love. It is the "you are in me and I am in you" of John 14:20 and the fruitful life of abiding and dwelling in Jesus of John 15, and the indwelling Spirit's baptizing fullness of love gifting and gracing for ministry (Acts 2; Eph 5:18). Having "tasted that the Lord is good" (1 Pet 2:3 NIV), his divine power enables us to participate in the divine nature (2 Pet 1:3-4). Moreover, as we put away the old self with its sinful, unhealthy patterns, our true self united to Christ emerges (Eph 4:22-24; Col 3:9-10). We live by the inner wisdom (Jas 1:4) that God generously supplies to mature and perfect us in our journey.

Attentive listening in silent prayer affords this quest for intimate connection with God. Henri Nouwen writes: "Every time you listen to the voice [of God] that calls you the Beloved, you will discover within yourself a desire to hear that voice longer and more deeply. It is like discovering a well in the desert."[3] Attentive listening is the means, or more correctly, the *non-means* to personal discovery of oneself as known and loved by an everlasting Love. This calls for a significant shift from active assertion of will and wit to a detached receptivity disposing and availing oneself to simply *be* before God. This is not something easily grasped by take-charge leaders responsible for motivating and moving the organizations they lead to the next level. Moreover, the reality of contemporary ministry in concert with the human condition usually mitigates (though it need not) against hearing this inner voice.

Barriers to Listening

Functionally-Driven Ministry Culture

Our ministry context reflects our North American culture; we are a doing, achievement-oriented people; doing in contrast to being. Being?—what's that? Picture this: two parents, two vehicles, multiple commitments, several times a week and all weekend. Drive-through meals and personal DVD players designed to alleviate highway boredom also pre-empt meaningful conversation. Chores and homework squeeze out family time. The latest techno-gadgets fill empty rooms and empty hearts with noise. Time for listening to one another's stories sounds like a nice value, but demands too much of one's energy. Invisible emotional barriers wall family members off from nurturing vulnerability. It's just easier to zone out in front of the TV (in separate rooms!). Parents and children become strangers living under the same roof separated by busyness and noise. We are a hi-speed, high-stress, low-touch, low-intimacy people. We Tweet hundreds of times per day, but we never share our hearts. No one has time for just being together.

Similarly, in church and ministry culture, we perpetuate an activity-oriented spirituality immersed in a culture of busyness, separated from meaningful prayerful listening. As a leader, with so many demands to juggle, it's just easier to allow ourselves to operate on auto-pilot. We run the risk of becoming disengaged from our churches, families, ourselves, and God.[4] We keep on preaching our sermons, running the church machine, putting out fires; and likely doing a good job, too. Then one day, an unsettling discovery: the inner fire is gone. Despite the successful parade of attendance increases and multiplying ministries or our perceived failures on these points, the inner glow borne of divine communion has evaporated. And we don't know how to get it back. What used to work does so no longer. Renewed efforts of consecration and surrender fail to recapture the fire. By no means have we intended to "leave our first love" but something's amiss.

Neither do we feel real, authentic, or human. Personal identity has long been intuitively linked to ministry achievements. Awareness of the divine energy of love (Col 1:28-29) motivating ministry is submerged under the impulsive need to satisfy ministry expectations through performance, perfectionism, or people-pleasing.

The Human Condition

Our cultural and ministry milieu is symptomatic of the intrinsic reality of the human condition. The real issue from a contemplative spirituality perspective is our innate drive to be masters of our destiny.

Generally speaking, the first half of life is spent building up the natural self (ego). Skills develop. Personalities emerge. Identities crafted. All normal development.[5]

We mark spiritual God-moments of conversion and consecration at altar calls and youth rallies. In preparation for a ministry vocation, we enroll in college and seminary. Haltingly, we progress toward establishing ourselves in the spiritual disciplines of Bible study and daily prayer. Precept upon principle we are discipled in the faith, crafting characters of integrity and godliness. We consecrate ourselves to advance the discipleship mission through our ministries. It's good. It's godly. It's biblical.

But there is another side to the human condition, the fallen side: the old self, the sinful, carnal self. Contemplative writers refer to this as the "false self." The false self refers to both natural expressions of being human as well as unhealthy, sinful, dysfunctional manifestations. We not only grow and develop; we get wounded too. We sin and are sinned against. Unhealthy coping patterns etch themselves into our psyche as we struggle to survive. To protect these fragile, wounded ego-selves, we craft masks of a preferred self—preferred by us or, the more likely, what our parents and peer community prefer according to prevailing social norms. Consider these masks of the false self operating below the radar of the pastoral persona.

The Performer: People-pleasing perfectionism for positive performance drives this pastoral personality. How often do we fret about congregants' response to our sermons, or buying into our leadership and vision? As much as we are loathe to admit it, our sense of self depends on the positive estimation of others.

The Tin Woodman: Early life experiences taught us to shut off unpleasant or culturally unacceptable emotions. As adults, leaders feel the pressure to present an image of having life well put together; a matter of mastering basic Christian life principles. Struggles are not simply kept hidden; they are ignored. Unacknowledged powerful emotions sabotage relationships, self-perceptions, and work performance. Unexamined fear, anxiety, or anger dominates us more than we perceive.

Rapunzel: Grimm's Fairy Tales' imprisoned damsel waited years for a rescuer when all along she possessed her own resources (her long hair) for freedom. We continually rely on external sources for rescue by validation—even God!—and cast blame on others when that validation is lacking. If only God would send revival. If only I could get my board to adopt this sure-fire program of evangelism. If only...

Little Red Hen: The self-effacing, compliant super-pastor who does it all with a smile. Underneath, resentment broils over the inactive malaise of distracted parishioners and denominational peers who value us only for our productive input to the organization. Pastors work out of the proverbial martyr mindset. Songs of lament sound off continuously: no one cares about God's work because no one can do it like me.

Chicken Little: These leaders are perpetually fearful of impending doom. Paralyzed by unnamed fears of failure and rejection, they coast in safe mediocrity, content with reciting self-justifying platitudes about faithfulness and heavenly rewards.[6]

Compulsions and dysfunctions shape us. What is human and normal is to some degree skewed by the sinful nature spinning out into unhealthy choices and unholy life patterns. The natural ego-self inevitably morphs into the "ego-editor," the Big I. Its agenda is self-preservation and self-validation at any and all costs.

While Christians speak of learning to depend on God, the self-reliance encoded in our DNA prevails. This explains why we are so susceptible to turning ministry into a venue for self-fulfillment, despite all our protestations and aspirations to the contrary. Like a powerful invasive computer virus attaching itself to every component and program of our computer's inner workings, self-centered preservation and self-aggrandizement subtly and subversively attach to everything we do, even in ministry and spiritual endeavors. This self-reliance learned in the first half of life becomes a liability for contemplative listening. The noise of our internal clutter restricts our ability to listen to God in meditation. Ego, therefore, must be deposed and dethroned.[7] Sue Monk Kidd invitingly writes: "Throughout our lives we create patterns of living that obscure [our true] identity. We heap on the darkness, constructing a variety of false selves. We become adept at playing games, wearing masks as if life were a masquerade party. This can go on for a long while. But eventually the music of the True Self seeks us out."[8] Our true self beckons. God sends us into our own purifying wilderness.

Threshold to Listening Prayer: The Dark Night of the Senses

Clearing out the Ear Wax

A period of restless discontent, aridity and anxiety prepares us to enter into the realm of listening contemplative prayer. Welcome to the Dark Night of the Senses (the 1st movement of the Dark Night of the Soul[9]) as identified by John of the Cross, a 16th century Spanish mystic. As the term suggests, our "sensory" perceptions of God at the emotional and mental level dry up.[10] Familiar patterns of praying that once nurtured our faith and renewed our assurance feel dry and boring. Bible reading is about as inspiring as reading a computer system manual. As a pastoral leader, this of course is quite disconcerting. Surely these tools for communion learned in an earlier stage of discipleship cannot be at fault? The problem must be with me. Our aridity contradicts and mocks our proclamation of the loving presence of a faithful God creates a bewildering, painful tension. Moreover, misunderstandings and mis-spoken words (unintentional and intentional) cut to the heart. Even physical sufferings contribute to the sense of darkness.[11] Yet, we long for God—if only we could find him. John of the Cross' famous line speaks the agony of this desert:

> "Where have you hidden yourself,
> Oh my Beloved, having left me in anguish?
> You fled like the deer,
> Having wounded me.
> I went forth searching frantically for you, and you were gone."[12]

Throughout the early period of the Dark Night, the individual suffers an acute awareness of one's wounded and sinful self. Usually one particular issue surfaces to consciousness:

- a besetting temptation to indulge the flesh for sensual pleasure and relief from the suffering (i.e., over-working, compulsive eating, sexual immorality, laziness);
- an old wound surfaces commanding our attention and consuming our energies and we wonder when or if we'll ever get beyond this deep hurt;
- a general loss of satisfaction with one's life in general, even though at one time it represented the fulfillment of one's dreams and ambitions;
- a deeply embedded anger since one feels that life, ministry, and relationships are out of control;
- anxiety that one has somehow fallen out of favor with God.

The aridity of the Dark Night of the Senses will likely strike at our identity as a leader. Accomplished goals, realized dreams fail to deliver a joyful satisfaction. Or conversely, we wrestle with feelings of inadequacy and failure with regard to our leadership effectiveness. The myriad of typical congregational challenges, internal conflicts, vision paralysis, volunteer malaise, threaten the justification of our existence. Everything starts pulling us into a downward spiral of exhaustion, anger and resentment. To our dismay, pent-up frustrations erupt behind the closed doors of the parsonage adding to our guilt and anxiety. In the stress of it all, sensual temptations may find fresh allure. An inner compulsive hunger drives us to compensate for the feelings of worthlessness and shame. What a mess! Unable to cope with the intensity of the turmoil, many ministry leaders fall into sexual immorality, leaving in the wake broken homes, disillusioned congregations and skeptical communities. Or as is more often the case, leaders quietly give up their dreams, numbing out or just bumming-out until retirement.

Take heart! This period of aridity and anxiety is God's preparation to lead you into deeper communion with himself through contemplative prayer. (You may want to take a deep breath and read that sentence again!) This is also why the ministry of spiritual direction can be so vital, since so few of us understand what is happening. Nor do the traditional answers to repent and change one's behavior/attitude prove a helpful solution.

In the Dark Night of the Senses, God is deposing the ego-editor as the driving force within us. But for this to happen, we have to come face to face with our ego-centricism. The many masks of our false self must be recognized before they can be discarded. Illusions about who and what makes life meaningful must be brought to the light of our conscious awareness. This false ego-self has been running amuck under the radar. Now God is exposing it in order to clip its wings and purify us and transform us by his love. God applies his sanctifying grace at deeper and deeper levels of our being.[13]

Employing biblical imagery of suffering as crucifixion, 19th century holiness writer George Watson writes:

> It does not matter what the occasion of the suffering may be. It may come from our own sins, or poverty, or ill-health, or loss of friends, or separations, or terrible and protracted temptations or assaults of evil spirits, or the hatred of others, or great disappointment, or divine chastisements; it may come from many of these sources; but let it come from any cause in the universe, if we give it over entirely into the hands of God, and sink ourselves into His will, with a perfect desire for Him to work His best will in us, He will make every pain, every groan, every tear, every particle of our suffering, work in us a death to sin and to self, and to all things on earth, which will be for our highest perfection and for His glory.

> When we suffer so severe and so long that we become dead to it, and divinely indifferent as to how much we suffer or how long it will continue; when the suffering soul reaches a calm, sweet carelessness, when it can inwardly smile at its own suffering, and does not even ask God to deliver it from the suffering, then it has wrought its blessed ministry; then patience has its perfect work; then the crucifixion begins to weave itself into a crown.[14]

In addition, God allows certain internal storms to surface which will seem to us a reversal of growth in holiness. John of the Cross vividly categorizes these as storms of blasphemy, fornication and dizziness. Blasphemy is related to the issue of control and manipulation: manipulating circumstances and people to force our preferred programs for happiness. As we experience a storm of blasphemy, God is working to increase in us the spiritual virtue of hope. Enduring the purifying storm of blasphemy, we will grow in hope. The storm of fornication targets our sensual desires and compulsions (i.e., eating, sex, shopping (!), work, laziness). As a purifying storm, the grace intended is that of love: finding our satisfaction in God's love alone. Most believers need to grow in this virtue especially. It's so easy to source our satisfaction in our relationships, achievements, reputation and status. Observe how uplifted you feel when you are applauded for your talents. Then observe when the stock market plummets or people ignore you. A favorite verse of mine when I'm going through one of these storms is Psalm 90:14 (NIV): "Satisfy us...with your love." Psalm 62:7 is another: "My salvation and my honor depend on God" (NIV). I've prayed these verses many times.

The third storm, dizziness, a general overall anxiety or uneasiness, unexpectedly comes over an individual. Quite often, we can't link it to any particular stressor. By this storm, God increases in us the quality of faith. Three storms produce three primary virtues of the Christian life: faith, hope and love. Only amazing grace could accomplish this.

The whole purpose of the Dark Night of Sense is to wean us off of our ego-self reliance and undergo a purification and transformation into our true self. The objective reality of justification through Christ by faith is that we live in divine favor (Rom 5:1-5). Subjectively, however, our perception of this loving favor has been clouded internally by all the noise of our false self with its unresolved wounds and myriad of self-generated emotional programs for happiness.[15] In the Dark Night of Sense, God weans us from these.

In relation to meditative listening prayer, with the unruly voice and energy of ego gradually being stripped of its power and influence, communion and divine union flow more freely! We enter into a gentler, quieter habitation of God and his love deep within the soul. God works more directly in our inner being by his Holy Spirit, although we will not always have awareness of this direct action of God. He prays within us by the groans of the Holy Spirit that supersede rational comprehension (Rom 8:26-27). Sometimes he will give us new insights. Sometimes we'll sense that we are praying. Sometimes we'll feel his presence. Many times we won't. Passing through the Dark Night of Sense, God weans us off the craving for and the clinging to these sensory signs of God's presence and action.

Toward Contemplation—The Daily Practice of Meditation

Following years of faithful engagement with God through vocal praying and Scripture reading and meditation, contemplative prayer is understood as a successive, deeper, intimate way of entering into and sustaining communion with God. It is a radically different way of praying since it is (or will become) a wordless communion from within one's own being. This is not to suggest by any means that we never express ourselves in verbal prayer or meditate on Scripture. God is adding a new dimension of prayer. In contemplation, God is understood as the primary pray-er, praying in us by his Spirit, at a level apart from our immediate perceptions. This explains why our natural ego self had to undergo the neutralizing process of the Dark Night of Sense.

For many active, faithful believers, this concept of praying without words can be difficult to grasp. But it's not so strange at all. A couple of observations may help. First, imagine sitting with a group of friends in front of a crackling campfire at night. Have you noticed how the conversation gets quieter? The warmth and glow of flickering flames centers your attention. You're content just to sit in the silence!

Or, imagine a senior couple sitting on their front porch watching the sunset. Five, ten, twenty minutes pass by with scarcely a word uttered between them. Another twenty minutes later, she gets up and goes into the house, shortly thereafter emerging with tea for two—hers with one milk and two sugar, his with just a drop of milk and no sugar. "Aaah, just the way I like it!" as he takes the first sip. They continue to sit comfortably in the silence enjoying one another's company, established on a firm, time-tested foundation of fifty-plus years of married life. (There's not really much to say, now, is there?) Just as the sun sets, he reaches over and adjusts her sweater over her shoulder moments before she notices the chill in the air. A little while later, they both get up at exactly the same time. "It's time for bed. Thanks for spending the evening with me." Silent, wordless communion of hearts. This is the essence of contemplative communion. I delight in the One who delights in me. I dwell in the love of the One who knows everything about me, and is working for my good. Wow! What really needs to be said?

In the early stages of the Dark Night and the concurrent transition toward contemplative prayer, seekers will be well-advised to first practice the *Lectio Divina* method of Scripture meditation. *Lectio Divina* has 4 movements to it: reading a Scripture text (*lectio*), meditating on a specific word/short phrase from within that text (*meditatio*), praying the text in response to one's life situation (*oratio*), and concluding with a time of silent waiting and listening before God (*contemplatio*). Immediately we understand how *Lectio Divina,* meditative prayer, and contemplation, prepare the way into full-fledged contemplative prayer as here described in this chapter.

As we now recognize, the listening of contemplative prayer requires something very different from the willful assertion of our natural (ego) self. Before the Dark Night we conceived prayer as what *we* thought, said, felt, imagined. Contemplation bypasses rational and affective processes. It is God's own grace that has moved us beyond the conscious awareness of his gifts and presence as experienced in the first half of life.[16] Thomas Keating explains, "The reason is that our thinking process tends to reinforce our addictive process—our frenzy to 'get something' from the outer world to fuel our compulsions or to mask our pain."[17] Now we listen in the silence to the silence. Prayer takes us to our inner-center, where God dwells by the Holy Spirit (Rom 5:5). Solitude has become our friend. In the simplicity of wordless meditation, we take time daily to seek God in the silence of our hearts. Teachers of contemplative spirituality, such as the Desert Fathers as early as the 4th century, the Cloud of Unknowing,[18] and contemporaries like Thomas Merton and Thomas Keating encourage us to make use of a prayer word[19] or short phrase while we wait before God. Keating's *Centering Prayer* is a popular contemporary form of meditative prayer that anticipates full-fledged contemplation. Some examples include: "Maranatha," "Jesus," "Love," "Shepherd," or the slightly longer Jesus Prayer: "Lord Jesus Christ have mercy on me."[20] It is a matter of personal preference as to what prayer word one chooses. By a quiet, and necessarily slow rhythmic repetition of the word we bring ourselves before God to wait in loving awareness. We're neither trying to empty our minds or to work up some feeling or arrive at some great insight. For a period of time (for beginners 20-30 minute sessions twice per day) we just hold ourselves before God in loving awareness.

Technically speaking use of the prayer word/centering prayer is not contemplation in the strict sense of the word. Contemplation as fully-developed wordless communion will evolve after a prolonged faithfulness to praying with one's prayer word. This happens exclusively within God's timing. For our part, we persevere in praying our word in season and out, in dry times and seasons of refreshment. Contemplation is commencing in subtle ways and will gradually increase over the years, and even decades.

People always ask about what to do with wandering thoughts. This does present a real challenge for our busy minds addicted to constant stimulation. (How many minutes has it been since you last checked your Blackberry for a tweet, your cellphone for a text, or your email!) Trying to stop our thoughts is pointless and is not recommended. When you become aware that your attention has focused on your thoughts or feelings (that elusive third point in the sermon, a sudden argument with your spouse, a memory of an old or current wound, tonight's Visioning Meeting), gently turn your attention to saying your prayer word. That's it! No guilt. No imposed discipline or panic. Just pray your word. Again, simplicity is the order of the day.

Prayer now becomes a general loving attention to God. The Desert Fathers and mystics speak of it as a resting in God, of being content just to be with God. Trust in God and God's unconditional love is the essence of meditation. Father Thomas Keating writes:

> Without trust in God, we cannot acknowledge the dark side of our personality, our mixed motivation, and our selfishness in its raw misery. Deep prayer increases our trust in God so that we can acknowledge anything and are not blown away by it. Without that trust, we maintain our defence mechanisms. We try to hide from the full light of that realization. Like Adam and Eve, we hide in the woods. On the other hand, as our dark side is confronted, it is removed. By our acknowledging it, God takes it away. The process of contemplative prayer is a way of releasing what is in the unconscious. The psyche has a need for evacuation the same as the body, and it does this as a result of the deep rest of contemplative prayer.[21]

As we are nourished and flourish in this new-found accepting love, purification and transformation are continued.

The Fruit of Listening Prayer

Letting the Real You Shine Forth

As we advance in contemplative listening and living, our true self gradually manifests. The true self is your basic personality or essence, the real "you" created by God and redeemed through Jesus. The theological term is "imago Dei"—the image of God in human beings. Each and every person bears the mark of the Creator; we are made in his likeness (Gen 1:26, 27; Jas 3:9). The Psalmist declares that we are "fearfully and wonderfully made" (Ps 139:14). Our capacity to think and love, explore and delight, create and serve reflect our Creator's parentage.

Scripture's witness is clear. Original sin rendered a permanent disfigurement of the divine image, evidenced in manifold sin and brokenness of the human family. Nevertheless, the divine image remains. When a person comes to God by faith in Jesus, their true identity is restored "in Christ." Paul uses this phrase repeatedly to name our new reality and new identity (Rom 6:1; 8:1; 1 Cor 1:2; Eph 1:3; Phil 3:9; Col 1:28; 2:10).

We don't invent a new image of ourselves. In the Dark Night, God has been working to liberate one's True-Self-in-union-with-Christ. Recall the story of Lazarus emerging from the tomb still hindered by stinking grave clothes, as Jesus calls out: "Loose him, and let him go!" (John 11:44 KJV). With great love and faithfulness, God recovers his likeness in us. We learn the way of "keeping in step with the Spirit" (Gal 5:25 NIV). Faith-union with Christ, facilitated and deepened through contemplative prayer, effects this transformation: "And we, who with unveiled faces all reflect the Lord's glory, are being transformed into his likeness with ever-increasing glory, which comes from the Lord, who is the Spirit" (2 Cor 3:18 NIV).

On-Going Purification and Transformation

There will be setbacks of course. Our internal default favoring the false self is constantly susceptible to the addictive urgency of the frenetic, frantic pace of our world (Rom 12.1). Too easily, we let the world squeeze us into its mold (Rom 12:2 Phillips). An analogy may be helpful here. Waiting before God in listening meditation is like the process of cardiopulmonary bypass surgery. In this medical procedure to repair a diseased heart, the flow of blood is diverted out of the body to a machine which cleans, oxygenates and returns it to the body. Contemplation is the machine that connects us to the purifying loving presence of God. Neglecting the silence of contemplation is like sending our blood back through a chronically diseased heart. We revert to the old patterns for security and meaning. Soon we feel the deadening effects of our old attachments. In another article, holiness writer George Watson provides further insight on these on-going purifications:

> There are a multitude of things which are not sinful; nevertheless our attachment to them prevents our greatest fullness of the Holy Spirit and our amplest co-operation with God. Infinite wisdom takes us in hand, and arranges to lead us through deep, interior crucifixion to our fine parts, our lofty reason, our brightest hopes, our cherished affections, our religious views, our dearest friendships, our pious zeal, our spiritual impetuosity, our narrow culture, our creeds and churchism, our success, our religious experiences, our spiritual comforts; the crucifixion goes on until we are dead and detached from all creatures, all saints, all thoughts, all hopes, all plans, all tender heart yearnings, all preferences; dead to all troubles, all sorrows, all disappointments; equally dead to all praise or blame, success or failure, comforts or annoyances; dead to all climates and nationalities; dead to all desires but for *himself.*[22]

Nevertheless, God persistently works to get our attention, allowing us to suffer our false self. Remember the three purifying storms John of the Cross identified: blasphemy, fornication, and dizziness. Lesser episodes of these will crop up as part of God's tools to get us back on track toward contemplation and a life of faith, hope, and love. Once we wake up and return to listening prayer, we continue on the path to emotional and spiritual health and holiness. Again, Watson's words speak powerfully:

> When the soul undergoes this deeper death of self, it enters into a great wideness of spiritual comprehension and love; a state of almost uninterrupted prayer, of boundless charity for all people; of unutterable tenderness and broadness of sympathy; of deep, quiet thoughtfulness; of extreme simplicity of life and manners; and of deep visions into God and the coming ages.... Such a soul looks back over its heartbreaking trials, its scalding tears, its mysterious tribulations, with gentle subduedness [sic], without regret, for it now sees God in every step of the way. Into such a soul the Holy Spirit pours the ocean current of His own life....[23]

Renewed Mission

Meditation is not a retreat from life. All the writers on meditation stress this point repeatedly. Liberated from subversively exploiting ministry to meet our own needs (now we can see it and admit it!), a compassionate sense for the other emerges. The fruit of our deeper communion will manifest in our living and loving and serving. More authentically human, a new inner freedom will serve the interests of God's Kingdom far greater than our ego-invented schemes. Henri Nouwen writes:

> When you are interiorly free you call others to freedom, whether you know it or not. Freedom attracts wherever it appears. A free man or a free woman creates a space where others feel safe and want to dwell. Our world is so full of conditions, demands, requirements, and obligations that we often wonder what is expected of us. But when we meet a truly free person, there are no expectations, only an invitation to reach into ourselves and discover there our own freedom. Where true inner freedom is, there is God. And where God is, there we want to be.[24]

From this authenticity and freedom we engage life and God and ministry. Imagine the attractiveness of faith communities composed of people entering into this freedom of true-self-in-union with Christ.

Our growth in contemplation allows us to become the person and the leader God created us to be. The old emotional programs for our happiness are seen for what they are: empty wells. God's love dwelling within is now the source of our security and identity (Rom 5:5; 1 John 3:1). With gratitude we rejoice as we witness within ourselves an increasing capacity of actually knowing the surpassing greatness of Jesus Christ in his resurrection power (Phil 3:8). Contentment from the living union of being "in Christ" flavors our engagement with life. From within us, we enjoy the breadth and length, height and depth of Christ's love, the fullness of God filling us (Eph 3:14-19). Faith, hope and love (1 Cor 13:13), the fruit of the Spirit (Gal 5:22-23), and the qualities of the Beatitudes (Matt 5:1-12) will manifest in our character and behavior.[25]

Moreover, we can anticipate fresh empowerment for life and ministry. In Reinhold Niebuhr's famous *Serenity Prayer*, we witness the progress that follows our many surrenders: "God, grant me the serenity to accept the things I cannot change; courage to change the things I can; and wisdom to know the difference."[26] We cease trying to change the past. Neither are we chained to old memories and survival patterns. By no means is the transition easy, especially for the early years. But with a practiced persistence to return to the silence of our hearts, God continues his transforming work. I'm free to accept who I am as I am: warts and bumps, yes, but gifts and graces, too.

Acceptance of what cannot be changed creates the inner space for courage to bring about redemptive change for the common good in Jesus' name. Our energies are harnessed for Kingdom work. New directions for ministry may surface. In her groundbreaking work, Janet Hagberg writes directly to leaders who undergo the transforming process of the Dark Night. She calls it "hitting the wall." Leaders who emerge from the wall (rather than reverting back to familiar life patterns) can anticipate lives of confident purpose and courage. Known for a wisdom borne of sensitivity and surrender to the Holy, they empower others for life and witness.[27]

Receptivity to the Word and will of God

Our renewed minds are more immediately disposed to receive truth from God for the ongoing work of personal transformation. I am amazed, when listening to a passage of Scripture, a sermon, a small group study, how many times just a brief word or phrase comes alive with fresh clarity as a particular word from God for that moment. The inspired written Word resonates within as God's good will; the wisdom of the Word imparts life-giving goodness. We embrace the truth in Christ Jesus and follow it more readily.

Loving Lifestyle

Love, the premiere virtue of the Christian spiritual journey, progressively manifests as the warp and woof of daily experience. We abide in Jesus' love (John 14). This love flows from our ongoing, abiding union with Love itself, the Trinity of God: Father, Son and Holy Spirit. Thomas Keating:

> The Trinitarian relationships, of their very nature, invite us to the stream of divine love that is unconditional and totally self-surrendered. This boundless love emerges from the Father into the Son, and through the Son is communicated to all creation. The invitation is given to every human being to enter into the stream of divine love, or at least to venture a big toe into the river of eternal life. As we let go of our false self, we move into this stream of love that is always flowing and bestowing endless gifts of grace. The more we receive, the more we can give. And as we give, we open the space to receive still more.[28]

To our amazement and wonder, we actually "live a life of love" (Eph 5:2; cf. Matt 22:37-39; 1 Cor 13; Rom 12:10; 1Thess 3:12; Heb 6:10; Jas 2:8; 1 Pet 1:22, 2:17, 4:18; 1 John 3:11, 18). Our spouses and our children will sense it, and so will those we lead. We perceive others with new eyes of compassion instead of assessing them for their effectiveness based on our standards! We learn to embrace fellow human beings made in God's image; people called to follow Jesus, too. God's love will move us out to find ways to practically minister to others in their needs (1 John 3:17).

The practice of listening prayerful meditation allows God greater access to us our inner worlds where genuine and lasting transformation will occur. It is all by grace; grace upon grace in increasing measure. We live out our lives and ministries from this favored place (Rom 5:1-5) with freedom to be and become what God created us to be: authentically human, increasingly holy, compassionately motivated. With Samuel we say, "Speak, for your servant is listening" (1 Sam 3:10 NIV). With Mary, we sit at Jesus' feet, ready to listen (Luke 10:39 NIV). And with Solomon (but with different results) we pray: "Give me a God-listening heart so I can lead your people well, discerning the difference between good and evil. For who on their own is capable of leading your glorious people?" (1 Kgs 3:9 *The Message*).

Notes

1. Brennan Manning, *Abba's Child: The Cry of the Heart for Intimate Belonging,* (Colorado Springs: NavPress, 1994), 38-39.

2. In contemporary usage, meditative and contemplative prayer are often used as synonymous terms, as in John Main. Others like Thomas Merton and Thomas Keating prefer the classical distinction between meditation and contemplation. In the latter, more traditional understanding, meditation is a quiet, nearly wordless reflective prayer that serves as precursor to contemplative prayer which is understood as wordless prayer. Contemplation refers to God's inner workings by his Spirit, akin to the process of sanctification. In this essay, I begin with meditation terminology, but gradually switch to contemplative terminology. See Paul T. Harris, *Frequently Asked Questions about Christian Meditation* (Ottawa, Ontario: Novalis, Saint Paul University, 2001).

3. Cited in Bruce Demarest, *Seasons of the Soul* (Downers Grove, IL: IVP, 2009), 113.

4. Sue Monk Kidd, *When the Heart Waits: Spiritual Direction for Life's Sacred Questions* (New York: HarperCollins Publishers, 1990), 192-3.

5. See the many Developmental Psychology models of human development as well as James W. Fowler's model of Faith Development. A comparative summary of these is found in Francis Kelly Nemeck & Marie Theresa Coombs, *The Spiritual Journey* (Collegeville, MN: The Liturgical Press, 1987), 228-31.

6. Sue Monk Kidd, *When the Heart Waits*, provided several of the labels which I recast in a pastoral-leadership perspective (58-73).

7. Notice, there is no suggestion of obliteration of the ego-self. Development of healthy ego is an essential aspect of normal human growth.

8. Sue Monk Kidd, *When the Heart Waits*, 47.

9. Readers may be familiar with the term Dark Night of the Soul which is often used of any period of intense and prolonged suffering. The term originates with John of the Cross. He perceived the Dark Night in three movements commencing with the Dark Night of the Senses, followed by the Dark Night of the Soul, and culminating in the Dark Night of the Spirit. The contemplative life is initiated by God through the Dark Night of Sense. Our sensory perceptions and experiences of God undergo a radical aridity. God weans us off our dependency upon our awareness of God through the senses: great comfort in prayer, enjoyment of corporate worship, even visionary and/or revelatory experiences. The two successive Dark Nights are further periods of intense aridity for greater purification and transformation.

10. Nemeck & Coombs, *The Spiritual Journey*, 104.

11. Ibid., 102.

12. St. John of the Cross, *The Ascent of Mount Carmel*, Canticle, stanza 1. cited in Francis Kelly Nemeck, *Receptivity*, (Eugene, OR: Wipf and Stock Publishers, 1985), 18.

13. In both the Old and New Testaments, the word groups for *holy* and *sanctify* are linked. To be holy is to be set apart for God. To sanctify is to make one's set-apartness to God a reality in worship, character and lifestyle.

When a person trusts Christ for the forgiveness of their sins, God *declares* that person righteous (justification). At the same time, the person is *made righteous* through regeneration; and s/he is set apart to God for his holy purposes, namely to renew us in his image, the image of love. But there is still much work to do! The residual effects of one's years lived in trespasses and sins (Eph 2:1) must be cleansed (1 John 1:9). In the ongoing process of sanctification, God continues to purify and transform a person into his image in actual day to day living. Christlikeness, particularly Christlike love, constitutes the essential nature of holiness and righteousness in principle and practice. Here we see the compatibility of vision in the theological traditions of contemplation and sanctification.

The urgency of the need for teaching on sanctification was keenly felt by John Wesley during the years of the Evangelical Revival (mid 18th Century). Converts were falling back into former unhealthy and unholy behaviors. Shaped by the Anglo-Catholic tradition of the Church of England's teaching on perfection, Wesley urged believers to pursue a radical inner transformation in holiness of motive and lifestyle.

14. George D. Watson, *How to Die to Self.* Excerpts available online at www.finitesite.com/ vesselsofmercy/excerpts.html.

15. Thomas Keating, *Intimacy with God* (New York: The Crossroad Publishing Company, 1994. 3rd Printing 2008), 60, 64, 163.

16. We of course still make use of all means of grace: Bible study and meditation, intercession and petition, corporate worship, etc. Now, however at this stage, our primary and priority means of communion and transformation is silent contemplation.

17. Keating, *Intimacy with God*, 68-69.

18. The Cloud of Unknowing (14th century) is an anonymous work about contemplative prayer.

19. Some use the term mantra. I avoid this term because of its associations with eastern religions.

20. John Main sees the role of this word to maintain our attention while praying. See Paul T. Harris, *Frequently Asked Questions about Christian Meditation*, 41, 79. Somewhat differently, Thomas Keating's *Centering Prayer* approach uses the word only as a signal of intention to wait in loving communion before God.

21. Keating, *Intimacy with God*, 51

22. Cited in Paul E. Billheimer, *Don't Waste Your Sorrows*, (Bloomington, Minnesota: Christian Literature Crusade/Bethany House Publishers, 1997, 2006), 69.

23. Billheimer, *Don't Waste Your Sorrows*, 70.

24. Henri Nouwen in a daily email reading for April 19, 2010. Henri Nouwen Society: email_lists@henrinouwen.org

25. Keating, *Intimacy with God*, 44.

26. This is the most popular of many versions of this poem by Niebuhr. The occasion for the poem is explained by Niebuhr himself. See *The Essential Reinhold Niebuhr: Selected Essays and Addresses*, (ed. Robert McAfee Brown; Yale University Press, 1986), 251.

27. Janet Hagberg, *Real Power*, (Salem, Wisconsin: Sheffield Publishing Company, 2003), 145-200. See also a companion volume Janet Hagberg & Robert Guelich, *The Critical Journey*, (Salem, Wisconsin: Sheffield Publishing Company, 1995) which is a contemplative analysis of the Christian life and the stages through which many believers progress.

28. Thomas Keating, *Intimacy with God* (New York: Crossroad, 1994), 150.

Chapter 11

The Role of Listening in Loving God: A Conversation with Julian of Norwich, Theresa of Avila, and Simone Weil

Nathan Crawford

I recently stood onstage during my local church's worship service; my capacity was as the bass player for the music team. The pastor stood up and spoke about the musicians leading worship onstage. He remarked about how each of us onstage seemed to be "doing our own thing" and, yet, somehow, it still sounded good, that somehow the music came out all right. Now, musicians will immediately recognize two problems with this statement. First, rather than doing our own thing, each of us was listening to each other and to the music. Though each of us did something different in the group, through listening we became a cohesive whole. Second, the music did not just somehow happen to sound good, but came through a lot of personal and group practice; practice that developed ears that could hear the music and play it well. We had each invested time personally and together so that we could make the best sounding music possible; we had participated in a series of practices that formed us into musicians that could play the music.

This story leads us into being able to explore what it means to listen to the Triune God and how this listening is developed through a believer's spiritual formation. Developing ears to hear God comes through a series of practices, the same way a musician develops ears to hear through practice. I want to explore the development learning to listen. Listening to God is the key of the spiritual life; being someone who is committed to listen to God is what distinguishes the spiritual masters from the everyday folk who struggle to connect with God. Spiritual formation is predicated upon one's commitment to listening to God and, through this listening, to develop the ears to hear and react to God.

As we take this journey into listening to God, we will follow three spiritual masters that can teach us much in the way of learning to listen to God through the development of a time of personal worship. Julian of Norwich, Theresa of Avila, and Simone Weil each spent considerable time developing the spiritual ears that allow one to hear God. For them, the hearing of God results in a deep love for God which then extends into all creation. It is their path that we set on in order to learn to love God through listening.

Refocusing Our Attention

The first part of learning to listen to God is to learn attach, or attune, ourselves to God. This is a refocusing of our attention which takes place as we tune ourselves into God. When we attach ourselves to God, we are then in the position to grow deeper into the love of God. This also allows us to store our treasures in Heaven rather than putting our treasures in things of the world (Matt 6:19-21).

Simone Weil helps us begin our journey by questioning at the outset what it is that we are attached to and whether we are rightly attached to God. She was born in France in 1909 to Jewish parents and died alone in 1943. She was a Jew who wrestled with whether or not to become Christian, involving herself in many of the activities of the church while in France. As France was occupied by the Nazis, she left the country with her family, only to return because she could not bring herself to abandon her fellow country people. And, while highly educated, she spent much of her time working in the factories and farms with other manual laborers, attaching herself to their plight in France at this time. All of this was because she was trying to attach herself to God by unattaching herself from the various niceties and pleasantries that she had become accustomed to. Instead, she worked to unify herself with God and neighbor through love.[1] Weil wanted to attach herself to that which infuses all of creation, the One who is God.[2]

So, how does one attach the self to God? Here, a fourteenth century English mystic named Julian of Norwich points the way in her meditation *Revelations of Divine Love*.[3] This text is Julian's account of a series of visions of Jesus Christ she received while in prayer. As she begins *Revelations of Divine Love*, we see her praying to God for closeness to God. But, after asking God for this, Julian simply waits and listens. Her preparation is to ask for closeness to God, to reach out, asking to experience God in the way that Jesus experiences in the Passion, but then she waits and actively listens for God to engage her.[4] The result of her listening is that God gives her visions of Jesus Christ and allows her to dwell in God's love. Thus, Julian shows us that the beginning of one's spiritual formation is listening that actively engages God so that God may engage us.

Theresa of Avila, a nun and mystic living in Spain in the 16th century, continues this line of thought on the spiritual life. In her famous work, *The Interior Castle*, she offers a meditation upon the movement of the person into the full experience and love of God.[5] Theresa tells us, "The whole aim of any person who is beginning prayer...should be that he work and prepare himself with determination and every possible effort to bring his will into conformity with God's will."[6] She tells her readers that the only way we can pray is if we are in conformity with God's will; or, as Weil has told us, if we are attached to God. As Theresa shows, though, there is no method for bringing oneself into conformity with God's will—there is no special prayer, no one way to meditate, no Scripture study, etc. The only way to attach oneself to God is if one gives oneself over to God completely, surrendering oneself to God so that the person is attached to God.[7]

To say that there is no one method or technique for putting oneself in conformity with God, however, does not mean that we should give up or not practice spiritual disciplines, like prayer, Scripture reading, meditation, confession, penance, and so on.[8] All of these disciplines work together in the life of the believer to tune us into the life of God: we read Scripture to learn about God; we meditate to draw close to God; and we confess to cleanse ourselves for God, to name but some of the multitude of spiritual disciplines. The goal of all the disciplines is conformity with God in such a way that our will is in tune with God's will so that we are attached to God.

The practice of listening, then, operates to draw us to God. An apt metaphor here would be the way that listening tunes a musician to his or her instrument. For example, when I first started to play the bass, I did not really know what I was doing. I did not know the keys or scales or modes necessary to play the bass well. However, I began to listen to other bass players intently and spent a lot of time working on scales, keys, and modes so that I could hear the possibilities of the bass in music. As I got better and more comfortable, I was simply *in tune* with my bass, playing well because I was comfortable with what was going on in the music and the possibilities open to me: I almost did not even have to think about playing. Similarly, when we try to listen to God, we cannot jump to being expert listeners. First, we must attach ourselves to God and unattach ourselves from those things keeping us from God. We do this through the practice of listening in things like Scripture reading, prayer, meditation, and others. These disciplines teach us to hear God so that we are in tune with God so that, eventually, our natural inclination is simply to do God's will because we just "hear" it.

Listening to God: The Priority of Attunement

The first section of this essay explored how we attach ourselves to God. The second section continued to expound upon this theme, spelling out a way that we not only attach ourselves to God, but become attuned to God.[9] To continue our musical metaphor, attunement is what happens when musicians or listeners begin really to listen and "feel" the music, grooving with each other. Attunement is a fuller attachment, where one chooses not only to participate, but to become immersed in something. As a musician, when I play with others our goal is to be completely tuned in to one another, anticipating each other's next musical moves because we have learned to listen to one another in such a way that we can always anticipate where each one is going. Or, to use another example, attunement is what happens in a marriage over time, where each spouse is so in love with the other and has given the self over to the other, that he can anticipate her needs and desires, her dreams and wishes, and she vice versa with him.

If we continue with this marriage metaphor,[10] we can see how attunement is a two-way street in that the life of the believer is grounded in the double nature of love: both God's love for us and our love for God.[11] Attunement first occurs because God reaches out and chooses us. The work of attunement is begun by God with God's choosing us through the decision to create, to give and sustain life, and through God's active involvement in creation. However, God's choosing of creation calls for a response, just as a lover wants a response from the beloved. The impetus on the part of the believer is to dispose ourselves in such a way that the work of God can take place in us. The way that this is done is through practices that form the believer in the image of God, most notably in prayer.[12]

Our Christian formation begins with God's decision to create and choose us as God's beloved. As Julian of Norwich says, "Before he made us he loved us, and when we were made we loved him...Thus man's soul is made of God and bound to God by the same ties."[13] God's decision to first love us is the beginning of our formation into the image of God. God's love calls out for our response even before we are.

As 1 John 4:8 and 4:16 make clear, the nature of God is love and it is from this love that God creates and extends Godself to all of creation. Simone Weil says that all begins in the love of God. This love springs from the very nature of the Triune God within the perfect relationship of the Father and the Son and the Holy Spirit. However, these three, as God, exist in an infinite distance from each other. This infinite distance is overcome through God's love, through the Father's love of the Son and vice versa, the Son's love of the Holy Spirit and vice versa, and the Father's love of the Holy Spirit and vice versa. The relationship of love that is inherent to God overcomes the infinite distance between the three persons of the Godhead through the complete self-giving of one over to the other, exemplified by the giving of the Son over to the Father in the Incarnation. This desire to love on the part of the Triune God leads to the springing out of creation, which is the result of God's overflowing love. However, the creation is always wholly other than God, only coming from God's love. There is another infinite distance between God and creation, but God overcomes this through God's love of creation. This unification is only able to be bridged through God's love.[14]

For the believer, the way that God loves us is overwhelming. There is a certain incomprehensibility in the fact that God has overcome this distance to love creation. Yet, this is what God does and this knowledge does something to the believer. When God overtakes this divide and chooses to love us, the soul is overwrought with God and does not know what to do, just dwelling in the light of God.[15] This person only desires God. God has "conquered" this soul by crossing the infinite distance between Godself and creation to embrace and love the soul. Simone Weil, though, believes God's love empowers the human to cross the same infinite distance that God has just crossed, searching out God because it loves God fully. The soul "makes the same journey God made toward it." For Weil, the ultimate example of this is the cross, where God traverses the distance between the divine and the created while also traversing the same distance between the created and the divine: Jesus is the one that can simultaneously bridge these gaps.[16] Here God teaches that love is the key. Everything God does is in love. This love tunes God into us so that we may be tuned into God.[17]

As we encounter the love of God, we are then empowered to become attuned to God. The way we become attuned to God is through the creation of a disposition that allows God to work in and through us. Our worship, both in the communal place of the church and in our personal moments, is our response to God. This teaches us to love God. This is like practicing to a musician: a musician sits down and practices by herself in order to learn the music and the ways of the instrument. This practice then allows one to "play" the music. Similarly, one's own personal spiritual formation is a private practice where one "practices" or, better, becomes formed so that she can "play" her Christianity well.[18] Simone Weil echoes this when she says, "The effort that brings a soul to salvation is like the effort of looking or of listening.... It is an act of attention and consent...."[19] Weil shows that the formation of the believer is concerned with having one's full attention being brought to God in such a way that one is tuned into God.

In bringing one's full attention to God in attunement, the three authors we have been conversing with believe prayer is the central practice attuning humanity to God. There are a variety of reasons for this. In what follows, we will mainly discuss prayer because this is a central practice to Christians, and has been used through the church's history to attach ourselves to God, along with being a practice that is both intensely personal and teaches us how to listen to God. I also focus on prayer because it is central to all aspects of spiritual formation. As we will see, then, prayer is the central component to the Christian life and the attributes of prayer work to help us listen to God so that we may become attuned to God in love.

The reason that prayer is so central comes through in Simone Weil's thought as she explains how prayer tunes her into God. She points to the centrality of prayer in her spiritual life. She says that it is prayer that develops our attention to God so that we can hear the voice of God in the creation. Prayer tunes us into the music that God plays in the creation. For Weil, the ability to hear this comes similarly to the way that one learns Latin. One learns Latin by practicing Latin, doing the exercises so that one is immersed in the language and can recognize all of the different aspects of the Latin language—like verbs and nouns, singular and plural, adjectives, adverbs, etc.—eventually coming to the point where one just "knows" the language because on has immersed oneself so fully in it. The way we become attuned to God is through similar commitment and practice. If we continue to practice listening to God, we can begin to see and hear God.[20] Prayer offers us a specific practice that tunes us into the voice and life of God. Weil relates this well in her meditation upon the Lord's Prayer. She says that she recites this prayer every morning. The recitation of this prayer, the prayer that the Lord Jesus Christ taught us to pray, brings her attention to the reality of Christ in the world. Christ becomes more real to her through the praying of this prayer.[21] For Weil, then, through these times of prayer, we make contact with God through the full devotion of our attention to God, bringing the experience and reality of God closer to us.[22]

Prayer, then, is the practice that tunes us into God because it develops the reciprocal love between God and person. The practice of praying is one that teaches us to listen, developing our ears to hear God. Prayer brings us into a closeness with God. We develop our ability to listen to God the same way that a musician develops the ability to hear different notes or patterns in a piece of music. Theresa of Avila shows that the closeness we feel to God in prayer comes through the development of the ears of our soul to listen to God, giving us the ears to hear the still small voice of God.[23] For Theresa, the way to not doubt whether a vision or voice is God's is to be so tuned into God that there is no doubt that the One we love is the One we pray to and worship. The development of the ears to hear God gives us the ability necessary to know when we are encountering God and when we simply meet an idol or human projection.

Learning to know God becomes the key to one's spiritual formation. This is because it is only in knowing God that the believer can listen to God. The type of knowledge talked about here is not like knowing a mathematical equation or scientific proof, but is more like knowing that one is in love or that something is beautiful. There is an intuitive knowledge that comes from being disposed correctly toward what it is that one is knowing, in this case God. Simone Weil points to the development of this type of knowledge, calling this the development of attention (as was discussed previously). More than this, though, Weil is interested in prayer as "the orientation of all the attention of which the soul is capable toward God."[24] When we place our attention on God, then we develop the desire for God along with the ability to hear God. Weil points out that this is not a method that guarantees the believer the ability to hear God; rather, the development of one's attunement to God brings a patience whereby one is willing to wait upon God.[25] Further, as one becomes more and more attuned to God, regular knowledge of things that are not God also becomes knowledge of God in that God created these things. All knowledge then becomes knowledge of God. Beyond this, though, knowledge of other things brings knowledge of God because God has infused all of creation with Godself. Thus, as we develop our attunement to God, we begin to hear God's "tune" in all creation.[26]

Weil continues this line of thought by arguing that prayer is the development of humility. As she defines it, "Humility is the refusal to exist outside God."[27] Humility is the understanding that one is not God but finite, human. This realization brings with it the subsequent realization that we are dependent upon God for our existence and that this God encounters us in God's love for us. The response, on our part, can only be humility, giving our full attention to God, attaching ourselves to God so that our wills may be conformed to God's.[28]

While Weil is concerned with describing how it is that we can come to be attuned to God, Theresa of Avila and Julian of Norwich are caught up in the problem of what kind of knowledge results from our attunement to God. Here, both of these mystics have some crucial thoughts. Julian of Norwich points to two different insights that she is able to acquire and begin to understand through attunement to God. The first refers to the three things that belong to prayer: God is the foundation of all prayer; the manner by which we pray should lead to us becoming transformed; and the end of prayer is to be like God, bearing fruit as God would bear fruit.[29] These three aspects of prayer teach us that it is God who initiates the contact but then it is our responsibility to respond, becoming transformed so that we can hear God's voice.

The second insight Julian newly understands is an awareness of the immanence of God who dwells in all of creation, infusing all things with the divine presence. Julian learns that all things have three properties: "the first is that God made it, the second is that God loves it, the third that God cares for it."[30] The Triune God, then, is immanent to our world, part and parcel of all of creation as God infuses it with the divine. The divine music, then, reverberates throughout creation. Julian, then, says that this develops in the soul a desire to be closer to the Triune God, "so bound to him that there is no created thing between [her] God and [her]."[31] The true happiness and complete rest that Julian seeks only resides in her becoming fully attuned to God, bound up with God so much that she loses herself in becoming one with God. This attunement to God brings with it the life of one who lives in the light of the love of God.

Theresa of Avila follows Julian, saying that attunement brings with it a different type of knowledge. Theresa says that the knowledge of God that comes through attunement is built around meditation. This meditation is a "discursive reflection" meant to train the mind of the believer to move beyond the obvious revelation of God into the deeper mysteries of God. Theresa wants to meditate upon the mysteries of the life of God; she wants to do this because of her belief that the more we immerse ourselves in the mysterious elements of our faith, the deeper our life in God. Thus, the meditation advocated by Theresa is one that is grounded in the biblical witness of God, whether of God's giving of the Son or the cross or the Passion or even the betrayal of Judas. All of these are available for Theresa to use as tools of meditation to bring her deeper into the mysteries of God. These narratives act as a place where prayer can occur as she immerses herself in meditation upon the stories. Her meditation leads to her being transported to the time and place and the thinking and feeling of those who were actually present, witnesses to the events. She wants to enter into a place where she can experience what they may have thought and felt. She is attuning herself to the way that God is working in these moments. As she continues to meditate upon these and upon the mysteries of God she learns to hear the voice of God as God has been revealed in these stories and how God continues to be revealed. This only comes through her time of prayer which leads to attunement to God.[32]

To this point, I have discussed spiritual formation and attunement to God. This was done through a meditation upon where our attention lays. I have also described the reliance of creation upon God along with describing how we respond to God. All of this has been done to show the centrality of attunement to God for one's spiritual formation as a believer and that this comes through prayer, the center of all personal worship. However, this account has not considered how attunement to God causes one to move outside of the strictly divine-human relationship to begin human-human relationships which seek to love people.

For Theresa of Avila, the entire purpose of the formation of the believer is that it leads to an attunement with God from which good works arise out of the life of the believer.[33] In fact, Theresa believes that the only way to "profit" from this path is to love much, doing the things that stir one to love. This "doesn't consist in great delight but in desiring with strong determination to please God in everything, in striving, insofar as possible, not to offend Him, and in asking Him for the advancement of honor and glory of His Son and the increase of the Catholic Church. These are the signs of love."[34] The life of attunement to God, then, is not one that is purely concerned with the interior, but with a transformation of the interior of the person made evident in the exterior. Part of this is learning, on the interior, to listen to God and going out in the world and hearing the places where God is. The site to begin hearing God in the world is to listen to the Jesus of the Gospels and learn where he saw and heard God, how he reacted, and what he did. If we begin to follow his example, our ability to listen to God will increase greatly.

As Theresa follows the life of Jesus, she realizes that for Jesus, if a person is in earnest prayer but has no compassion or love of neighbor, their devotion is lost: they have forsaken what the outcome of a life of contemplation, which is a life of love toward all people and all things. The life of compassion that arises from this contemplation will be one where one does what God wants in response to others, which is a willingness to suffer with the other person, showing love no matter the consequence.[35] God asks us to be people of love, both of God and our neighbor. And Theresa tells us that she believes that the way to tell if we are actually following these two commandments is if we are engaged in love of neighbor. For her, these two go hand in hand, but love of neighbor is more apparent and also is a way of teaching us to love. The more we love our neighbor, whoever that neighbor may be, the more that we are able to grow in love of God.[36] And, for Theresa, the real payoff of the love of neighbor is that no one, not even ourselves, can doubt it because it is evident in our outward lives; and, if people cannot doubt the love of neighbor, one can also not doubt where that love arises from, which is love of God.

Simone Weil continues this line of thought in regards to loving our neighbor, which she explicitly links to her meditation upon Jesus Christ. She says, "It is true that we have to love our neighbor, but, in the example that Christ gave as an illustration of this commandment, the neighbor is a being of whom nothing is known, lying naked, bleeding, and unconscious on the road. It is a question of completely anonymous and…completely universal love."[37] If we remember that Weil was the one who forsook more "cushy" jobs in order to work with laborers in factories and farms, often to her own detriment,[38] we see the type of love that she believes is advocated by Christ. Here, she is pointing to the Parable of the Good Samaritan in Luke 10:25-37. In this parable, Jesus is responding to what it means to love one's neighbor. For him, as for Weil, the answer is that we love in a way that overcomes all differences and boundaries. The love of neighbor that Jesus advocates does not worry about anything other than actually encountering the neighbor. Weil believed that following this was necessary in relation to being attached to God. If one was going to claim to love God, one also had to be engaged in loving one's neighbor, remembering that the neighbor was anyone who needed help. Weil exemplified this in her life and asked for it to be exemplified by any claiming to love God.

The imitation of this love exemplified by Jesus comes from the fact that Weil is actively trying to attach and attune herself to God. She believes that loving one's neighbor is a place where we can "imitate the divine love which created us and all our fellows. By loving the order of the world we imitate the divine love which created this universe of which we are a part."[39] Thus, the imitation of the divine in loving one's neighbor is the ultimate goal of a life committed to being attuned to God. In her understanding, the more that one is attuned to God in love, the more that this love springs out to those who we encounter without prejudice. This is similar to the way that the divine love in the Trinity erupts to bring creation into existence. Love, when God is involved, cannot help but go forth to encounter others. And, the more that we are attuned to God in love through our personal worship, the more that one's love goes beyond the self to encounter all those around us. This is to truly imitate the divine life exemplified by Jesus Christ, the Incarnate Word of God.

This section of this essay, then, has brought us to a point where we are immersed in the love of God, both as God loves us and as we love God. The section began by outlining how God first chose us through the love that existed in the Godhead. I, then, explained how this love of God asks for a response on the part of the human, that the person might respond in such a way as to fully attach oneself to God, tuning into God so that one can hear the voice and music of God as it reverberates throughout creation. The way that attunement is brought to fruition is through the practice of prayer, which exemplifies what it means to listen to God by tuning the believer into the life of the divine. As one becomes attuned to God, then, the natural outcome is a life that is spent loving one's neighbor. This love of neighbor is an outflow of the love of God by the person, as this love of God is made evident in the world. The place where we see this attunement to God overflow into love of neighbor is in the life of Jesus Christ, the one whose life exemplifies what it means to have love of God flow into love of neighbor.

Conclusion: Practices for Implementation

The goal of this essay was to enter into a conversation with Julian of Norwich, Theresa of Avila, and Simone Weil, three masters of the spiritual/ mystical tradition in Christianity, about what it means to love God. A central aspect of this is developing a way of listening to God in the world. In order to listen to God, the three laid out a way of attuning, or attaching, oneself to God so that one was immersed in the divine love of God. As this immersion in the divine love grew, one was able to grow in one's ability to respond to the divine love. Eventually, we came to the place where the flowering of this life of being attuned to God occurred when one was engaged in loving one's neighbor. The goal of the life of contemplation, of being attuned to God, is to be a person of love, a love that extends to both God and neighbor. Now, the question becomes how we implement this in our lives. Let me briefly point to four suggestions for attuning oneself to God.

First, make prayer central to one's life. In 1 Thessalonians 5:16, Paul says, "Pray continually." This means that our entire life is a prayer to God. In the words of Brother Lawrence, we "practice the presence of God."[40] The presence of God rings throughout the creation and praying continually means our entire life is about connecting with that presence. This also means that there is no amen to our prayers, but that everything we do is a prayer to God, whether it is reading Scripture, meditating, walking the dog, playing with our child, or seeing a movie—all of our life is a prayer to God. So, making prayer central to one's life is the first step to being able to be attuned to God so that one can listen to God.

Second, it is necessary to practice (and practice and practice). To evoke a metaphor I have used throughout, the spiritual life is like a musician. A musician who just walks onstage to play without practicing is going to fail; this is true even if the musician has practiced for hours and hours in the past. There must be a continual practice of one's instrument and music in order to play well. Similarly, the spiritual life is built around practicing our faith. If one does not practice, then it is impossible to perform one's faith well; similarly, if one has spent much time practicing faith in the past but not recently, the believer will be "rusty" and will not be able to "play" the faith at its best.

Now, one may ask how it is that we practice our faith. In the Christian tradition, the way that this is done is through works of piety and works of mercy. Both of these are concerned with forming the person in such a way as to be attuned to God. The works of piety are those spiritual disciplines meant to shape the interior of the believer, tuning her into God. These include Scripture reading, meditation, confession, simplicity, frugality, and others in this vein. Works of mercy, on the other hand, are concerned with extending the love of God to love of neighbor through the practice of extending mercy to the neighbor. Some of the disciplines that exemplify works of mercy are giving to the poor, serving others, washing feet, peacemaking, and submission. For the spiritual life, it is necessary to practice both of these together as the love developed in both works of piety and of mercy is meant to deepen both one's love of God and one's love of neighbor. They work together to form the believer in such a way that love is the central component of her life, attuning her to the work of God so that she may listen to God.

Third, it is important to hear God in the world. If one makes prayer central to his life and then practices works of piety and works of mercy, one should begin to be formed in such a way as to connect with the God that infused the divine throughout creation, hearing the still small voice of God in all things. One of the ways that a believer can do this is by picking one day a week and carrying a notepad and writing down the places one hears God reverberating in the creation. Or, one could spend a few minutes before going to bed to reflect on the day and to try and see where God was in the day, the moments that the believer encountered God. Through this practice, one will be shaped in a way as to learn to practice the presence of God in the world, eventually naturally hearing God instead of needing to reflect actively and find those life moments where God was present. This will help one's life reflect the love that is at its center.

Fourth, look for opportunities to worship God by loving one's neighbor. If one begins to see the moments where God's love has been extended into creation, then one should also be able to see those places where it is necessary to extend love to one's neighbor. By being tuned into the God of love, one's life should naturally flow with love in such a way that the extension of love to the neighbor happens. However, it is also important to be mindful and intent on extending love to one's neighbor. This is the outcome of the spiritual life and stretches us as well as teaching us greater ways to love, not only others who may be our neighbor but also God. The goal of all of the Christian life is to develop this life of love that extends beyond ourselves to all other places. This is what it is to imitate God made possible by developing ears to hear.

Notes

1. For a more thorough biography of Simone Weil, see Leslie A. Fiedler, introduction to *Waiting for God*, by Simone Weil (trans. Emma Craufurd; New York: G.P. Putnam's Sons, 1951), vii-xxxiv.

2. Simone Weil, *Gravity and Grace* (trans. Arthur Wills; Lincoln: University of Nebraska Press, 1997), 195.

3. Julian of Norwich, *Revelations of Divine Love* (trans. Elizabeth Spearing; New York: Penguin Press, 1998).

4. Julian of Norwich, *Revelations of Divine Love*, 42-3.

5. Theresa of Avila, *The Interior Castle* (trans. Kieran Kavanaugh, O.C.D. and Otilio Rodriguez, O.C.D.; Mahwah: Paulist Press, 1979).

6. Theresa of Avila, *The Interior Castle*, 52.

7. Theresa of Avila, *The Interior Castle*, 86.

8. For a fuller treatment of the spiritual disciplines, see two classic studies: Richard Foster, *Celebration of Discipline: The Path to Spiritual Growth* (rev. ed.; San Francisco: HarperSanFrancisco, 1988); and Dallas Willard, *The Spirit of the Disciplines: Understanding How God Changes Lives* (San Francisco: HarperSanFrancisco, 1988).

9. For a fuller treatment of the nature of attunement, see my "Pursuing an Ontology of Attunement through St. Augustine's Christology," *Wesleyan Theological Journal* 45 (Spring 2010): 179-196.

10. This metaphor of marriage is an important one for many in the mystical tradition in Christianity, drawing from the idea in Revelation 19-21 of the church being the bride of Christ. To see this metaphor at work, one need only look at the following passages from Theresa of Avila, *The Interior Castle*, 52, 108, 173, 174, and 190.

11. Julian of Norwich, *Revelations of Divine Love*, 112-3.

12. Theresa of Avila, *The Interior Castle*, 91.

13. Julian of Norwich, *Revelations of Divine Love*, 129.

14. Weil, *Waiting for God*, 74-75. See also Julian of Norwich, *Revelations of Divine Love*, 179.

15. Theresa of Avila, *The Interior Castle*, 116.

16. Weil, *Gravity and Grace*, 140-1.

17. Julian of Norwich, *Revelations of Divine Love*, 179.

18. This is not to deny the communal nature of personal worship or music making. In neither is the person isolated, completely alone; rather, the person practices in order to come together with a group and play rightly. This is the goal of the time spent practicing. Personal worship allows one to be shaped and formed in such a way that one can be part of the church rightly.

19. Weil, *Waiting for God*, 126.

20. Weil, *Gravity and Grace*, 173-74.

21. Weil, *Waiting for God*, 29.

22. Weil, *Waiting for God*, 57.

23. Theresa of Avila, *The Interior Castle*, 123-4.

24. Weil, *Waiting for God*, 57.

25. Weil, *Waiting for God*, 59.

26. Weil, *Waiting for God*, 57-58. An image that is reminiscent of what I am evoking here is the beginning of the movie *August Rush*. The first time the audience meets August, he is standing in a field "hearing" the music of the wind and is just dwelling here in this moment. The type of attunement I am advocating is similar to this, where one is just tuned in to the music of creation, played by the Creator.

27. Weil, *Gravity and Grace*, 87.

28. Weil, *Gravity and Grace*, 182.

29. Julian of Norwich, *Revelations of Divine Love*, 101.

30. Julian of Norwich, *Revelations of Divine Love*, 47.

31. Julian of Norwich, *Revelations of Divine Love*, 47.

32. Theresa of Avila, *The Interior Castle*, 147-8.

33. Theresa of Avila, *The Interior Castle*, 190.

34. Theresa of Avila, *The Interior Castle*, 70.

35. Theresa of Avila, *The Interior Castle*, 100-1.

36. Theresa of Avila, *The Interior Castle*, 100.

37. Weil, *Waiting for God*, 50.

38. Weil suffered from terrible migraines, many of which were brought on by her commitment to the working classes in France as she lived on lower means, meaning that she was under-nourished and did not get other forms of support she needed to keep the migraines in check.

39. Weil, *Waiting for God*, 99.

40. See Brother Lawrence, *The Practice of the Presence of God* (Grand Rapids: Revell, 1967).

SECTION 4

LISTENING AND THEOLOGY

Chapter 12

Theology and Listening: Considering Job

Ephraim Radner

Theological Listening: Job the Theologian

Theologians are fundamentally listeners, but in a particular way. That theologians are fundamentally listeners is a fact affirmed by both Catholic and Protestant traditions, which understand the theological vocation as primarily linked to "hearing". If "faith comes by hearing" (Rom 10:17 NKJV; *ex auditu* as the standard Latin rendering put it), so too does the *understanding* of our Christian faith derive from "hearing" as well, given its primary origin and focus in the Word of God, who *is* God.

So, theologians are listeners, at least in this general sense. But is it so general as to be a platitude? Almost, but not quite! Not quite, for the rather simple fact that, as many of us know, theologians have a hard time listening to anyone but themselves! And this rather personal (though universal) characterization masks something more challenging: actual listening to the Word of God is neither straightforward nor common. If it is pride that often blocks true hearing of God, and if pride is a besetting sin peculiar to theologians—why that may be the case is another matter—then *auditus* (hearing) joined with *humilitas* (humility) must be the central form of theological discipline. It is a coupling that people as disparate as John Calvin and Pope Benedict XVI have each stressed.[1]

And it *is* a point worth stressing. "Theology" as a discipline or activity refers to thinking about God, articulating these thoughts, and ordering them for the service of the whole Christian life. Thus, when people say that "every Christian is a theologian", it is, of course, true insofar as a Christian engages such thinking, articulating, and ordering for service. But those who do such work specifically as a vocation thereby offer themselves as examples of this broader Christian activity, and in so doing must face a special scrutiny as to the relationship between thinking about God and Christian faithfulness in general: hearing and humility, or their clear contradiction, become the "witness" (good or bad) of the theologian on behalf of the Christian Church. To put it plainly, the theologian's task, beyond all other Christians, is to demonstrate the Christian faith through his or her own life and work in theology. What does the theologian say of God unless he or she listens to his word in utter humility? The truth about God is shared in no other manner. Theological wisdom is not merely published: "Unless your actions uphold your words, you have spoken falsely."[2]

So the theologian's vocation is not only saying the right things about God, but in coming to say them rightly. In this sense, right listening is not the means by which to grasp the truth, but rather the very act of truth-telling, the very showing forth of the truth as true, when it comes to God. One does not teach this in theology doctoral programs! Nor even in seminaries, to be honest. Still, it is a reality that cannot be avoided, if the truth about God is to be apprehended and shared. Hence, we can say confidently—if with trembling—that theology takes its shape in the midst of a life of listening and that such listening must tell us what theology itself is all about.

How shall we describe this life that provides the very contours to theology itself? Listening to God, to be sure, is not something that has been left unexamined in the Christian tradition. Until recently, reflection on this has centered on two areas of activity, Scripture and prayer. Western and Eastern Christianity have both described them as meditation and contemplation--the external and internal Word. The character of human authority within the church community has also emerged as an object for "listening," particularly within monastic communities where "obedience" has been viewed as somehow bound to a divinely providential mission through the ordering of monastic superiors. To this authority has been joined, even if more self-consciously in the wake of the Reformation, a consideration of ecclesial "traditions" or Tradition, each with their own kinds of human and institutional authorities attached. Doing theology was, in these developing contexts, a matter of listening to and within such networks of practice and authority. As we submit to and are formed by these networks, our proper or truthful listening is enabled.

The range of these networks has expanded in the 20th Century. So, for instance, the scope of divinely providential instruments (i.e., monastic superiors, ecclesial traditions)—may we call them "sounds" or echoes of God?—has broadened to include all people of the Church—not only formally acknowledged authorities. So, too, Bonhoeffer sought to instill in his seminary students a practiced sense of the "obligation of listening" to a "brother," an obligation that was properly paired with that of "preaching the Word." "It is little wonder that we are no longer capable of the greatest service of listening that God has committed to us—that of hearing our brother's confession, if we refuse to give ear to our brother on lesser subjects"—something that Bonhoeffer believed reflects our "relationship with God" more fundamentally.[3] To one's brothers and sisters in the church, however, must be joined one's neighbors and even enemies within the world: does not God speak to us even there as well? So, in Barth's famous remark, that he had long "advised young theologians 'to take your Bible and take your newspaper, and read both.'"[4]

Mixed up in this widening range of authorities which become for us listening objects is the question of how one might listen to them. How might we hear the spiritual ancestors, the Christian tradition(s), our brothers and sisters in Christ, but specifically our neighbors and enemies, so that *humilitas* as it is joined to the *auditus*, enables such listening to be the "hearing" of God's word? Certainly a precise treatment of the topic of theological listening is difficult, because the reality itself is so multi-faceted and malleable insofar as persons and contexts inevitably vary. There is no template that can define proper theological listening to God, yet at the same time take into account the actual forces that divinely shape such listening. So, rather than provide a systematic analysis, let me simply *describe* a lived engagement, a *life* of theological activity with a single exemplar: the person Job. Job, according to Gregory the Great, is commended as a teacher of God to both Jew and Gentile, for he is a man "without the Law" who witnesses to God's righteousness before all people, both those under the Law and those outside it. In doing this, Job is acknowledged as righteous by all accounts, and, perhaps as a person through whom others might be saved (cf. Ezek 14:14).[5] Job is the Theologian *par excellence*, but not simply because of his stature as universal exemplar of righteousness (indeed, a cosmic exemplar, if we take seriously his role as witness before the "sons of God," including Satan [Job. 1:6]). Rather, this stature is granted through a peculiar *posture* of theological pursuit—he is the one whose listening has shaped his speech such that truth is its lived residue. It is Job's *life* that becomes the organ of his listening to the words of God. So Job fulfills the famous prayer with which Augustine begins his *Confessions*: "For your mercies' sake, O Lord my God, tell me what you are to me. Say to my soul: 'I am your salvation.' So speak that I may hear, O Lord; my heart is listening; open it that it may hear you, and say to my soul: 'I am your salvation.'"[6]

"I am your salvation:" this is ultimately the word of God that Job will hear. In his book there is no discussion of the Law or of the Gospels. The book is, in a sense, a single word that is uttered and received. But it is the word on which Law and Gospel together build their foundations because the book comes down to this end: God speaks and Job listens, a listening that moves to vision itself, yet through a process in which Job's own mouth is stopped (Job 40:4f.). Job is an odd kind of theological model, but he is the model, indeed the core, of all theological listening, and the subsequent fruit of such listening, for Job's last words to God are ones of repentance. Yet from this repentance, his life continues in a new and restored manner. Not in silence, for his mouth is opened again, but this time in prayer, first on behalf of his friends (Job 42:9-10), and then in the naming of his new children (Job 42:13-15), an act of procreative blessing. Even more than this, as a book in the Scriptural canon, Job gives way to the Psalms, with their profusion of voices now turned to God in focused and exclusive clarity.

So Job is Theologian. In an unfolding life of speech, listening, realization, reformed speech, his existence becomes the posture of humbled reception that issues forth in the ongoing fruit of prayer and praise. I often tell prospective doctoral students that their vocation is a rich one, but one geared not to a profession but to a kind life that is bound to the service, devotion, and delight of God. *This will come in many ways and mixtures.* And so Job the Theologian offers a life worth examining.

Job's Existence

What shall we say of Job's life? Only that it is small, regular, pious, and suddenly tragic. Yet in the midst of this life does Job's listening unveil itself in its variegating and enfolded experience. This is important to grasp: Job listens *from* and *within* this existence, not outside of it. So, however neatly his life is given, we must acknowledge its contours as the arena of Job's wisdom. To the extent that the arena seems constrained, we must inhabit this constraint as the sounding chamber of God's truth. Here is a man, otherwise unknown, who is "blameless and upright, one who feared God and turns away from evil" (Job. 1:1 ESV). This, in a sense, is no more than what Job will also come to understand as the sum of his struggles (Job 28:28). Yet it is just this *coming* to understand something already lived that marks the character of his listening.

The context of Job's life here is familiar enough: a blessed family and the fruit of fortunate labors. Yet, like all lives, Job's is also one that lies in the hands of others—of family, of servants, of strangers and criminals, of enemies and brutes. It is a life thrown into the midst of a wider world of winds and storms, and of course, of sudden deaths and losses; of physical assault and corruption, of disease and suffering. It is a life, we are told, put into the hands of Satan himself, to wrench and twist, to batter and to test. Job's life is like many lives, from the heights of their vaunted description, to their depths, a life given over to others. All this is the life Job himself is given—given, ultimately, we are told, by God himself.

As Job's life is drawn out in this initial, common movement from blessing to suffering, we are presented with one who, though righteous in all respects, begins his words before the reader and before God—before the world—with a *refusal* to listen, in this case, to his wife's bitter counsel to "curse God and die!" (Job 2:9 NIV). It is a righteous refusal, to be sure, a refusal to sin with his mouth, as it were, but it is also a refusal, as we quickly come to see, that Job himself must return to and explore over and over again. In this case, his refusal to listen is based on his own deep knowledge, still unshaken it seems, that God is the giver of all things and deserving still of Job's devotion.

This conviction is not an endpoint, however. It is rather an unstable belief with which Job must reckon in his listening to God, for the book begins to unveil Job's conviction as less settled than it at first appears and increasingly open to a deep questioning. Through Job we learn that refusals are rarely final; convictions, even those of the righteous, demand kneading.

Job will not listen to his wife, though he will later be forced to in a way. Yet others now join him—his "friends," as they are described. These he will listen to at first, although he will also react against them. But the very reality of the later part of the book, when the fourth friend, Elihu, finally speaks and sounds much the same message that God's own voice will offer in conclusion, reveals that Job will hear God *only insofar* as he has heard and struggled with these friends. So, wife and friends, although starting at different points of acceptance, become *partners* to Job's hearing. Indeed, the first two chapters tie Job down to a place and time wherein he has no choice but to make them partners. It is as if by dramatic emphasis the voices of his friends, and Job's own unfolding words, await a kind of etched engagement in this context, as they emerge only after seven days of silence and of grief, sitting together. *Here*, we are told, just in *this* place and with *these* people do ears and mouths, and hearts and minds, take their form before God.

The theologian is a person, who is bound to what is *given*, first of all, in his or her person. That includes a received faith that cannot be gainsaid. But the givens are not the whole story, nor can they be allowed to stand for it. After two chapters of a given life, the book unfolds as a long and subtle process of change. Do theologians "change"? Do they learn anything? They must! But not as neatly as we like to think, imagining that by simply studying and thinking, by praying and reflecting, they can draw conclusions that are then fit to be announced. Theology cannot be about gathering data and then coming to the truth. Hardly and never! We misread theology if we think this is happening (and should be suspicious if theologians claim this!). Job will change his mind, but like all people, that changing will take place in a non-linear fashion.

The Christian faith is bound up with this odd kind of change. We repent, for instance, in a way that allows us to *keep repenting*. We believe in such a way that we can renew our coming to belief over and over, through a kind of *ongoing* renewal of the mind, as Paul writes (Rom 12:2; cf. Col 3:10). These are not instances of data gathering and conclusion. As scholars like Howard Gardner of Harvard have begun studying the way in which people "change their minds," it has become clear that it is rarely as clear-cut as we like to think, especially in religious terms.[7] It takes time, and often the "data" are long lodged in the mind without any transformative effect. Other elements, often personal ones, must come to bear. One must, for instance, become *open* to thinking about something new. One must be able to *receive* new things, take hold of them for oneself, with one's own hands, and try them out somehow—like playing a new musical instrument, or trying on new clothes, although with ideas and attitudes and even faith itself, it is often a surreptitious and unconscious set of attempts. And only then, after all this trying out that takes time and is frequently unconscious, one has to be honest—or *brought* to a point of such honesty—and *recognize* and acknowledge that in fact one has changed: I am not what I once was. Christian devotional traditions have actually understood this, with their various "orders of salvation," processes through which individuals are humbled, rendered penitent, converted, confess, and are sanctified. But in actual practice, these are difficult matters. Most people get stuck at one point or another, but they are bound to the kind of listening that the theologian does, and that Job himself does so deeply. Job changes, it seems, without realizing it; but the realization, in the end, is the unveiling of a truth that once heard, is only then received.

This is what Job's "life" is all about. God's business is not necessarily to upend the "given," the forms of life through which we exist (although God may!). Rather, God works to transform this givenness, a transformation that marks the temporal passage of our lives. And all of these givens and their pressing and scattering, constitute the "dust" of the theologian's being, shaped by God, and reshaped again and again, as the case may be (cf. Isa 45:9; 64:8).

Job's Transformation: Listening and Conversation

How does Job change his mind (or find God changing it for him!) and in what way? Chapters 3 through 31 offer a massive description of this process and its contents. The process itself is a kind of spiraling repetition, as each friend speaks and Job responds, focusing ever more closely upon key elements of truth that Job must hear. But in many respects the chapters go back over and over the same territory, the drive forward in understanding only making itself apparent by the end of the book in retrospect. In what follows, I will sketch only the first round of discussions between Job and his friends, indicating broadly only some of the dynamics involved here.

First, we hear Job's initial complaint, bursting forth after the initial laying out of his life and the week-long silence that ended chapter 2, like heaven's pause before the breaking of the last seal (Rev 8:1). Now, with a fury unexpected, the force of what Job has been given obtrudes upon our consciousness, not as a gift received in resignation, but as a terrible problem and burden. This is the first word of Job the Theologian *at work*. Circumstances, searing in their destruction of Job's loves and well-being, force this upon him, and he speaks in response to this force. Whether Job-like or not, this is a primary theological task that arises out of a given faith: attending to the power of circumstance within the world as it weighs upon oneself or others. As I have argued elsewhere, it is just this impinging reality of the world that marks the "natural way" (*via naturae*) towards God, and we cannot escape it.[8] In this case, a dark shadow has cast itself upon Job's life, and his words in chapter 3 speak out of and about it. So he cries out what appears to be at least itself a shadow of his wife's advice that he had earlier rejected, "May the day of my birth perish" (Job 3:3 NIV). So brutal is the "cursing" of this day of God's creation, that early Christian writers, like Gregory, felt compelled to explain its meaning as a veiled allegory unhitched to Job's own heart. Yet the heart, for all that, is his; and the words are evoked by the voices of his own world.

When Job's first friend, Eliphaz, responds, he does so with a gentle, but firm reminder that God's chastening is to be welcomed (Job 5:17). If Job has suffered, he indicates, then take this with the endurance of a chastened child of God. That is enough, and enough too of God's own self-giving to receive. Eliphaz himself is not without a wealth of knowledge and an ear and eye to perceive. Receiving visions in the night (Job 4:12-17), he knows well enough through such revelations that human beings are nothing before God, in justice or anything else. This appeal to ultimate mystery, ensconced within the heart of God, as well as to God's ultimate justice, is hardly off the mark, is it? Again and again, it is so written in the Psalms (cf. Ps 143:2) all the way to Paul in Romans, whose voice will be given in the Scriptures long after Job's. Eliphaz, even, in Psalmic fashion, anticipates the *Magnificat*, like Mary singing that "[God] sets on high those who are lowly, and those who mourn are lifted to safety" (Job 5:11). If we are so certain that something is missing in Eliphaz's words, we cannot at this point say clearly what it is. Like Job, we too must listen.

To be sure, Job's reply (Job 6-7) is unsatisfied, although he too will reiterate Eliphaz's points in his own way. But here Job must first protest his innocence—hence Eliphaz's implication that Job is being "corrected" doesn't make sense to him. Rather, he wishes to die, given the miserable character of his own life and of human life in general. His response is not that God is not mysterious; it is that God is uncaring and cruel. Should he not say this, given that he has learned this, *heard* it in a fashion that he cannot escape? Here (Job 7:17), he takes the words of Psalm 8—"What is man that thou does make so much of him...?"—and applies them to their opposite purpose. In the Psalm it is a statement of wondering gratitude; in Job's mouth, it is a statement of human pointlessness. Even though human beings are sinners, God's power is made cruel in that simple forgiveness does not lead to relief.

We begin to see a pattern emerging in these interactions: Job the righteous must allow his righteous thoughts to be buffeted by both the world's impinging weight and the responsive capacity or incapacity of his own (and others') theological understanding. He must *allow* this in that he must learn to gauge the force of this buffeting and measure its outcome, the shape of what is left standing. That is, he must *listen*. So then, the second friend, Bildad, takes up Eliphaz's argument, but now uttered with greater urgency: Job *must* have sinned somewhere (Job 8). Own up to it! God will reward Job's admission. And Job's reply (Job 9) carries on where he had earlier left off, now going further too, in asserting that human justice is meaningless before God's uncaring cruelty. If God *were* to speak aloud, such that human ears could hear, it would do nothing but make matters worse! (Job 9:16f.). For God treats the good and bad alike.

Yet we must note something now that begins to emerge, a kind of small reordering of attitude, a shifting, however slightly, of posture. The deliberate pressing of these forces of life and conviction grind to a small change. For already here, Job now seems pressed in a new direction: he pleads for knowledge of God (Job 10:2); he wonders how God *could* be uncaring, given that he has made Job with his own hands (Job 10:3); God is *not* a "man of flesh," he sees the truth, and searches hearts (Job 10:4ff.); he has shown actual grace just by creating and preserving (Job 10:12), and this act and truth must somehow inform God's own being (Job 10:13). Still, having raised these questions, as if depleted by the effort, Job then falls backwards, and wishes he were spared a moment and then allowed to die. If Job's vision of God has opened a bit, it is an opening he cannot yet sustain.

Like his predecessors before him, Zophar now challenges Job to confront his own sin (Job 11). But, more even than the others, Zophar speaks of God's inscrutable ways (cf. Job 11:7-9), now using words like Isaiah 40, not to mention Paul (Rom 11:33), in describing the unreachable heights and depths of God's wisdom. Can you find out God by searching?, Zophar asks. It is the theologian's question! The answer is no, of course. Yet Zophar inadvertently states what will become the theologian's redemption: that the height and depth of God's ways become God's own gift to us (Eph 3:18; 1 Cor 2:10), just as the "eyes of flesh" (Job 10:4 NIV) that Job cannot attribute to God, are yet taken up by God as his own (cf. 1 John 1:1ff.). And here we begin to apprehend something of the divine process of listening at work, as the Gospel itself emerges, if only as the hint of an infant's crown, through the travails of its mother.

With Job's final reply to this first round of his friends' remarks (Job 12-13), he provides a key summation that is then built upon as the chapters further unfold. It concerns the nature of false wisdom as against true wisdom. On what is the distinction based? Judgments are being made in the course of this conversation, in the course of this life and its burdens. A person is forced into such judgments, if only by the words of another, and the heart's turn in envy or fear towards another. Thus Job assumes such judgments – his own of others (Job 12:3ff.) and theirs of him, however dangerously they may be aimed (Job 13:9). But God's ultimate power over all things, as creator and sustainer, must overtake all such judgments: this Job now asserts, as a kind of desperate claim to gain coherence out of the welter of human judgments he has been testing. Look to the beasts, he says, who know these things! God's providence is ordered to all of this, and we can perceive it in just these terms, as we survey the world more broadly: God rules over earth, over nations, over persons. What need is there to justify or contend for God (Job 13:8)? So Job articulates one of his clearest evangelical claims, stating that he "trusts in" God and in his "justification" (Job 13:15-18), though God "slay me."

What is going on here? For Job, having said these things, will quickly return to his complaint about human life's misery (Job 14), even as he begins to argue God's forgiveness, justification, and vindication as something *after* the "grave" (Job 14:13ff.), anticipating the famous chapter 19. He is as one pulled in his own heart and mind in violently antagonistic directions. What is going on is this: we are seeing laid out before us the motion of his "hearing," and each element is important to note. Over time, over its reiteration in existence, this pulling and wrenching becomes the form of Job's own theological opening and truth-telling.

The interplay between friend and resistant yet beleaguered self, between accusation and demanded innocence, between resignation and tremulous praise, is, from this point on in the book, repeated over and over, in a kind of twisting recapitulation, much like the book of Revelation, in the early readings of Victorinus and Tyconius: an image of truth and time taken up again and again, though from different angles and moments so as to belie linear progression, yet provide the shape of a transformed heart before the world and its Maker. This fact about the book is demonstrated in Job 13:1, where Job anticipates his final wisdom before God's self-revealing: he sees and hears and understands! Already? Yet the book is not yet half-way completed! Still, we must agree: Job does understand after a fashion, insofar as he is called now to know, and insofar as he is a part of a knowing existence whose end has not yet come. He sees and hears and understands, because he has given himself over to the lived turbulence of such questioning, such listening; though, if he understands, it is not quite as seems to think! Meanwhile, his friends become more entrenched in their views, as Job's impassioned response pushes further against the boundaries of his own knowledge. Bit by bit, Job is being thrust upon several realities that play themselves out as the book carries on:

- God *does* hold concern for his creation, for Job himself; and it is just *here*, in such care, where his mystery is located. It is not that God is mysterious first, and therefore his lack of care may be a part of this, as Job at first seemed to believe.
- Second, this divine care is bound into the very nature of things. It is because of this slow realization that Job is able to return to the world around him, observing it and considering it as the book progresses in an ever deeper way, seeing things he did not quite see before.
- Third, this fundamentally "loving" character of God, is indeed a "strange" love, in that it is wrapped up in death and suffering, in divine "slaying", yet with a new wisdom offered through it.
- Fourth, Job begins to understand that only God's self-revelation can bring him to the final resolution and explication from the manifesting person of God himself.

As the book progresses, then, and the spiraling conversational repetitions of Job and his friends unfold, these four points emerge with greater and greater profile. But they must *emerge* from the context of a life; they cannot be wrested whole.

The Way of Wisdom

There are at least two important points to note here. The first is that Job both moves to these understandings, and reaches out to grasp them, without reference to the Scriptures themselves, either Law or Prophets, or the Gospels themselves. But, in a sense, he *knows* of them already (leaving aside speculations as to his purported historical locale), and he begins their very utterance, such that *he too*, the man from Uz, joins in the chorus of the Spirit's words. This is part of the reality by which Job himself becomes "the word of the Lord" *within* the Scriptures. But how does he do this? He does it through the engagement of his convictions—convictions grounded in the righteousness of God—with the world of God's own making, which includes the details of Job's own existence. For Christian theologians, this passage through which Job's convictions move indicates something important: that is, the point of theology isn't to define our authorities, but rather to put these authorities which we presuppose to work, and learn their meaning by testing them reflectively within our own lives. The true character of theological study as "listening" must go beyond the "milk" of organizing authoritative doctrine, and actually learn that doctrine's meaning and its divine impulses as they engage our lives within time.

The second point to note is that just this movement of *coming* to wisdom, as it were, marks wisdom itself in her substance. That is, theological wisdom is the form of one who is *driven* to such a context and landscape of listening and perseveres in inhabiting it and moving through it until such light as God would give is indeed given and received. This movement and perseverance is the *humilitas* of the theologian of which so many have spoken. It is a *movement* rather than a static condition, in that there is indeed a growth in knowledge, understood in terms of the theologian's own transformation in the hands of God's providential gifts. It necessarily includes perseverance because this growth is not a simple linear progression. Rather, the theologian's progression must be able to circle back on itself, not so much out of fear of going beyond the presuppositions of, for example, Scripture and the authorities of the Church, but in order to apprehend their truth in the form of one's own body and life. And this is something that requires the continual subjection of the self to God's time.

So we can move to the end of Job's discourses, granting this movement and this perseverance as the shape of the book's unfolding. Thus, by chapter 26, we find that Job is now taking up the ongoing reality of God's inscrutable mysteries, already long established by both his friends and himself, yet now expressing this in a way that almost explodes their previous enunciation. The very ground of Sheol is "naked" before God (Job 26:6 NASB), and this plumbing of the depths and heights, ones already spoken of earlier in the book, signals a moment before the breaching of the limits.

Thus Job evokes the terrifying image of the dangerous and futile work of mining in the tunnels of the earth, in order to affirm that wisdom is truly hidden (Job 28). Wisdom is hidden even from the wise, even from those who seek God with all their heart and soul. So that finally, Job articulates, here at the border of human capacity, a word from God: "And he said to man, 'Behold, the fear of the Lord, that is wisdom; and to depart from evil is understanding'" (Job 28:28 NASB). This is the summit of human faith that nonetheless looks down into and across an abyss. And it is a central claim of the entire bible, as we know (cf. Ps 111:10; Prov 1:7; 2:5; 9:10; Eccl 12:13; Isa 11:3; Jer 32:40; Jonah 1:16; and over and over again in various formulations). "Fear" of God (deriving from the Hebrew cognates of *yar-* but also, in some instances of the formulation, from other Hebrew words), in its root meaning of terror and reverence both, is made the universal standard of theological truth, both in its content and in the posture of the knower: to "fear God" is to know who God is; and such knowledge is articulated in the form of reverence. Yet while Job had begun as a God-fearing man (1:1), has something now changed? What has Job learned that could be described as new, fuller, or more true? What has changed is the nature of Job's fear itself. Job the Theologian now fears as he has not feared before. Who will tell him of this? Who will tell us?

If we turn to the New Testament, we see this same progression in fear. From shepherds before the angel's announcement (Luke 2:10), to people before the works of Jesus (Luke 5:26), to disciples before his power over the natural world (Matt 14:26), to thieves on a cross shared with God (Luke 23:40), to a centurion (Matt 27:54), to women disciples before an empty tomb (Matt 28:8), and ultimately to the Church's own mission in the world (Phil 2:12), we see the progression to a better and wiser fear. While "perfect love casts out fear" (1 John 4:18)—that is, the fear of those who stand without hope before God's judgment—the "fear of the Lord" *rightly* marks the new disciples of Jesus the Christ (Acts 9:31) precisely because now this godly fear is grounded in hope, and such fearful hope will continue to mark their life in the world as a life that is true to God's own life given in His Son. A strange love of the theologian it is, who now fears the one he or she would understand! Yet, Job's fear is no longer that of one who knows that his master is "hard," "reaping where he does not sow" (Matt 25:24), but of one whose fear, like Peter's by the lake, melts with joy before the Lord's own coming (John 21:7). Though Job finally asks what he has asked before, that *God* listen to him (Job 31:35), he is now ready from his side to listen directly to God. And when he does, he falls silent! But here, it is no longer a demand or a need—it is the mark of having opened all aspects of his own being to God. God can listen, because Job has nothing left in his own possession to be seen: his words are "ended" (Job 31:40). God can "hear" Job's silence, a sign finally of his readiness, of his crossing of the threshold of wisdom.

Job the Theologian

So we come to the end of the Book. Elihu, the youngest of Job's friends—and should he not listen to the young as well, though Job is the elder?—remarks what Job himself has already mentioned: who can understand the mystery of God, even as that very mystery must form the beginning of all our thinking? Where shall we find it? As if to lead Job on to the use of his opened hears, Elihu insists that God *does* speak to us (Job 33), though we often do not "perceive it" (Job 33:14 NIV), and does so for our good, somehow bringing us back from the edge of the Pit, even if we do not realize the precariousness of our beings. Does this not reveal our primordial dependence upon God's grace, even for our breath and life, so that all *is* grace (cf. Job 34:14ff.)? Even "righteousness" means something other than we thought, in such a light as this (Job 35:7f.).

Yet Elihu presses this point clearly: God speaks and the wise one will listen. "Surely God does not hear an empty cry, nor does the Almighty regard it" (Job 35:14 ESV). Who now is wise in this way? Is it not Job himself, through this long passage? For God opens the ears of the afflicted to hear him (Job 36:10-12). The wicked will not hear, to be sure, but only the afflicted who have turned to the Lord. Elihu says no more here than the other friends, but now with a deeper sense of God's prior being than theirs, and a more willing sense of Job's place in this work of grace. And so Elihu begins again—like Job earlier!—to extol the mystery and unsearchable character of God's work in the universe (Job

36:24-26). "Hear this, O Job; stop and consider the wondrous works of God" (Job 37:14 ESV).

Stop here. And God now answers (Job 38-41). But there is no new information that God gives! Surprisingly, God only *carries on* with Elihu's description of his marvelous works, as if to underscore the point that God indeed speaks all the time in multiple ways though we may not hear. Still, it is *God's* voice that is finally recognized by Job at this point, though he has been hearing God speak throughout the book. This is what is new: God speaks, and Job now "hears" in truth. And doing so, *he* ceases to speak: "Behold, I am of small account; what shall I answer you? I lay my hand on my mouth. I have spoken once, and I will not answer; twice, but I will proceed no further" (Job 40:4-5 ESV). So the Lord simply continues, into the ears of one who, though ever closer to hearing, had not yet gone as far as he was called to go.

What is the difference between the Job of chapter 2 and the Job of chapter 42? This is the question of our reflection. Is it information? It does not appear so. "I have uttered what I did not understand, things too wonderful for me, which I did not know" (42:3 ESV). Job spoke, perhaps truly enough, but without the depth of God's own presence before him. And here we see the failure of so many so-called theologians. The work of ordering true sayings is something they can do well enough perhaps; but it is only preparatory to their real task. There is no need to find *new truth*, or to uncover new authorities. Nor is there need to argue more cogently about the Scriptures or the traditions of the Church: these are *all already given*. Theologians have wasted too much time and energy in this, breeding only controversy. Indeed, it is only the dissatisfaction with the givenness of these truths that fuels the constant search for wisdom in the bowels of the earth, as Job remarks! To *hear* the truth *already* given, is to be given over *to* its press within the world, to be shaped *by* it, and finally to articulate a witness to its power from within such pressing shapes as it has given. So God speaks at the end of the book of Job, not with a new message, but simply with his own voice. The voice is present, as is the truth it bears. And before it, all crumbles. That is the conclusion of the whole matter (Eccl 12:13).

Conclusion

I have described the theologian's "listening" in terms of Job's life and discourses. But it can be put in other ways. "Recognize yourself as a sinner, and you will be acquainted with truth," wrote Stephen of Muret, echoing the deep tradition of his Christian monastic discipleship.[9] Or again, to expand on our earlier citation from St. Augustine:

> For your mercies' sake, O Lord my God, tell me what you are to me. Say to my soul: "I am your salvation." So speak that I may hear, O Lord; my heart is listening; open it that it may hear you, and say to my soul: "I am your salvation." After hearing this word, may I come in haste to take hold of you. Hide not your face from me. Let me see your face even if I die, lest I die with longing to see it. The house of my soul is too small to receive you; let it be enlarged by you. It is all in

ruins; do you repair it. There are things in it—I confess and I know—that must offend your sight. But who shall cleanse it? Or to what others besides you shall I cry out? From my secret sins cleanse me, O Lord, and from those of others spare your servant. Amen.[10]

The ruined soul that lies before God who alone would come to "repair" it, is a Christian claim. But it is not "theology" until it is spoken by the one who hears its truth as his or her own, something that cannot happen without the work of subjecting oneself (and being willingly subjected) to the gifts—the "givens"—of God's own work in the world. And this is the theologian's listening. We tend to stress the truth of the Christian claim as spoken, but not the form of its emergence in speech. It is the last, however, that is truly theological, for it describes the primordial, and ever repeated and renewed listening to the God who unveils our complete dependence upon him.

It is interesting to read Gregory the Great describe his own work in writing on Job,[11] a task that became the massive multi-volume work now known as the *Moralia* on Job. He speaks of his own struggles in vocation, the weariness of his pastoral duties, the longing for God, and the anguish of life in the world. So, to please his friends, but even more to make sense of his own life, Gregory embarks on this long engagement with the book of Job, which itself produced a work that arguably became the single-most influential theological treatise of the next 700 years in the Christian West. What will he do by reading Job? He writes that he will be entering the river of God's word, in the midst of the stormy oceans of this world's existence, battered by secular demands and depletions, grasping at the solace of friends, seeking the depth of God's life as through a passage within Job's own journey. So, Gregory goes on to say, he will seek to uncover, however strenuously, the various levels of meaning in the text: history, faith, moral action, testimony, explication and a constant moving back and forth into the corners of Gregory's own life, that it might be pried open by the word itself. Yet in all of this, Gregory admits, he will always be brought back to this point of grateful receipt, as a poor man, from the infinite store of God's grace. "He who has ears, let him hear!" (Matt 13:9 NIV), Jesus calls out to those who would receive God's word. But ears are themselves given, in the course of a life that knows itself as God's, and is thus lived.

Notes

1. On the richness of Calvin's understanding here, see Randall Zachman, *Image and Word in the Theology of John Calvin* (South Bend, IN: University of Notre Dame Press, 2007). See also "What in Fact is Theology?", in Joseph Ratzinger, *Pilgrim Fellowship of Faith: The Church as Communion* (San Francisco: Ignatius Press, 2005), which is a very Roman Catholic take on this topic, but one that is deeply colored by the pope's Augustinian and Franciscan theological roots.

2. Stephen of Muret, *Stephen of Muret: Maxims* (trans. D. Van Doel; Kalamazoo, MI: Cistercian Publications, 2002), 57. Stephen may seem an obscure authority here. But his small foundation in Grandmont exerted enormous influence, far beyond the meager remembrances of his teaching or unstable history of his monastic descendents: Stephen was seen to represent the unadulterated "Gospel lived." Hence his few recorded words carried, for a long time, an aura of the purest Christian wisdom.

3. Dietrich Bonheoffer, *Life Together* (trans. J. Doberstein; New York: Harper & Row, 1954), 98.

4. "Theologians: Barth in Retirement", *Time*, May 31, 1963. Available online at http://www.time. com/time/magazine/article/0,9171,896838,00.html.

5. Gregory the Great, *Morals on the Book of Job* (trans. J. Bliss; 4 vols.; Oxford: J.H. Parker, 1844-1850), 1:5.

6. Augustine, *Confessions* (trans. J.G. Pilkington; First Series, vol. 1; *Nicene and Post-Nicene Fathers* repr. Peabody, MA: Hendrickson, 1995), 46.

7. Howard Gardner, *Changing Minds: The Art and Science of Changing Our Own and Other People's Minds* (Boston, MA: Harvard Business School Press, 2004).

8. Ephraim Radner, *The World in the Shadow of God: An Introduction to Natural Theology* (Eugene, OR: Cascade Books, 2010), 14-26.

9. Muret, *Maxims,* 74.

10. Augustine, *Confessions,* 46.

11. Gregory, *Morals,* opening Epistle.

Chapter 13

Becoming People of Character: Learning to Listen to Scripture

Timothy J. Furry

My argument is with Christians who congratulate themselves on a knowledge of the holy Scriptures gained without any human guidance and who—if their claim is valid—enjoy a real and substantial blessing. But they must admit that each one of us learnt our native language by habitually hearing it spoken from the very beginnings of childhood, and acquired others—Greek, Hebrew, or whatever— either by hearing them in the same way or by learning them from a human teacher.[1]

But if anyone reads and understands without any human expositor, why does he then aspire to expound it to others and not simply refer them to God so that they too may understand it by God's inner teaching rather than through a human intermediary?[2]

~St. Augustine

Introduction

My wife and I recently had our first child, a son, who we named Ezekiel. One of the many things I learned throughout the pregnancy is that more unsolicited advice is given to soon to be parents than any other demographic. Some of the comments and suggestions were very useful but others not so much. Of course, the difficult part is discerning the good advice from the bad. Which advice do we listen to and which do we simply nod, smile politely, and allow to go in one ear and out the other?

Discerning good and bad advice and guidance is not easy and requires trained ears and experience. I remember hearing experienced parents talk to us about how they learned to distinguish the different cries of their newborn; there were hungry cries, painful gas cries, dirty diaper cries, and I-am-just-mad-at-the-world cries. Before Ezekiel was born, all baby cries sounded the same to me: annoying. Though it only took my wife a few days, after a couple weeks I was able to listen and discern his cries just like other parents had told us. It took me time to hear Zeke's cries *as* something more than an annoying cry. To be sure, his cries never really changed; what changed was my hearing. I had to learn to hear his little whimpering cry *as* a dirty diaper cry; to hear his cries bordering on screams and kicking legs *as* painful gas cries.

So it is with the reading of Scripture for Christians. The key difference is that we never have to worry if what Scripture is telling us is good or bad. The language of "Scripture" already presumes that Christians hear the reading of our canonical books *as* divine revelation. By definition as the Word of God and as 2 Timothy 3 asserts, "All Scripture is inspired by God and is useful for teaching, for reproof, for correction, and for training in righteousness, so that everyone who belongs to God may be proficient, equipped for every good work" (2 Tim 3:16 NRSV). Scripture should always be listened to and heeded. However, just because we trust that Scripture only speaks truth and goodness to us does not make it any easier to discern what Scripture is saying. In other words, we know *that* Scripture will not lead us astray and *that* we should obey and believe what it teaches, but this is quite different from knowing *what* Scripture is saying. After all, the Pharisees failed to rightly understand *what* Scripture was saying while holding steadfastly to its authority. Jesus held his sternest rebukes for these religious leaders who believed in the authority of Scripture but failed to listen to what it had to say. Enter the practice of listening and having ears that hear.

In what follows, I will discuss listening to Scripture in two contexts. First, I will discuss listening to Scripture in worship or in the liturgy. Next, I will address listening in the context of the church classroom (bible studies, Sunday school, small groups, etc). While both of these contexts are relatively distinct from each other, the order in which I address them is quite intentional and will become clearer as the chapter progresses. However, before we get to listening to Scripture in these various ecclesial contexts, we must properly understand what Scripture is, what it is primarily for, and the general characteristics of those who can hear what Scripture is saying.

Scripture: What is it and what is it for?

To inquire about the nature of Scripture is a much deeper question than to ask about its empirical composition. In other words, the answer to the question, "What is Scripture?" requires more than "A book made from paper" or even "The sixty-six books that make up the Old and New Testaments." So what is Scripture? A deceptively simple and traditional answer is that Scripture is God's revelation about himself to humanity. Of course, the ultimate revelation of God to us is Jesus Christ—God incarnate. However, since we do not live in the first century A.D., we have to learn about Jesus somehow and that somehow is Holy Scripture and the Church. I said this understanding is deceptively simple because divine revelation comes with certain demands; it puts us into a certain kind of relationship with the God who desires for us to call him "Father." Thus, Scripture as divine revelation is not simply facts written down, like a modern history or science book. While real and factual truths are conveyed in Scripture, their intent is to bring us closer to God by revealing the truth about him and his creation.

Most Christians are probably familiar with the nature of Scripture as God's revelation to humanity, even if only intuitively, but that awareness often disappears when the question moves to the purpose of Scripture. Too often Christians use Scripture in ways for which it is not intended. While a baseball bat makes a fun golf club and could even aid in one's golf game (especially off the tee!), that is not what it is intended for. Hence, a professional golfer would be instantly disqualified for using a Louisville Slugger as a golf club because a baseball bat is not, in fact, a golf club. A baseball bat is for hitting baseballs pitched toward home plate, not for teeing off on the eighth fairway.

In order to understand what something is, it is helpful to consider what it is for. If I was from a remote tribe in the Amazon jungle and came across a wooden baseball bat, there is no way for me to understand what this long cylindrical piece of wood really is. I would probably recognize it as a humanly altered piece of wood, but that is not what it is or what it was made for. Even if I use it to hunt wild boars for food successfully, it is still a baseball bat because that is why it was made and even its physical characteristics are tailored specifically for this purpose. In other words, just because I use the bat for other purposes other than its intended use (and even successfully) does not mean that I know what it is. Not until I watch a baseball game, understand the rules of the game, and learn about the science that goes into making wooden baseball bats do I begin to understand what a baseball bat is. I must learn what a bat is used for in order to know the nature of the bat. Only after I learn that a bat is for striking a white ball with laces thrown from a pitcher in order drive in runs to win a baseball game do I learn that an inappropriate use of it is beating wild boars in the jungle—not to mention there are many more effective ways to slay a wild boar.

So, what is Scripture's purpose? The answer to this question will go a long way in helping us better understand the nature of Scripture. Let us begin by recalling the 2 Timothy passage that says that Scripture is for correcting, reproof, teaching, and training in righteousness to prepare disciples for good works. Scripture understands itself to be an inspired book used for spiritual guidance, moral exhortation, and discipleship training. The shorthand Christian term for all of these is "salvation;" the purpose of Scripture is to bring people to salvation and to grow us into that gift. While it seems silly to say, we do need reminded of it: Scripture has a specific purpose. It is not a general book about general things. If you wanted to learn how to fix an internal combustion engine, Scripture would not help. If you wanted to learn how to play the piano, Scripture is not the book you need. If you want to understand quantum mechanics, you will search Scripture in vain. The key is to remember that Scripture's purpose is to point people towards God. To paraphrase St. Augustine in *On Christian Teaching*, Scripture is a sign that signifies another reality, the Father, Son, and Holy Spirit. Scripture should not be confused with the Triune God to whom it points or else we become idolaters. Ultimately, this "sign status" of Scripture is why Augustine says that any interpretation of any Scripture that encourages one to love God and their neighbor cannot be called a wrong interpretation.[3] Not exactly what most seminaries and colleges teach as "responsible" exegesis!

It will be helpful to understand Augustine in detail. More specifically, Augustine breaks the world down into two categories, things and signs. Everything that exists is a thing: birds, pencils, denim, humans, words, letters of the alphabet, etc. However, not all things are signs because a sign is something that signifies something else; it directs our attention away from itself and to another reality. Words are always signs because they seek to communicate something besides themselves.

This can be confusing since at one moment a thing could be a sign and at the next it is not. However, I think we already implicitly understand this and use it quite regularly in the church. Think of sermon illustrations or object lessons in children's Sunday school. Pastors tell stories to illustrate a broader and deeper spiritual truth. Therefore, the story is a sign that points beyond itself to something else. However, if the pastor read the story in a history book, the story might not have been intended to be a sign but simply a piece of information. Now, if a pastor opens a sermon with a joke simply intended to "loosen up" the audience, then it is not a sign; it is only a thing. Later on, if that joke comes to have a point beyond or outside of itself or to illustrate a greater truth, then it is a sign. One last point of clarification: if a word or thing is a sign, this does not mean that the object itself is unimportant and can be forgotten. So, if Scripture is a sign, it points us beyond itself in a way that does not diminish its own status as God's revelation. Scripture as divine revelation is entirely good and infallible but its point is not to draw attention to itself but to the Triune God it reveals. Even the traditional language of "revelation" presupposes this sign status of Scripture, because the word "revelation" implies an object used to show something else.

Now that I have sketched out a basic outline of the purpose of Scripture (to bring us to salvation and to help us grow into that gift) and what it is (primarily a sign that points to or reveals the Triune God), I will begin discussing general ways to hear what Scripture is teaching.

The Ears that Hear Scripture

Whether we like it or not, understanding Scripture is not easy or immediate. Understanding seems easy because we forget the common things in place that even enable us to read Scripture, let alone understand it. Think about everything that goes into reading; everything you learned at a young age that you no longer even think about. We need to know the English alphabet, all the parts of speech, and how they function; to assemble a working vocabulary; to know how to follow a train of thought and series of sentences, etc. So, there needs to be certain skills and attributes in place before one can even read anything, let alone the Bible. If we want to understand what Scripture says, we need basic reading skills as well as other attributes or virtues. We need to become certain kinds of people. This is both good news and bad news. The good news is that if we can acquire these skills and virtues we can better understand God's Word. The bad news is that one of the ways we acquire them is through the reading of Scripture itself, which transforms us. So, if we lack these attributes and cannot therefore understand Scripture properly, how do we read it, understand it, and then acquire these virtues? It is the proverbial chicken and the egg conundrum in a different context. Once again, Augustine will help us find our way.

We often think that knowledge is the most important part of acting in the world. We treat knowledge as a way to control and tame our world. Undeniably, knowledge can and should be used in such ways. Cancer treatments, for example, are such controlling uses of knowledge. However, this very specific type of knowledge is not the only kind of knowledge. The fact that I use the word "know" in both of the following sentences does not require that both mean the same thing. "I know my wife" and "I know that $2 + 2 = 4$." Those are two very different kinds of knowledge. The relational knowledge I have of my wife does not (or at least should not) have anything to do with controlling her, while mathematical knowledge can be used for such good things like safe bridges and overpasses, which is a kind of (good) control. Augustine understood that knowledge has purposes, which means that we have antecedent reasons for why we come to know what we know. We do not come to knowledge about the world neutrally; we have reasons for knowing what we do. Most of those reasons have to do with our desires. For example, I do not see cheeseburgers as neutral objects. I see them as pleasing to the eye and good for food (Genesis 3 allusion fully intended!). Humans are naturally inclined toward food; we desire it and therefore see it as a good to be pursued because if we did not we would die.

Our desires orient us toward things in certain ways. We usually perceive food as a good and jumping out of airplanes as usually bad. As a result of sin, our desires incline us in the wrong ways toward the wrong things. For example, our good and created desire for sex is perverted into uses of pornography, adultery, and fornication. Anyone who has known an addict of any kind knows the power desires can have over us and how they can even make us blind to the obvious lies we tell ourselves to justify our behavior. The seven deadly sins (wrath, greed, sloth, pride, lust, envy, and gluttony) are illustrative examples of the perversion of desire. Wrath is an inordinate amount of anger; sloth an overextension of rest; pride is loving oneself too much; etc.

Augustine argues that our most fundamental desire or inclination should be the fear of God. "It is therefore necessary above all else to be moved by the fear of God towards learning his will: what it is that he instructs us to seek or avoid."[4] Desires guide us in what to seek and avoid. However, sometimes our desires or initial reactions are wrong, like being fearful of someone because of the color of their skin. Hence, we cannot just rubber stamp our initial reactions or desires. They, along with everything else in our lives, need to be redeemed and perfected by grace. Furthermore, while commenting on the first beatitude,

Augustine states, "And the 'poor in spirit' are rightly understood here, as meaning the humble and God fearing...."[5] Thus, we should come to Scripture understanding our lowly status as sinful humans in need of God's guidance. If we do not approach Scripture in a posture of humility, then we are setting ourselves up to misread and misinterpret God's sacred Word because our desire is not be transformed, which is precisely what we need.

The fear of God is the first of seven stages/virtues that Augustine says are required to hear and understand Scripture properly. He bases his list of seven on Psalm 111:10 and Isaiah 11:2-3. Psalm 111:10 says, "The fear of the Lord is the beginning of wisdom; all those who practice it have a good understanding" (NRSV). And Isaiah 11:2-3, "And there shall rest upon him the spirit of the Lord, the spirit of wisdom and purity of heart, the spirit of good counsel and strength, the spirit of knowledge and loyal obedience; and his heart will be filled with the spirit of the fear of the Lord."[6] Augustine also integrates these gifts of the Spirit in Isaiah with the Beatitudes in his commentary on Matthew's Sermon on the Mount. For the sake of brevity and clarity, what I offer below will be a synthesis of Augustine's understanding of the gifts of the Spirit in Isaiah and his sermons on Matthew 5.[7] Quite intentionally, I will not spell out all the connections between Isaiah, Matthew, and Augustine's reading, in order to encourage the reader to look for these connections themselves and contemplate them.[8]

The second stage is piety or holiness. "After [the fear of God] it is necessary, through holiness to become docile, and not contradict holy Scripture—whether we understand it...or fail to understand it—but rather ponder and believe that what is written there, even if obscure, is better and truer than any insights that we can gain by our own efforts."[9] In other words, part of fearing God and approaching him humbly is being docile and teachable. If we think we know better, there is no way to progress in holiness because our own arrogance blocks the way. We will not be able to understand Scripture and God's holy teachings if we fail to submit to them and be willing to be made holy.

Knowledge is the third stage. Augustine highlights two specific pieces of knowledge at this point. First, "This is the area [knowledge] in which every student of the divine Scriptures exerts himself, and what he will find in them is quite simply that he must love God for himself, and his neighbor for God's sake, and that he must love God with his whole heart, his whole soul, and his whole mind, and his neighbor as himself."[10] Notice that the first piece of knowledge is not a doctrine, e.g. that Jesus died for you. Instead, it is a moral understanding that we should love God and love our neighbor. To be sure, this moral knowledge is intimately connected with such essential Christian doctrines as the atonement, but Augustine is saying that only by loving God and our neighbor can we come to understand what Scripture is saying when it tells us that Christ died for us. The second important instruction in knowledge is recognizing our sinfulness and that we are "entangled in a love of this present age."[11] In short, we must know that our perverse desires have made us idolaters who love the world inappropriately. As Genesis says, the world was created as good by God, but we must recognize that we fail to see the world as a sign pointing to God and take it only as a thing for us to use for our sake. Other forms of knowledge are important for understanding Scripture as well, such as knowledge of Hebrew and Greek and the ancient Christian tradition. However, in the end, the knowledge that Augustine wants us to learn is personal and specific to growing in holiness and salvation. Without it the seed of the gospel, even read in the original Greek, may fall on infertile soil.

Fortitude is the fourth step. Fortitude helps provide the strength necessary to help us extricate ourselves from our illicit love of transient things. Augustine also connects it with the hunger and thirst for righteousness in the Sermon on the Mount. We cannot simply decide not to love the world. We need fortitude to help us persevere because the journey into godliness is difficult and requires patience and persistence. Tied directly to fortitude is the fifth stage, counsel which leads to "the resolve of compassion."[12] Counsel and compassion help one to put the knowledge of loving God and neighbor into practice. This is not easy since we love ourselves more than we should. If we love ourselves too much and/or in the wrong ways, we will not seek out counsel from others. When one begins to love even his enemy as Christ instructed, then one has ascended to the fifth stage.

The sixth stage is purification. Here, Augustine is noticeably different from the Isaiah 11 text, which mentions understanding. However, for Augustine understanding and purity of heart go hand in hand. In his commentary on the Sermon on the Mount, Augustine says that since God can only be seen with the heart, as opposed to with outward eyes, then only the pure in heart are able to see or know God.[13] Thus, Augustine is not eluding the text but instead clarifying it through another passage of Scripture. Hence, Christians need the Spirit to purify their hearts if they are to see and understand God as he is revealed in Scripture. Augustine describes this person as such: "So this holy person will have a heart so single-minded and purified that he will not be deflected from the truth either by an eagerness to please men or by the thought of avoiding any of the troubles which beset him in this life."[14]

Wisdom is the seventh and final stage in the journey of knowing God and properly understanding Scripture, which are one and the same. Augustine equates this stage with the peacemakers beatitude because where there is peace there is no opposition. In other words, the wise are those who do not resist or oppose God. Their entire way of life is subjected to the rule of the Father, Son, and Holy Spirit. Their desires are rightly ordered and used in order to pursue holiness and the knowledge of God. A good example of someone who has reached the stage of wisdom is the martyr. They do not let the fear the death deter them from obedience. Their good and natural desire to live has been perfected and made holy through obedience and service to God because they know that death is not the worst thing that can befall a Christian.

These stages of spiritual growth are the ways that we can hear Scripture *as* the Word of God revealing Christ to us. They help us know that we are not deceiving ourselves and making Scripture say what we want it to because, left to our own devices, sin will pervert our understanding and reading of God's holy Word. For that reason we cannot read Scripture in isolation or simply trust that the Spirit will tell us what a specific passage means. After all, and as Paul says,

Satan masquerades as an angel of light (2 Cor 11: 12-15), and we must be able to discern if it is Satan twisting Scripture or it is the Spirit's illumination of God's Word. It is imperative to remember that as Isaiah says these stages are gifts of the Spirit. We cannot progress through these stages of spiritual growth and understanding of God on our own. Our progress is the direct result of the Spirit's activity in our lives guiding us deeper and deeper into an intimate friendship with the Father through the Son (John 15:15-16).

Listening to Scripture in Worship

Just as a baseball bat has a "home" context in a baseball game, so does Scripture have a home context in public worship. The primary context for Scripture is the gathered community of worshipers, not the classroom and not even in a favorite chair or in bed for personal devotions. Every book of Scripture was written with the community of faith in mind. The Torah was read in the Temple and in synagogues, as Jesus demonstrates in Luke 4, and Jewish synagogues continue to read the Hebrew Scriptures aloud as part of their worship. The gospels were written to preserve the memory of Jesus' life, death, and resurrection with the intent to be read aloud in early churches. Likewise, Paul's letters were written to early Christian gatherings and read aloud in them. From the time the ink began drying on its autographs, Scripture was written for the community of faith and intended to be read aloud. For the early Christians and throughout the Middle Ages, to read Scripture meant to listen to it read out loud in worship.

To listen (and even merely to hear) is not the same as to read. For your next personal devotional time, read Scripture out loud to yourself. If it makes you feel like you should be diagnosed by a psychiatrist, ignore that thought. Know that you are in good company because the monks throughout the ages, the few who actually had the physical books of the Bible to read from, read Scripture out loud to themselves in their cloisters.

While Scripture's primary locus is audible reading in the gathered community of faith, unfortunately, church worship services are probably the hardest places for church leaders to listen to God's Word. Like the Pharisees, we all too easily know what Scripture says but fail to listen to it. I struggle to hear Scripture in worship for two main reasons. First, as a trained theologian, my brain is always in evaluation mode. I am constantly listening to the preacher to see if I agree with her; to see if she handled the biblical text responsibly. This critical posture reveals my sinful desire to already know what Scripture is saying and therefore to have no need to hear it again—not exactly the fertile soil the gospel seed hopes to fall upon.

The second reason my ears fail to hear in worship is because there are so many other distractions and things that demand a church leader's attention on a Sunday morning. If I am preaching that morning, I am rehearsing what I am going to say. If I help serve communion, I am checking to see if the others who are scheduled to serve are there. I am looking for visitors who might be in attendance. I might be going over the names of some people I just met to ensure I can recall them after the service. I am looking and listening to discern if everything is going well with the worship team. I could go on and on. Quite frankly, however, this is all rubbish compared to listening to and being transformed by the Word of God. What good is it if I recognize visitors and even remember their names but cannot connect meaningfully with them later on because my heart is cold and unchanged by God's love? Anyone else hear a resounding gong or clanging symbol? I might have helped them become a more regular attender (at least for a while) by my initial and perfunctory hospitality, but should they come to me in the future with a crisis or for authentic Christian friendship my hardened heart will have nothing to offer them. I am still a long way off from helping them become a true disciple of our Lord because I, myself, am not listening to the call of Christ proclaimed in the Word. If we allow ourselves to be distracted by many things, our primary desire is not the fear of God but something else.

Before we let ourselves off the hook too easily, we need to ponder how disconcerting and disturbing an inability to listen to Scripture in worship actually is, especially for those in ministry. As church leaders, we are called to help people progress in salvation and holiness—to help others progress through the stages sketched by Augustine—but in our context this call requires much of us during the very time we should be hearing God's sacred Word. If we are going to hear Scripture as God's Word as discussed above, how is that possible if we are deaf to communication with God through Scripture in its primary context of worship? If we are deaf to of Scripture in its home context, how can we teach it properly others?

If we cannot listen to Scripture in its primary context, we run the risk of forgetting what it is all about: calling people out of the world and into salvation and the Church. Mindless of what Scripture is for, we use it inappropriately as a battering ram to get our way and/or to reinforce what we already believe or want to believe. We forget that it is intended to be for the church to build her up and make her holy. To be sure, there will be difficult times that Scripture calls us to repentance, but the Church is there to offer the support and community that a sinner seeking holiness needs.

We cannot be saved or become holy by ourselves. God uses others to sharpen us and form us more into the image of the Son. I have learned fairly quickly that being a good parent requires me to be holier than I was before. I never knew how selfish I was until we had our son. Scripture calls children "blessings" not simply because they are wonderful gifts of God, which of course they are, but also because they are part of God's more ordinary way of making people holier. Of course, we are free to be horrible parents who are selfish and obvious examples abound. However, those who recognize that there is a cross to bear in being a good parent end up being more godly as a result. We need others, warts and all, in order to become the people that God wants us to be. Failing to hear Scripture in the community that it is for and which Scripture calls together will stunt our spiritual growth and make us unfit to lead others into the gospel's call to salvation and holiness.

We must break through the distractions to have ears that hear on Sunday mornings or whenever the community is gathered. I can offer no "how tos" that guarantee church leaders will listen to Scripture in public worship. I can only offer some advice based on my own success and failure in properly attending to God's Word.

For starters, recall Augustine's starting point of fearing God and remember what worship is all about. Worship is where the people of God come to meet God, which includes ministers and church leaders. While we might be involved in leading worship in various ways, it is still for us. There should be no lay-clergy distinction when it comes to one's worship mindset. There are no parts of worship specifically for the laity and no parts specifically for the leaders. While there might only be one person speaking during the sermon or the consecration of communion, the proclaimed Word and the sacrament is also for the preacher and leader. We all stand under God's and Scripture's authority. One small way to test and see how well you do with understanding that worship is for church leaders too is to look back at your sermon notes or remember and reflect upon the words you speak in front of the congregation. Ask yourself, "What kind of pronouns do I use? Do I say 'you' or 'we' when addressing God's people?" Of course, just because one uses "we" does not ensure they are listening to Scripture as they speak or preach. However, it can be a small first step towards reflecting more substantively on how we see ourselves and our role in the worship service as church leaders.

Second, be prepared and organized for worship. Of course, last second adjustments and changes will occur, but the more last minute solutions that need to be found will only detract from the purpose of worship and our attitude. While some people think that God only works in spontaneous acts, I completely disagree. He certainly can and does act through more spontaneous circumstances, but planning and organization are not intrinsic hindrances to the gospel. God is not in heaven wringing his hands powerless to move and act because we planned a worship service. God already knows who will be present at each and every worship experience and works in the planning process to reach them. While planning and organizing are essential nothing can curb one's ability to hear like being rigid. So, be flexible as well. Ultimately, the order of how candles are lit, whether or not the congregation stood at the appropriate times, if the rocking praise band missed a verse, or if the soloist was off pitch does not make or break worship.

Listening to Scripture in the Classroom

Classroom settings vary greatly, even within churches. There are fellowship oriented small groups who do some Bible study to in depth discipleship groups and classes that meet weekly. I will offer more general advice that is applicable in multiple classroom settings. More specifically, I describe someone who practices Augustine's second stage of understanding Scripture, having piety and being docile and teachable.

In response to some friendly banter on Facebook, I recently sat down with a friend to talk theology and politics at local restaurant. He is not a trained theologian, so I thought I would be the one imparting most of the insight and wisdom.

At one point, our discussion turned to a reading of Jesus' post resurrection appearance to the disciples on the shore of Tiberias in John 21:1-14. My friend claimed that Peter jumped in the water because he was ashamed. I countered by saying that that is not in the text and that Peter swam toward the Lord to see him more quickly. After looking up the passage right there in the restaurant, it turns out his reading is completely legitimate. The reference to putting on a garment (very strange indeed if one was going to jump in the water) could be harkening back to the shame of Adam and Eve in Eden when God made them garments, and Peter had every reason to be ashamed since he had not yet been "reinstated" by Jesus. Whether we "solved" this passage or not is debatable, but the point is that because I am a trained theologian and church leader I thought I had the answers.

My desire was not be docile and teachable, as Augustine recommended, but to "be right" or to be the one with the answers. Here is a primary example of how our desires influence our thoughts and actions and can inhibit our ability to hear. It turned out that eventually I was able to hear my friend and God's Word because God has fostered in me an ardent desire to know the truth and pursue it relentlessly.

In reality, those of us who have formal training should know better and should never assume that "the experts" have the corner on hearing God's Word. Think of all the examples of God working and speaking in unexpected ways: Balaam's donkey, the sound of sheer silence to Elijah, the conniving of second-born Jacob, and, the most important of all, a Jewish carpenter born in a manger. I think it is all too easy for pastors and church leaders to think we have all the answers or at least believe that we know better than those we are serving. As a result, leaders often assume the role as knowledge imparters and can easily be closed to input and insight from others. We do the Church (and God) a great disservice if we treat those we serve as if they are our ignorant students in need of our wisdom. To be sure, a very important role of being in ministry is to teach and there will be times where we impart knowledge and wisdom to others. I am not disputing that, and I am certainly not advocating some kind of anti-intellectualism. Far from it! My point is that we can become hardened in certain roles, apply unnecessary pressure on ourselves to get it right every time and thereby unknowingly pervert our desires and fail to listen to Scripture speak through those we are serving. Therefore, in the classroom everyone's opinion and ideas matter and are worth consideration. Class participants should not assume a merely passive position because they have valuable knowledge and insight to offer. If everyone sits and listens to the expert, there is a much lower chance for fresh readings and insights to be gleaned from God's robust and plentiful Word.

Note that above I did not say everyone's opinion is right. All opinions and thoughts are not created equal and some are simply wrong. In fact, one of the most difficult parts of teaching is correcting someone's wrong thinking or opinion. While it may be difficult, correcting is also one of the most important components of effective teaching. However, if we want to listen to Scripture and speak the truth in love, leaders must correct gently.

In order to correct someone lovingly, we first have to listen to them because they might not be saying or affirming what we think they are. Recently, my denomination made headlines for all the wrong reasons. The Evangelical Lutheran Church in America opened the path for the ordination of persons in monogamous same sex relationships. As expected, it is causing major problems within our tradition of Lutheranism. In response to the denomination's decision, our local church decided to have listening post forums to let people express their thoughts on what our denomination did so we as leaders could gauge where our congregation was. Somehow, I was given the task to moderate some of these forums and my job was simply to facilitate and listen. While I strongly disagree with what my church did, I had to listen to some who supported it without saying anything—a *very* tough task for me because one of my primary desires that needs constant transformation is the desire to be right and to prove that I am right. Moreover, we also laid out ground rules that disallowed our disciples from arguing with each other in order to avoid unnecessary conflict. However, that discipline of listening was quite good for me and for all who attended. It made us discipline our initial reactions and desires and be quick to listen and slow to speak (Jas 1:19).

The best outcome of this mostly painful experience was that it made me listen for understanding. I learned that this divisive issue is very personal for many folks. For most, it was not simply a matter of being right and being wrong. They have family members or good friends who are homosexual. After hearing their thoughts and stories, I did not change my position on this issue, but I did come to better appreciate and understand many of the people I serve. Once I understood their circumstances and why they thought what they did, I could engage them in a more substantial and honest fashion at a later time. We could discuss each other's actual thoughts, perspectives, and arguments, while avoiding mere Scripture quoting and yelling. That is how correcting should take place because no one wants to be told they are wrong and then promptly forgotten or ignored. Sometimes God takes indirect routes for speaking to us and transforming us. Therefore, we should always be listening to everyone and how they read the Bible because God might be trying to tell us something only tangentially related to the specific topic or passage at hand. While I do not think God was trying to change my mind about the ordination of homosexuals, (though we must be extremely careful in saying what God wants to communicate to us because we must remain teachable), he definitely was trying to teach me something about docility through discussing it. Remember Augustine's maxim that is based on Scripture's purpose of salvation: any reading that fosters authentic love of God and/or love of neighbor is not a wrong interpretation. I have found that very useful in my teaching through the years.

Ultimately, what I have been arguing is that listening to Scripture requires us to be certain kinds of people. This should not surprise us, since the Triune God who meets us in his holy writ asks us to come as we are but to never stay that way. Listening to Scripture is a transformative practice, and Augustine's stages are good ways to judge our own transformation and how well we are leading others into saving transformation. Writing this piece has been transformative for me, and I hope and pray that it is of some small help to others seeking to serve our Lord, Jesus Christ.

Notes

1. Augustine, *On Christian Teaching*, (trans. R. P. H. Green; New York: Oxford University Press, 1997), 4.
2. Augustine, *On Christian Teaching*, 6.
3. Augustine, *On Christian Teaching*, 27.
4. Augustine, *On Christian Teaching*, 33.
5. Augustine, "Our Lord's Sermon on the Mount," *Nicene Post-Nicene Fathers* (ed. Philip Schaff; Grand Rapids, MI: Christian Classics Ethereal Library), 6:15. Available online: http://www.ccel.org/ccel/schaff/npnf106.html
6. This is a translation of the Latin Vulgate from which Augustine worked. It differs slightly from our modern versions. Isaiah 11:2-3 (NRSV) says, "The spirit of the Lord shall rest on him, the spirit of wisdom and understanding, the spirit of counsel and might, the spirit of knowledge and the fear of the Lord. His delight shall be in the fear of the Lord."
7. For a readable summary that details more clearly how Augustine's sermons fit with *On Christian Teaching* see John Sheila Galligan, "The Augustinian Connection: Beatitudes and Gifts" *Spirituality Today* 38 (1986): 53-62.
8. Access to most of Augustine's writings is widely available on Christian Classics Ethereal Library. Available online at www.ccel.org.
9. Augustine, *On Christian Teaching*, 34.
10. Augustine, *On Christian Teaching*, 34. The Scripture reference here is to Matthew 22.
11. Augustine, *On Christian Teaching*, 34.
12. Augustine, *On Christian Teaching*, 34.
13. Augustine, "Our Lord's Sermon on the Mount," 6:17.
14. Augustine, *On Christian Teaching*, 35.

Chapter 14

Words, the Word, and the Triune God

Kenneth F. Gavel

He humbled you and let you be hungry, and fed you with manna which you did not know, nor did your fathers know, that He might make you understand that man does not live by bread alone, but man lives by everything that proceeds out of the mouth of the LORD. (Deut 8:3 NASB)

God's Word is the most important communication ever given to humans. Humans are saved by hearing the Word of God, the Gospel of Christ. As Paul says, if no one proclaims the Word of life, then we cannot hear the Word, and hence cannot respond to the Word with faith and repentance. Moreover, once we are saved, we are told to immerse ourselves in God's Word (Col 3:16), for this is the chosen means by which God enters and shapes our lives into the image of Christ. Paul clarifies the mechanism by which faith comes by hearing the Word of God: "my message and my preaching were not in persuasive words of wisdom, but *in demonstration of the Spirit and of power*, so that your faith would not rest on the wisdom of men, but on the power of God" (1 Cor 2:1-5 NASB; italics added).

For this reason, it is essential that we rightly understand why God has put his words in our hands as well as in our hearts; to understand why he expects us to study and hear (obey) his written Word. Wrong understandings of God, salvation, means of grace, and the role of the Word in our lives can profoundly cripple our life in Christ. I learned this from my own initial stumbling in the faith.

183

I grew up in an evangelical church where I was told that salvation was by faith alone. But I had erroneously come to understand that faith was something *I* had to generate before God would save me. As hard as I tried, I could never believe, *without doubt*, that God would save me. I could never drum up a sure trust and confidence that God *now* saved me. Passages such as James 1:6-7 frequently came to mind, condemning me for my doubt.[1] I just knew I could never obtain such faith, such certainty. Thus I was caught in a catch-22: I could only be saved by faith in God's free grace in Christ, but I had no way to get this faith. If salvation was by grace alone, then how could God demand of me that *I* must *first* produce saving faith? Didn't that turn salvation into salvation by human effort? The Bible clearly affirmed that wouldn't work (Eph 2:8-9 NASB).

Again, I was taught that in order to grow spiritually, you must read your Bible and pray every day. And the clear implication was that if you did not grow, you'd backslide and lose your salvation.[2] Thus, the same dilemma appeared in a new form. If salvation is by grace alone, then how could God require me to read the Bible and pray as the means to keeping my salvation? Didn't that amount to keeping *myself* saved?

Perhaps others have had a similar experience. As a result, let's reflect upon the nature of the Word of God and how it is a means of spiritual life. After all, it is precisely because life in Christ (salvation) is *all of grace* that God has provided his written Word as a means of receiving and keeping that life.

As we enter a discussion surrounding God and his Word, let's start with a few reflections on our relationship to God. First, God created us for his own enjoyment. As the *Westminster Shorter Catechism* expresses it, "Man's chief end is to glorify God, and to enjoy him forever." C.S. Lewis adds: "In commanding us to glorify Him, God is inviting us to enjoy Him."[3] God's creative design ensured people would be self-conscious, personal beings with whom he could dwell, and with whom he could personally interact. God communed with the very first humans "face-to-face"—at least until Adam and Eve rejected his plan and presence (Gen 3:8-9). God's stated goal for Israel, and for all of humanity, is summed up in these words from Leviticus: "Moreover, I will make My dwelling among you, and My soul will not reject you. I will also walk among you and be your God, and you shall be My people" (Lev 26:11-12 NASB); and is repeated in Revelation: "And I heard a loud voice from the throne, saying, 'Behold, the tabernacle of God is among men, and he will dwell among them, and they shall be His people, and God Himself will be among them'" (Rev 21:3 NASB).

This is a goal made possible by the mediatorial work of Jesus Christ, whose name, Immanuel, literally means, "God with us" (Matt 1:23 NASB). It is this reality, God dwelling with us in the close intimacy of family, which makes the Christian's approach to his chosen means of "family communication" so centrally important.

In view of God's longing for us to commune with him constantly and intimately, he provides everything we need in order for that to be our daily experience. We do not have to wait for heaven. Through the work of Christ, God has provided his Holy Spirit and his written Word to be the means of our intimate conversation with him.

Communion with God, thus, is much more than having warm fuzzy feelings or a vague sense of wellbeing as we think about our kind Creator. Rather, this communion can be highly structured, and follow certain guidelines which ensure it remains communion between the one true God and ourselves, and not communion with an undefined "spiritual realm."

God's status as our Creator, Redeemer, and Sanctifier requires that any contact we have with him must come about as the result of *his* initiative and through the means *he* has provided. The "means" we will focus on is the written Word. Of course, one can already see that this written Word is not something we can take in isolation from its Author. This Word has a divine purpose (2 Tim 3:16), a divine Source, a divine structure (Christ, who is the enfleshed Word), and a divine power (the Holy Spirit).

God takes the initiative in communicating himself, his will, his love, his law, his good news of salvation to us, through the medium of words. And God can also read us like a book—God can encode the truth about us in words so accurate there is no room for error. For these reasons, the Bible takes the business of words very seriously.

As Eugene Peterson puts it,

> Language is sacred at its core. It has its origin in God. 'In the beginning was the Word, and the Word was with God, and the Word was God' (John 1:1).... This Word, this Jesus...both was the language and spoke the language that reveals God not from the outside but from the inside, God's heart, God's comprehensive way of being personally and relationally with us as Father, Son, and Holy Spirit.[4]

God's written Word serves as God's voice to us in concrete, specific form. How then, might we approach this Word with most benefit?

As we reflect on God's Word, let's first address the nature of the Word of God as his personal communication, for only when we understand the connection between God, his Word, and ourselves, will we properly understand how we are to receive and interact with it. We will then briefly suggest a few basic principles for "rightly dividing the Word of truth" (2 Tim 2:15 KJV). Finally, we will introduce a few guidelines for hearing God speak through his Word.

God's Personal Word

Words are not magic, but they are powerful tools. Words, the building blocks of coherent communication, are fascinating creatures. We use them to create contracts that only death or divorce can break; we use them to define sophisticated philosophical concepts; we depend upon them to identify the parts of the body and the complex medical procedures involved in brain surgery. Words on a piece of paper can bring you a promotion or fire you; make you a millionaire or take away your house. Words can make you feel good: "I love you, honey." Words can heal: the little phrase, "I'm sorry," can restore a broken relationship. The words "I forgive you" can release someone from an unbearable load of paralyzing guilt. Words can also make you feel like dying: "I hate you, and I wish you had never been born." Such words destroy your spirit, and can bring on life-shortening depression.

Words can connect spirit-to-spirit and heart-to-heart. And since in the very core of our being we are "spirit," what we do to each other's spirits profoundly determines what becomes of our souls and bodies. The heart, the spirit, is an exceedingly sensitive and malleable reality. Hearts can, of course, become "hard"—closed off from the world outside. The unavailable heart is a dying heart, for God designed us to be most fully alive, most fully ourselves, when we are most intimately connected to God and to others. God himself established these various functions of words. Thus, words must be treated with care and explored with reverence, especially as we explore God's Word.

In addressing the personal word of God, then, we must reflect on the Son. Because Jesus *is* the Word of God, God has no other Word for us. The Father does not speak without the Son, for it is precisely by speaking through or by his *Son* in these last days that God's new covenant is shown to be God's final, perfect, saving Word. In fact, all that came before the incarnation of the Son—the Sabbath rest, the Old Covenant (with the Law as its expression)—all derived their significance from their future: Jesus Christ, the Word incarnate. Jesus Christ, the Logos/Speech of the Father, is the focal point of all that the Father does in the created realm. Therefore, in reflecting on Christ as the Word, we do well to do the same as the Father said to Peter, James, and John: "Listen to him!" (Mark 9:7 NASB). A call to the Word, therefore, is not merely a call to the written Word, but through the written Word, as applied by the Spirit, and received in faith, a call to the Word is a call to the Son, the Logos, the Word of God, he who is *the* way, *the* truth, and *the* life (John 14:6 NASB; italics added). The written Word, as beautiful and profound as it is, if read as merely *human* words (if read without faith), carries no more *significance* than Shakespeare's plays. But the written Word is not *by itself*; it is not just human words, even though humans wrote them and can understand them: the written Word was authored by the living Word of life, through the life-giving Spirit, as directed by the will of the Father. For this reason, the Bible is often referred to as living and infallible. As Kevin Vanhoozer describes it, the biblical "text has an identity that is more like a person than a thing."[5] This is why James is so emphatic about listening to, and doing, what the Word says (Jas 1:22-25 NASB).

The Word as God's Personal Communication to Us

Even though God, through his Spirit (2 Tim 3:16), has chosen to communicate with us through the medium of human authors who wrote under his guidance, this does not mean these are the inspired writings of *only human* authors. Rather, God retains ultimate control of what is communicated. This gives the text both an historical anchor (the life-world of the human author) and a continuing impact. Kevin Vanhoozer puts the point this way: "The text is both a completed communicative project and a projectile that has the potential to enter into and make a difference in the life-world of its readers."[6]

Scripture captures this reality by referring to God's Word as "living and active":

> For the word of God is living and active and sharper than any double-edged sword, piercing even to the point of dividing soul from spirit, and joints from marrow; it is able to judge the desires and thoughts of the heart. And no creature is hidden from God, but everything is naked and exposed to his eyes to whom we must render an account [lit. *logos*, word]. (Heb 4:12-13 NET)

God's Word is God's personal, active, and present communication. Thus God's communication is not just about single words. God expresses his active, creative *will* through the medium of words that humans can understand. And it is God's own power that makes the communication of his will take effect. God's Word, as expressive of his will, gives direction and shape to the divine power behind creation.

The Powerfully Shaping Word

The powerful nature of words embodies both a potential blessing and a potential curse for us. Because God has sovereignly established what words can do, he himself gives words their ability to bring about effects. Thus when his saving word is preached, it actually makes receptive hearers righteous and thereby it becomes the power of God unto salvation (Rom 1:16-17). When we turn away from his saving word, when we are careless about the condition of our heart, we cut ourselves off from the Vine (the Word) who is our life (John 15:1-4).

The living God himself, in his written Word, describes the *power* of his living Word. For example, when God created the world, he did so by commands (Gen 1:3ff)—he commanded the light to shine out the darkness, and it was so (see Gen 1:6, 7; Ps 33:6; Ps 148:5; John 1:3; 2 Pet 3:5). Hebrews asserts: "By faith we understand that the worlds were set in order at God's command [word], so that the visible has its origin in the invisible" (Heb 11:3 NET). Through these commands God's creative will found expression by delimiting and differentiating the previously uniform chaos and by establishing the different rules, laws, and properties which, for example, forever define birds as a species different from that of rabbits. Even humans had a part in this process, for Adam creatively applied names to the different animals, thus *telling* them apart. God granted Adam a share in the creative process. And God continues to allow us to share in the creative power of words.

When God speaks, things happen. For example, when God sends forth his Word, people are healed (Ps 107:20; Matt 8:8). Both God the Father, and Jesus the Son, speak the creative Word: we are created (John 1:1) and sustained (Heb 1:3; Col 1:16-17) by the Word of God.

When the Son speaks storms are stilled, the dead are raised, sins are forgiven, and people are reborn: "You have been born anew, not from perishable but from imperishable seed, through the living and enduring word of God" (1 Pet 1:23 NET; cf. 2 Cor 4:6).

The Author of the living Word is the living God. Thus, the Word has a distinctly Trinitarian shape: The Father speaks his Son-wise Word to us through his

Spirit. The Son, through whom the Word is spoken, also himself speaks the Word and is the Word, and is also Creator, Sustainer, and Revealer (Heb 1:1-3; cf. John 1:1; Col 1:16-17), and this Word is applied to us by the living Spirit (Eph 6:17), the same Spirit who sustains us in being. Through this Trinitarian source, the dynamic Word has life-giving properties. As such it reveals God himself to us, and to coin an awkward phrase, "It discovers us to ourselves," transforming us into the image of Christ (cf. John 6:63).

The Word is living, therefore the "foolishness" of preaching *works* (1 Cor 1:21 NASB). When we preach, we are participating in the Father's and Son's speaking of the creative, redemptive, dynamic divine Word. He has entrusted to us the message of reconciliation (2 Cor 5:19-20).

That is why the Gospel is liberating. It is God's Word of good news to us, a covenant-establishing, re-creative Word spoken by the Spirit from heaven (1 Pet 1:12; cf. vv. 23, 25). God's Word carries the same power as expressed by the divine Son—through whom all things were created (1 John 1:1-2). This power is not ours, but rather is always sovereignly exercised directly by God. He allows us to be his mouthpieces, although the power of the Word is always God's, and always made effective in and by the sovereign Spirit.

Because it is the living Word, when we open our minds and hearts to the Divine Author of the written Word, we invite the Living Word himself (the Son) to enter our hearts and begin to reshape us into his own image (Rom 8:29)— "Sanctify them in the truth; Your *word* is truth" (John 17:17 NASB; italics added).

Precisely because it is God himself who speaks his Word, who does things through his Word, this Word is our only and all-sufficient source of life.

The All-Sufficient Word:
The Word and the Sabbath Rest

God's original creation was perfect, at least to the extent that it could achieve God's good purposes. It was so perfect that God stopped creating, and called this state of perfection the Sabbath rest.

Neither God nor humans needed to add anything material to creation to enable it to fulfill its proper functions. It provided the completely sufficient basis for a full life of unmediated fellowship with God, each other, and the rest of creation—as long as Adam and Eve obeyed the words of the covenant which protected the harmony of the Sabbath rest. However, rejection of God and God's role as Creator and Lord and Provider violated the Word of the covenant, and destroyed the perfect basis for full fellowship with God—which was and is God's purpose for us. So God eventually inaugurated a new covenant, a new creative and defining Word, established in the flesh of the incarnate Son, the same creative Son of the first creative sequence.

This second and final Sabbath is absolutely perfect; nothing now needs to be done by God or humans to make eternal salvation possible. This is why the Son now sits at the right hand of the Father. If we obey the rules of this new covenant by trusting God alone for salvation, by faith, eternal Sabbath rest and unmediated fellowship with the Father and the Son in the Spirit is ours. This time there is nothing better to come. This is God's final provision. Nothing more will ever be needed. This provision meets our deepest need and highest aspirations. When this new creation has become fully present, the Kingdom of God will have arrived fully—the new heaven and the new earth (Rev 21:1-6).

The Revealing Word

We have said that the same creative Word that gave us *being*, is the same creative Word that *re-creates* us. This God who speaks is the living God. Because he *lives*, so do his words. No human words can fully capture this living Word; they can only tell *of* it, they can only point *to* it. God alone remains in sovereign control of his words. He applies his Word in our lives through his Holy Spirit.

This reflects the essential illuminating work of the Spirit. Take, for example, the written Word. This Word is never just ours; it is never just at our disposal. In fact, we do not so much read the Word as it reads us. It is not so much a matter of us coming to this Book and asking, "What are you?"; rather the Book asks, "Who are *you*? *What* are *you*?" If we dare to open ourselves to truth and therefore to the Book, we find it lives. Through the Spirit's agency we encounter the Author of the Word, in person, and because this is a contact with the living God, with the living Son, through the life-giving Spirit, there is nothing *safe* about it—but how exciting, for there is hope in self-discovery and truth! It discovers us to ourselves as we really are—as God sees us!—and the revelation carries in itself its own judgment or approval.

This living Word, just because it is not *our* word to *ourselves*, is not exactly "safe." In the passage quoted above from Hebrews 4, the Preacher[7] wants to stress that any *real* encounter with the Word is an encounter with the living God, and therefore with the living Christ. In such an encounter, there is no room for pretence; there is no hiding behind a plea of ignorance, because God himself shines into our hearts, and in him all is light without any darkness at all (1 John 1:5 NASB). Encountering Scripture is not safe because all is exposed.

It isn't just *conscious* hypocrisy the Preacher is aiming at, although that is included, but *anything* in us that is not Christ-like, even though we may not now be aware of it. The Preacher is worried lest any of us "be hardened by the deceitfulness of sin" (Heb 3:13 NASB). This hardness can involve a closing of the heart to uncomfortable truth. Such closing is disobedience; it is what God calls "unbelief" (cf. Heb 3-4 RSV). But even if we have already begun to lose the ability to recognize truth, if we will turn, even now, toward the light, no blindness or deception is any match for the living Word!

We have seen that God's Word is personal, powerful and transformative, all-sufficient, recreative and redemptive, and revealing. This is what makes God's Word a means of grace.

The Sustaining Word—A Means of Grace

God wishes to remain in constant relation with his people. To that end he has created humans as persons with the grace-enabled power to choose to love and obey God freely. This is the divine pattern demonstrated by Jesus. One of the ways God empowers our personhood is through the divinely appointed means of grace.

A means of grace is any activity or sacrament which God has especially designated as a place or practice where his enabling grace is especially present. Participation in the Lord's Supper (a sacrament), and such activities as prayer (private and public), worship, and scripture reading, are designated means by which God extends extra grace into our lives.

God sustains our spiritual vitality through these means of grace in a way analogous to the way he provides for the sustenance of our bodies. God enables us to work, earn money, buy food, and feed ourselves. While it is true that God's enablement makes all this possible (Deut 8:10-20 RSV), he does not do it *for* us, but rather requires our full *participation*. He does not, for instance, actually fork the peas into our mouths. He has given us the ability to do this for ourselves. This is part of what it means to be a person. God delights to enable our freedom. He therefore requires that we use the gifts, graces, and means of grace that he has provided (cf. Phil 2:13 RSV). Paraphrasing John Wesley, the basic spiritual principle here is, "Use the grace you have, and you will receive more grace; neglect the grace you have and you will lose even *that* grace."[8]

When we apply this principle to the reading and study of scripture, we find that God enters into conversation with us through his Word, and in so doing imparts spiritual strength to our souls. We find ourselves increasingly able to love others as ourselves; we discover a deeper sensitivity to the Holy Spirit's guidance; we enjoy an increasing freedom over sin; we find greater joy in loving, obeying, and serving God. We are enabled to become our *true* selves.

Learning to listen closely to God as he speaks to us in and through his Word becomes the means by which the personal God communicates grace to us through the Holy Spirit. God has chosen *his Word* as a primary means of grace so that: 1) through the inspired Scriptures there will be consistency, truth, and reliability in what we hear from God; 2) through the illumination of the Holy Spirit we can see, understand, and appropriate the message; 3) through the Word and Spirit, God's goal for us can be achieved: transformation into the image of Christ.

Therefore, a call to the Word = a call to the Living Word = an invitation to life—a life ordained by the Father, patterned in the Son, and empowered by the Spirit.

Now that we have explored the nature and role of God's Word as a means of grace in our lives, how do we ensure that we hear *God* speaking through his Word, that is, how do we avoid turning *his Word* into *our word*? How do we truly *listen* to *God* speaking through his Word?

Accurately Interpreting the Word of Truth

The purpose of the present volume is not to provide a handbook on how to study the Bible.[9] However, in order to provide a context for our prayerful response to the Word, it may be helpful to review some basics as they relate to prayerful, receptive reading of and listening to Scripture.

In spite of our best intentions, it is impossible to read the Word (or any other document) with complete objectivity. Therefore, it is important to be aware of our presuppositions and try not to let them control how we read.

When reading Scripture, it is easy to miss the canonical context—the context of a passage from a book in a series of books. Thus it is important to keep stepping back, seeing the passage in its immediate context, and in the context of the book as a whole. As you gain increasing familiarity with the content of the Bible, keep trying to see each passage in the context of the whole of Scripture.

Continually ask: "What was the author trying to say?" "To whom?" "Why?" "To what effect?" This keeps us from reducing the Scripture to a series of timeless propositions that can be plucked out of their original context and applied arbitrarily to our personal situation today.

Kevin Vanhoozer lists three "interpretive virtues" ("qualities or habits of the spiritual reader") which we need to bring to the Biblical text: *"justice, understanding, vitality."* *Doing justice* to the passage means letting the text "'be what it is,'" "rather than trying to shape it into an image of oneself or one's desires," it means examining the text "as fully as it demands." *Understanding* means studying and praying over the text to the extent that one is confident she has grasped the "intention and information" invested in the text by the Author. And as we noted above it is the Spirit who makes the Scripture come alive in us, giving it a *vitality* it could not otherwise have: "It is the Spirit that enlivens the text...that...makes the Word come alive by inciting readers to *love* it," who enables a variety of readings and applications without compromising the correct meaning or "the literal sense."[10]

After we have prayerfully read and studied a passage of Scripture, using such tools as different versions and Bible study guides, we also need to submit our interpretations to the Bible itself, and then to the larger community of interpreters (such as commentaries and the theology of our faith community). Neither biblical interpretation, nor the theology based upon it, should remain an individualistic enterprise.

The very fact that two Spirit-filled Christians can arrive at very different interpretations of a portion of scripture demonstrates that God does not normally overpower our normal means of understanding. He has left room for our individuality, our different perspectives and life-situations, precisely because he wants us to communicate with him *freely*, even at the risk of our mistaking his meaning. The fact that with our limited vision we sometimes find God's ways strange to us, the fact that we are embodied creatures whose emotions do not always allow our minds to synchronize with reason and recognize truth, accounts for many of the errors in our interpretation of God's Word, and explains why we sometimes disagree with each other. This fact reminds us to cultivate a spirit of humility when interpreting God's Word.

In order to avoid turning God's Word into our word, it is important to remember that Scripture is not "a manual of magic" which we can memorize in order to manipulate the divine powers. The very mystery involved in Scripture as a means of grace can make it susceptible to being twisted into something *we* control, a mantra repeated until we have a mystical encounter with God. There are those who think that by "praying Scripture," by quoting God's promises back to him, somehow forces God to "come through" for us; that by giving us his promises in print, God has somehow put himself under obligation to us. Praying the Word without understanding "what it meant then" and "what it means now" is to treat the Word as if it works by itself. It separates the written Word from the Living Word. It is precisely because God is the Sovereign, loving, personal God of Abraham, Isaac, Jacob, and Jesus that mere repetition does not work (Matt 6:7-8).

Following the rules of responsible Bible study and reading does not lead to use of the Bible as a book of magic, does not give us access to some "power" we can manipulate. Rather, the Bible is a playbook, an invitation to join God's story and to allow God to make us into one of the characters in his story. Hence there is an *ethics* of reading/hearing/obeying, of *attending* to what *God* is saying. It is the reason there are both requirements *that* we read, and also requirements about *how* we read, and most importantly, how we *respond* to the reading (Jas 1:22-25 NASB). For just as a book by a human author speaks to us personally (even after the author is dead), even more so with God's book. God's book is an ongoing, personal communication.

Eugene Peterson notes that it is a mistake to reduce the Bible to an "impersonal authority" which we use to define or others.[11] Rather, "[t]he words of Scripture are not primarily words, however impressive, that label or define or prove, but words that mean, that reveal, that shape the soul, that generate saved lives, that form believing and obedient lives."[12]

The theology of Scripture described above informs our prayerful/worshipful exercise of listening to the Word. There is a way of listening to the Word that goes back to the early church, to the *monastic* order of St. Benedict. It is known by the Latin name, *Lectio Divina*.

Lectio Divina

Richard H. Schmidt notes that *Lectio Divina* (literally, "divine reading"), or holy reading, "is more than merely reading sacred books. It is reading in order to listen to God and listening in order to respond to God, which means reading slowly and meditatively."[13] *Lectio Divina* is not a substitute for a careful study of scripture, but is rather an important complement to thorough study.

Think of "listening" as a basic spiritual posture, a spiritual discipline, and thus *a means of grace* to be applied in all of these contexts. There is an important sense, then, in which *Lectio Divina* involves prayer, personal worship, and retreat. Remember, the Bible is God speaking to us. God opens the conversation. We have been invited into the conversation, in fact, we have been summoned. Therefore, we are obligated to insert ourselves into this conversation. Prayer ensures we keep it a two-way communication. For that reason we should read prayerfully: before, during, after our time in the Word.

The attitude one adopts in *Lectio Divina* is one of humble submission to the sovereign Word of God. When we come to the Word with our full attention, we are acknowledging God's sovereign lordship over our lives. Full submission recognizes God's requirement of our full engagement with him: "You will seek me and find me when you seek me with all your heart" (Jer 29:13 NIV). *Lectio Divina* is a means of offering our body, mind, and soul to the sovereign guidance and enabling power of the Holy Spirit. It is the "livingness" of the Word that makes it especially apropos for us to *listen*. "When we engage the text intentionally, it can give birth to new insights and possibilities in our lives.... [A]s we gather the wisdom of scripture in, it becomes knit into the very fabric of our being."[14]

Kevin Vanhoozer has likened our response to Scripture as a "performance" in which God has, through human authors, established the books of the Bible (the canon) and in which the church is called to faithfully order its life according to this divinely authored script, that is, the church is called to faithful response and performance of God's playbook. Thus, *"the canon is a script that both records key moments in the drama of redemption and summons the reader rightly to participate."*[15]

The focus of *Lectio Divina* is to allow God, through his Word and Spirit, to transform us into the image of Christ. Thus it is as much about *transformation* as it is about *information*. It would be a mistake, however, to reduce these two emphases to an either/or proposal. God has chosen to create us with minds, through which we communicate with each other. Thus God's chosen means of communication is through the written Word. Our obedient, informed, intelligent response to that communication allows God to shape us into Christ's image.

Lectio Divina is not just another method of reading the Bible. Rather, it describes a biblical and habitual *attitude* of remaining open to God's voice, of enjoying God's presence, of delighting in following his will. The attitude required for *Lectio Divina* is identical to the attitude required in order to "pray without ceasing" (1 Thess 5:17 NASB). It means that we consciously and continually hold our lives open to God with no reservations whatsoever. It is a mode of absolute trust and, therefore, of rest.

In a world where we value *doing* over *being* and *becoming*, prayerful listening is the proper response to God's address. Such listening gladly embraces God's Lordship, acknowledges God's all-sufficiency for all aspects of our lives, and ensures that we keep in step with the Spirit (Gal 5:25 NASB). Terence Kardong notes that "desire for God, not intellectual sharpness, is the primary requisite for fruitful *Lectio Divina*."[16]

While various models of the practice of *Lectio Divina* follow a similar pattern,[17] I would suggest a couple of cautions. Some models seem to lead toward a kind of mysticism, a merging with God that implies a divine possession of our body and soul and mental faculties. While there have been those in the history of the Christian church who emphasized losing oneself in a blissful merging with the divine, the Bible maintains a clear distinction between Creator and creature, even in the closest of relationships.

Similarly, there has been a long practice of "praying scripture," which can be a legitimate part of *Lectio Divina*. However, as noted above, we ought not to construe this as a means of manipulating God (cf. Matt 6:7 NASB).[18]

Conclusion

When we open a Bible, and read it with a receptive, prayerful attitude, we enter into an ongoing conversation with our living Creator, Lord, and Savior. Listening to the Word is the chief means by which God communicates to our minds the truth about himself and ourselves, and by which he transforms our character into the character of Christ. This truth, revealed to us and applied to our hearts by the Holy Spirit, becomes *very* personal and alive. We find at work in us the same creative power as spoke the worlds into being, as brought Lazarus forth from the tomb at Jesus' spoken command, and as raised Jesus from the dead. Since the written Word has its source in the Living Word, and since through this Living Word all things have their being, there is no better or more sufficient source of life for us. The Word of truth, therefore, precisely because it is *truth*, requires our careful study, dedicated obedience, and prayerful listening.

Notes

1. I should point out that this was a misapplication of these verses. James is not speaking here of honest doubts, but of willful vacillation between, on the one hand, faith and obedience, and on the other hand, unbelief and disobedience.

2. J. Kenneth Grider, *A Wesleyan-Holiness Theology* (Kansas: Beacon Hill Press, 1994), 511.

3. C. S. Lewis, *Reflections on the Psalms* (Glasgow, Scotland: William Collins Sons & Co. Ltd, 1961), 82.

4. Eugene Peterson, *Eat This Book: A Conversation in the Art of Spiritual Reading* (Grand Rapids, MI: Eerdmans, 2006), 137.

5. Kevin Vanhoozer, *Is There Meaning in This Text: The Bible, The Reader, and the Morality of Literary Knowledge* (Grand Rapids: Zondervan Publishing House, 1998), 461.

6. Vanhoozer, *Is There Meaning*, 226.

7. There is debate and uncertainty about who is the actual author of the book of Hebrews. I will simply refer to the author as "The Preacher."

8. John Wesley, *Sermons*, vol. 2 of *The Works of John Wesley*, vol. 6 (3d ed.; Kansas City: Beacon Hill Press of Kansas City), 513.

9. There are excellent resources for the reader who wishes to pursue a better understanding of how to interpret the Bible, such as the following: Howard G. Hendricks and William D. Hendricks, *Living by the Book: The Art and Science of Reading the Bible*, (rev. and updated ed.; Chicago: Moody Publishing, 2008); Gordon Fee and Douglas Stuart, *How to Read the Bible for all its Worth*, (3d ed.; Grand Rapids: Zondervan, 2003).

10. Vanhoozer, *Is There Meaning*, 419-20.

11. Peterson, *Eat This Book*, 139.

12. Peterson, *Eat This Book*, 140.

13. Richard H. Schmidt, *God Seekers: Twenty Centuries of Christian Spiritualities* (Grand Rapids: Eerdmans, 2008), 74.

14. Christine Valters Painter, and Lucy Wynkoop, OSB, *Lectio Divina: Contemplative Awakening and Awareness* (New York/Mahwah, NJ: Paulist Press, 2008), 23.

15. Kevin Vanhoozer, *The Drama of Doctrine: A Canonical-Linguistic Approach to Christian Theology* (Louisville, KY: Westminster John Knox Press, 2005), 180-1 (italics original).

16. Philip Sheldrake, ed. *The New Westminster Dictionary of Christian Spirituality* (Philadelphia, PA: Westminster John Knox Press, 1983), s.v., "*Lectio Divina*," by Terrence Kardong.

17. A typical pattern or procedure is outlined by Teresa A. Blythe (*50 Ways to Pray: Practices from Many Traditions and Times* [Nashville: Abingdon Press2006], 46-47) as follows: "Step one: *Silencio*" (silence). After reading a short passage of scripture, wait in silence as you consciously "turn all your thoughts and desires over to God. Let go of concerns, worries, or agendas." "Step Two: *Lectio*." Read and reread your short passage, perhaps aloud. "Be alert to any word, phrase, or image that…invites you…puzzles you, [or]…intrigues you." "Step Three: *Meditatio*. Take…[the] word, phrase, or image…and allow yourself to ponder it in your heart…. Let it speak to your life." "Step Four: *Oratio*." With this personal word filling your mind and heart, be in prayer to God, allowing him to apply it to your inmost being. "Step Five: *Contemplatio*. Read silently [and contemplatively] in the presence of God."

18. For example Teresa Blythe suggests that, in the *Meditatio* step of *Lectio Divina*, "we ruminate over our chosen text. Repeat it to yourself like a mantra" (*50 Ways to Pray*), 47. In some spiritual practices mantras may actually lead to a disengagement of the mind.

Conclusion

Becoming the Church that Listens: Listening, Narrative, and Atonement

Aaron Perry

Is it too bold to say that reflective listening, with its underlying attitude of acceptance, gives the person an echo of God's love?[1]

~William Miller and Kathleen Jackson

Introduction

Listening matters. In spiritual development and pastoral ministry, listening matters. In your home and in your church, listening matters. In a fragmented, broken world, where patches of narratives are desperately strung together in the vain attempt that this story-meld will eventually make sense, listening matters. Stories of sexual license, materialism, and elitism begin to fall apart in the presence of a skilled and caring listener. I have sat with friends and parishioners whose storied-worlds crumble as gently and irreparably as clods of sand when they finally have someone listen to the story the world has been telling and they have been repeating.

Yet Christians listen not just to deconstruct false stories, but to develop new narratives, make mature disciples, and heal broken people. Listening provides the space for people to reorient and reconsider the most important stories of their lives, thereby shaping new identities. The patchwork story is seen for what it is in the presence of a skilled and caring listener *so that* a true narrative may be started—indeed, so that the narrative God has been weaving in this broken world can start to take prominence in the life of one more broken person. All of these benefits have implications for the life and work of the church as this community helps to orient people in reconciliation to God and his mission.

Because God has given the church the ministry of reconciliation (2 Cor 5:18), listening is a defining role of the church that invites others to join this community. Listening is a practice that can achieve reconciliation because it allows the participants of a conversation to share a mutual story that is vital to the order and sense of each of their lives. This is a challenging thought, so let's tackle it in stride. First, we will consider how God shares a story with humanity. Second, we will think of God's method of achieving this shared narrative using the metaphor of interpersonal communication, in which God's listens to humanity. To wrap up these thoughts on listening, we will consider listening, especially as it plays a role in the practice of conversation, and its role in the mission of the church, in light of what God has done to bring us into relationship with himself.

Atonement as a Shared Story

Christians have good news to share. The message of reconciliation, that God has adopted sons and daughters into the family of his Son Jesus is a powerful and transforming message. The exploration, development, and clarification of this teaching is typically gathered under the doctrine of atonement. Put simply, the doctrine of atonement discusses how people are put at-one with God; hence, at-one-ment. Thus, the doctrine has implications for the church, the community gathered together by God.

A community already has a sense of at-one-ment because a community is formed by sharing. Augustine noted that a community "is a gathered multitude of rational beings united by agreeing to share the things they love."[2] In all its diversity across time, space, and culture, the community of God, the church, shares the story of Jesus Christ. The church participates and orients its life around this story.

This sharing is not simply in the mind, however. Rather, having been made flesh, Jesus enters into communion with all of humanity.[3] In the Incarnation of Jesus, God and humanity begin sharing a story because Jesus is the God-Man and his story belongs both to God and to humanity.[4] His story is open to all because Jesus, the second Adam, represents all of humanity.

Jesus' representation involves two features. First, Jesus' representation is unique in that he alone represents humanity.[5] No one else has been like him and no one else will ever take his place. He alone represents humanity. Second, the ones whom Jesus represents are present in Jesus and participate in what he has done.[6] As was noted about Incarnation, Jesus is so fully human that his experience covers and entails the human experience of all other people.

While Jesus is the fullest picture of representation for the Christian, the phenomenon of representation is common. For example, governments and government officials represent their electorates when they make appearances at social functions, offer official remarks, and extend appreciation for gifts. Another biblical example of representation is Abraham. Outsiders to the Israelite family could claim the story of Abraham as their own in word and deed (cf. Deut 26:5-11). Insofar as Abraham's election and subsequent story represented the non-Israelite, Abraham's story became the outsiders' own[7] and was the means of effecting their relationship with God. Because of Abraham's election, Abraham's story is a representative story, and the *story* of Abraham is the word of God's grace that enacts oneness between God and even the non-Israelite insofar as they claim that story as their own.

Just as an outsider could enter the story of Abraham and enjoy the benefits of that story, so can humans, in Jesus, enter the story of God. Likewise, so can God enter the story of humanity. Because God has entered our story in Jesus, people can be reconciled to God. Both God and humanity participate in the story of Jesus.[8]

This brief discussion around atonement, representation, and narrative has been to serve as a theological basis for considering the work of the church in reconciliation as communication. Let's turn in this direction.

Interpersonal Communication

Community and communication both have origins in the Latin word for "common." Just as community meant to share common objects of love, so does communicate mean to impart knowledge or share with another. To share a story, we communicate with others. Sometimes we *tell* the story; sometimes we *act it out*. (If you are like me, you can't possibly tell a story without using your hands!) Sometimes we communicate via email, sometimes by telephone. Sometimes a face-to-face communication is necessary. We share information with a spouse differently from how we share with a colleague. Likewise we share information, we communicate, with a telemarketer differently from how we share with a cabbie. Have you ever noticed how some people can shape the way you tell a story or a joke; give a sermon or a lecture; ask a question or make a comment just by their presence? Of course! Communication is tailored to the people with whom we are communicating.

This means that communication and identity are wrapped up in each other. In fact, identities are negotiated in communication exchanges of all sorts, no matter their size or length. Ordering a pizza, saying "No" to a telemarketer, and depositing money with a real-life bank teller all involve the negotiation of identities—who the other will be in relation to you and who you will be to them. Thus, communication differs when the pizza-delivery person is also a friend, the telemarketer reminds us of *Slumdog Millionaire*, or the bank teller attends your church! How you share, how you communicate, in these instances changes. It becomes *personal*.

Interpersonal communication accounts for the uniqueness of the other person in conversation by "[emphasizing] the presence of the personal."[9] This is why you don't always tell a story the same way to every listener. You know which words will bring about a stronger reaction and which words will fall on deaf ears. Interpersonal communication takes seriously that other people will be affected differently by types and content of communication.[10] This is why you telephone your closest friends with news of a pregnancy rather than sending an email! Essentially, communication that is interpersonal takes great care for the identity of the other with whom there is sharing.[11] Thus, listening is a key aspect to interpersonal communication.

God Listens

Earlier we looked at God's act of sharing himself. We saw how God shared the story of humanity in the Incarnation. This act of sharing, or communication, can be illuminated using the idea of interpersonal communication, especially the act of listening. In taking on flesh, God listens to humanity.

To see what it means for God to listen, consider Carl Rogers' definition of listening. He defined empathic listening as entering the private perceptual world of the other and becoming thoroughly at home in that world. Doesn't this sound like what happened in Incarnation—that God entered our world in a real way and made it his own in Jesus?

God's listening is redemptive and healing because God's presence transforms the narratives and the private worlds in which he listens. The Incarnation communicates that God has given his full attention to the world. Entering the world of another through listening conveys the deep value of the other and "can transform all of our relationships."[12] One such world of broken relationship is the life of the outsider. Frank Lake writes that Christ must be a "listener to every item of painful shame that is recounted, so that its power to bind the soul in the iron chains of condemnation and alienation is manifestly overcome."[13] This is especially important in the context of shame. As Norman Kraus writes, "[O]nly insofar as [Christ] was identified fully with those suffering the debilitating stigma of shame could his own 'despising the shame' enable them to live above the existential circumstances in which they were trapped."[14] The presence of God in Christ provides a relationship of listening that transforms those who identify with Christ.

This transformation can be described in light of three benefits made possible through listening.

1. Listening gives the speaker space for interpretation of his or her narrative;

2. Listening allows the speaker's life to be re-narrated and reinterpreted; and

3. Listening empowers the speaker.[15]

We will consider these in order. First, listening gives the speaker *space* for interpretation of his or her narrative. Listening allows for one's story to be removed from complete subjectivity thereby allowing an alternative consideration that remains existentially vested. Communication of one's story, sharing one's interpretation of it with the listener, gives it the space for new meaning.[16] In God's presence, events can be reexamined and reinterpreted, and some must be condemned as unjust, evil, abusive, etc. This judgment, perhaps facilitated by the listener as the story becomes more existentially objective, can communicate alternative interpretations of such events to the listener that would otherwise have not been available.

Second, listening allows the speaker's life to be re-narrated and reinterpreted. Listening facilitates a coherent and thematic shape to memories. This is called a life story schema. The development of the life story schema happens as a residue of speaking, thinking, and reasoning about events in one's past. So, we can say that speaking enables one to narrate the events of life and work out the narrative template which they use to consider these events and new ones.[17] The role of the therapeutic listener is to alter how "sufferers are engaged in stories of suffering sustained in their ways of conversing."[18] Life stories can be re-narrated through listening.

Let's look at this idea of reconstruction in a different way. Psychology tells us that autobiographical memories, the memories humans have about themselves, are malleable and can get worked out in the presence of a listener[19] because a listener opens the story of an individual to the constructive abilities of both *speaker and listener*.[20] Just as we tell jokes differently based on the other with whom we are sharing, so do listeners help shape the story the speaker is telling about their life.

Who better than God to listen to humanity and thereby open this story co-construction? Have you ever seen a crime show where some misguided counselor or therapist was blamed for giving a patient false memories? Well, consider God as the counselor or therapist who doesn't facilitate false memories, but who facilitates a redeemed and rescued interpretation of our life's events. With God listening, no event is beyond his willingness to hear, and therefore beyond his ability to engage in its reconstruction and healing.[21]

One can easily imagine, however, how a speaker may share a story with a listener that is not really the story she believes about her own life. Consider this in the context of shame. In the face of such false sharing, or false cover stories,[22] "the chronically shamed person is in reality a 'silent' being…. Though the real self exists, it lives the life of a mute, never daring to speak its name, barred from doing so by the crippling power of shame."[23] This real self, the real story, is covered by shame. In the face of such false sharing, is the listener bound? Partially. The story narrated, however, even if a cover story, can still be listened to with new narratives slowly offered and practiced for the speaker.[24] Listening may embolden the speaker to share more of the real story. Since each communicator is unique, the cover story offered bears insight into the speaker. Why have they shared *this* story in *this* way? Is there a kernel of truth to this narrative that is inherent to the real narrative?[25] As the listener presents a new narrative, it can be adopted and applied by the speaker. "Even without a 'real' self being present [as the cover story hides the real self], there can be healing and transformation."[26] This transformation of the speaker is by the re-narration of their own story, which can be started even if they only present cover stories initially.

Another element to listening to stories is hearing silent stories. Parin Dossa writes that subordinate groups wait for the "appropriate time and context before speaking; otherwise they risk the possibility of not being heard."[27] Dossa cites studies concerning bombed Japanese women (from Hiroshima and Nagasaki in 1945) and how they remained silent about their suffering until they could express themselves through the accepted status of motherhood. They were then able to describe their sufferings in the context of "tainted bodies."[28] But even in the silence, the group was sharing. Dossa's point is that, though lacking the ability to communicate verbally, the body will communicate in other ways. Once we understand that "silence can be recognized as language, we can learn to read 'the cadences of silences, the gaps between fragile words, in order to hear'" what is being said.[29]

Of course, while silence and false stories do present challenges to human listeners, grounding the practice of listening in God's work of atonement, we know that God sees through all pretense and that God hears each individual when no words are shared.

Finally, listening empowers the speaker. Telling one's story provides the speaker a "way out of inherited authoritarianisms...."[30] Once someone is listening, then tyranny's grip loosens. Gabriel Fackre captures this benefit well by saying, "The right to tell one's own tale is a weapon of the marginalized in the struggle against their cultural captors or a preserve of identity in a world of uniformity. Narrative in this mode is a way of giving voice to the voiceless...."[31] Arthur Frank writes, "In stories, the teller not only recovers her voice; she becomes a witness to the conditions that rob others of their voices."[32] In one person telling, many gain a voice. Perhaps listening to the least is listening to Jesus. Time and again, Scripture affirms that God is on the side of the poor and marginalized.[33] God's listening gives voice to those Christ most identifies with in their unique settings.

The story of humanity is open to reconstruction by God's listening presence in Jesus. When God communicates with us, God takes into account who we are and who he wants us to become. God is the ultimate interpersonal communicator! Because God inserts himself into our story in Jesus, our identities are up for reconstruction and our stories are up for retellings.

The Church Listens

God listens and the result is at-one-ment, a shared story with creation. This story is one that provides new identities to all its participants because of the healing, empowering presence of a listening God. While this idea is abstract, it has very practical implications for the church and the communication practices of its members. Just as God has created a community through his listening, bringing healing to the lives of those to whom he listens, the church can find her identity in providing this same listening service. Let's track with this idea using our previous thoughts of interpersonal communication.

Communicating communities provide the opportunity for change. Social processes like dialogue and conversation allow processes that provide psychological change.[34] The church can be the community oriented around these social processes and practices of story-communication because God has communicated with her. Thus, as God has made new identities possible, the church can become the community of this story's communication in which individuals are able to negotiate new identities and new selves.[35] The church becomes the real, flesh and blood community of communication because the listening God has first listened in the real, flesh and blood life of Jesus.

As the church lives out its calling to be a new culture, being a community created by God's communication, the communication practices of its members will both impact and describe who she is. By having similar ways of speaking and listening, individuals show that they belong to the same culture.[36] Christians can become known as being a community marked by their practices of conversation, faithfully embodying the atoning work of God in their practice of listening and entering into private perceptual worlds. In so doing, the private perceptual world is no longer private and may be reformed, in part, by the practices of the one now listening.

Could this service and ministry be thought of as deep friendship? Brad Kallenberg suggests we think of friendship as "the embodiment of conversation: the character and durability of a conversation *is* the character and durability of the friendship."[37] Speakers and listeners can embrace one another and their narratives in these very acts.[38] The invitation to the church, the community established by the listening and speaking of God in Jesus, is initiated by the listening community.[39] As the speaker is listened to, her narrative is presented with a new narrative, a new culture that practices listening to other narratives. The speaker's own narrative can be judged, considered, and re-appropriated by this new community. The church finds not only her story (the content of her speech) changed, but the manner of her communication as well—she can now become a listener.[40] The process of change for the speaker now becomes, in part, the responsibility of the church, as the speaker is engaging in deeper and more frequent conversations.[41] The church begins to bear burdens because they are "social spaces where we engage in atoning practice 'in that we acknowledge that an individual's sin is never his alone, that its endurance harms us all, and therefore its cancellation is also the responsibility of all.'"[42]

In seeing Christ as one who listens, our own eyes are first opened to learning that there are people needing a listening character in their private perceptual worlds. As the listener carries presumptions to the act of listening, they may be "intimidated" by the speaker's content.[43] This shortcoming can be transformed in the presence of Christ who listens first and along with us. The news of the speaker does not hold eternal consequences if the listening of Jesus ends in resurrection. No story that you will ever hear is beyond redemption, healing, and God's transformative work.

So, with this Good News of a listening God and this opportunity to listen and converse with others in our world, why would Christians, even mature ones, shrink from listening? Because some stories are hard to hear. Peggy Penn writes that in listening to the one who is chronically ill, the well person often acts in self-protection and so "avoids or downplays the true content of the story. The listener feels they must intuitively protect his or her own immune system against the personal impact such a story could have."[44] Arthur Frank describes one type of story told in the experience of deep illness[45] as the chaos story. One example of a chaos story is when there is illness which has thus far resisted diagnosis. The feeling of this chaos narrative is that the "disability can only increase, pain will never remit, [and] physicians are either unable to understand what is wrong or unable to treat it successfully."[46] The story feels as though there is no coherence and no end. The potential disintegration of a person's story in this condition presents a threat to the listener that the same possibility exists for his or her own life.

Phrases that counteract the speaker's narrative might include, "Well, look on the brightside," or "It's not so bad." We even baptize such language: "You haven't learned the lesson God is teaching you." However, simply listening to the chaos story means that if the chaos story can be told, then there is an opening for it not to be chaotic.[47] Once words capture the experience, its chaos is already attacked and is begins to weaken.

A willingness to listen to such chaos stories points to the depth of Christ's work and lordship. Graham Ward argues that as the church listens to the events and stories of the world the church tunes itself to the world.[48] Ward describes this theologically: "as [Christians] dwell in Christ and Christ in [them], then [events and stories] pass through Christ also."[49] Could we not say that these stories pass through the church as she listens? Is it possible, then, to consider as Christ is listening through the church that these events and stories become types of prayers and may be brought under the authority of Christ? Thus, even while the stories feel chaotic, they become less threatening and harsh in the midst of a listener whose own story is marked by the death and resurrection of Christ. What story dares to threaten in the face of a listening God and the resurrection of Christ?

Conclusion

Listening holds implications not only for your ministry and spiritual life, but for the mission of the church. By listening, the church may reflect the work of God that re-opens humanity's narrative to be shared with God and thereby invite an outsider to participate in this narrative. For this reason, it matters that you listen. It matters that you grow in skill, depth, and knowledge of listening. May the church follow our lead and become a community that reflects the gospel of a listening God with ears to hear.

Notes

1. See William R. Miller and Kathleen A. Jackson, *Practical Psychology for Pastors* (2d ed.; New Jersey: Prentice-Hall, 1995), 56.

2. Augustine, *City of God,* book XIX, article 24, in *From Irenaeus to Grotius* (eds. Oliver O'Donovan & Joan Lockwood O'Donovan; Grand Rapids, MI: Eerdmans, 1999),

162. For a contemporary consideration of Augustine's thought, see Oliver O'Donovan, *Common Objects of Love* (Grand Rapids, MI: Eerdmans, 2002).

3. Irenaeus, *Irenaeus Against Heresies*, in *The Ante-Nicene Fathers* (eds. Alexander Roberts and James Donaldson; vol. 1of *The Ante-Nicene Fathers*, eds. Alexander Roberts and James Donaldson; repr., Peabody, Mass.: Hendrickson, 1994), 1:527.

4. This sharing of narrative could also be fleshed out as *participation*. Philip Quinn ("Aquinas on Atonement," in *Trinity, Incarnation, Atonement* [eds. Ronald J. Feenstra and Cornelius Plantinga, Jr.; Notre Dame, IN: UND Press, 1989]) mentions this participation as one of Aquinas' benefits to the Incarnation: "[W]e are brought to fuller participation in the divine life because God has participated in human life" (155).

5. This line of thinking is completely owed to Oliver O'Donovan, *Desire of the Nations* (Cambridge: CUP, 2003).

6. See O'Dovovan, *Desire of the Nations*, especially 125. O'Donovan's work is sensitive to the political aspect of representation. For a Wesleyan consideration of representation, see H. Ray Dunning, *Grace, Faith, and Holiness* (Kansas City, MO: Beacon Hill Press, 1988), 373-6. Dunning also believes that Irenaeus' work is an antecedent to the Wesleyan affirmations of reconciliation and sanctification in the atonement (380-1).

7. See Joel B. Green, "Narrative Theology," in *Dictionary for Theological Interpretation of the Bible* (ed. Kevin J. Vanhoozer; Grand Rapids, MI: Baker Academic, 2005), 532.

8. The doctrine of atonement has further implication for all of creation, however for the purposes of this essay we will focus on oneness of God and people.

9. John Stewart (ed.), *Bridges not Walls: A Book About Interpersonal Communication* (9th ed.; New York: McGraw-Hill, 2006), 16.

10. Stewart, *Bridges not Walls*, 34-38.

11. Stewart, *Bridges not Walls*, 63.

12. Kay Lindahl, *Practicing the Sacred Art of Listening: A Guide to Enrich Your Relationships and Kindle Your Spiritual Life* (Woodstock, VT: SkyLights Paths Publishing), as quoted in Stewart, *Bridges not Walls*, 199.

13. Frank Lake, *Clinical Theology* (unabridged ed.; Lexington, KY: Emeth Press, 2005), 1:52.

14. C. Norman Kraus, *Jesus Christ Our Lord: Christology from a Disciples' Perspective* (Scottdale, PA: Herald, 1990), 218, as quoted by Joel B. Green and Mark D. Baker, *Recovering the Scandal of the Cross* (Downers Grove, Ill: IVP, 2000), 164.

15. Monisha Pasupathi ("The Social Construction of the Personal Past and its Implications for Adult Development," *Psychological Bulletin* 127:5 [2001]) writes that "people may recall the past in the service of solving a problem" (656). Each of these problems—the need for reinterpretation and re-narration, and powerlessness, is a problem that can be solved in cooperation with the listener. Pasupathi points out that, when faced with a "listener who does not display appropriate emotional responses at key points in [the speaker's] story. . .[that] speaker finds it difficult to end the tale coherently" (655). The result is a "shorter, less detailed, and less coherent" story (655).

16. Oliver O'Donovan, *The Ways of Judgment* (Grand Rapids, MI: Eerdmans, 2005), 250: "To communicate anything, material or spiritual, is to give it a meaning." Sharing one's story, in verbal or written form, is still to give it meaning.

17. This sharing also impacts the memory. Pasupathi ("The Social Construction of the Personal Past and its Implications for Adult Development") writes, "Socially shared memories are held with greater confidence and certainty than those not shared" (655). It should be noted, however, that not all memories are narratives.

18. Tom Strong, "Poetic Possibilities in Conversations about Suffering," *Contemporary Family Therapy* 24:3 (September 2002), 460.

19. Pasupathi, "The Social Construction of the Personal Past and its Implications for Adult Development," 651-72. The participants in the social construction of the personal past include the speaker, the listener, and the combination of both, which is not simply formed by the sum of memories between the two (656). As autobiographical memories are malleable, so is their meaning dynamic. Peggy Penn ("Chronic Illness: Trauma, Language, and Writing: *Breaking the Silence,*" *Family Process* 40:1 [2001]), when considering the impact of metaphor on interpretation, captures this well. She writes, "Meaning is not a stable entity, but an outcome of relational negotiations in a particular context. When those negotiations change, meanings change as well" (44).

20. Pasupathi, "Social Construction of the Personal Past and its Implications for Adult Development," 654.

21. Pasupathi, "Social Construction of the Personal Past and its Implications for Adult Development," writes, "Whether an event is evoked by a conversation at all can be viewed as one aspect of co-construction," 654.

22. Alan Mann, *Atonement for a Sinless Society* (UK: Paternoster, 2006), 43. Cover stories are those a shamed person may present to a listener that are not actually the ones that reflect his or her own considerations of him- or herself.

23. Mann, *Atonement for a Sinless Society*, 43.

24. Mann, *Atonement for a Sinless Society*, 85. This presentation of a new narrative may be irritable for the one hearing it. This is because, against the narrative of Jesus, their own narratives will be seen as inconsistent and incoherent. The question for presenters of the gospel becomes whether they are "willing to endure, even augment, this tension until the Gestalt of conversion occurs." Brad Kallenberg, *Live to Tell* (Grand Rapids, MI: Brazos), 61-62.

25. Bluck & Habermas, "The Life Story Schema," *Motivation and Emotion* 24:2 (2000), 139. Stories told multiple times often have a "kernel story," and parts of the story may remain stable while new information is added.

26. Mann, *Atonement for a Sinless Society*, 86.

27. Parin Dossa, "The Body Remembers: A Migratory Tale of Social Suffering," *International Journal of Mental Health* 32:3 (Fall 2003), 53.

28. Dossa, "The Body Remembers," 54.

29. Dossa, "The Body Remembers," 54.

30. Gabriel Fackre, "Narrative Theology: An Overview," *Interpretation* 37:4 (October 1983), 347.

31. Fackre, "Narrative Theology," 347.

32. Arthur Frank, *The Wounded Story Teller* (Chicago: University of Chicago Press, 1995), xii, as quoted by Dossa, "The Body Remembers," 56.

33. This attitude of God is captured by Hans Boersma's phrase, "preferential hospitality." See Hans Boersma, *Violence, Hospitality, and the Cross: Reappropriating the Atonement Tradition* (Grand Rapids, MI: Baker Academic, 2004).

34. E. E. Sampson, *Celebrating the Other: A Dialogic Account of Human Nature* (Boulder, CO: Westview), 103, as found in Stewart, *Bridges Not Walls*, 69.

35. See Stewart, *Bridges Not Walls*, 27-28. Although Stewart is not working in a church context.

36. Kallenberg (*Live to Tell*) writes that "...religious conversion necessarily includes the acquisition of the appropriate conceptual language" (41) and that "becoming fluent in a language involves participation in the grammar of the language, that is, participation in the form of life of the language's speakers" (57).

37. Kallenberg, *Live to Tell*, 61.

38. Kallenberg (*Live to Tell*) writes that "a friendship formed with an insider of a rival community may be the handrail that assists one's ascent into the new community" (61).

39. Consider the simple phrase, "Tell me a little about yourself." The self is relayed in short episodic stories. As such, a schema of the life story "serves in the development and maintenance of social relationships" (Bluck & Habermas, "The Life Story Schema," 137). Of course, the church does not *have* to be the one to initiate this conversation, but by practicing such initiations, she better lives God's first steps toward sinners.

40. Inasmuch as listening is part of the "language" of the church, Kallenberg's (*Live to Tell*) words are most appropriate: "Language can only be learned by participation" (87). One learns to listen, first, by being listened to. Hence, the cross of Christ begins the whole process of listening. We, as the church, listen because God first listened to us.

41. To enter into conversations, the entrant must gain in language and topics of conversation. Kallenberg (*Live to Tell*) addresses the language aspect of this by saying that "becoming fluent in a language involves participation in the grammar of the language, that is, participation in the form of life of the language's speakers" (57). Sehulster ("Things we Talk About") remarks about the need to develop common ground in order to converse: "The suggestion is that people whose favorite topics are clustered in the same factors will find communication easier. Conversely, those whose favorite topics are clustered in different factors may find little in common to chat about except experiences of the present moment" (430). One must acquire a new language and a new set of topics in order to properly converse with the new community.

42. William C. Placher, "Christ Takes our Place," *Interpretation* 53:1 (January 1999), 17.

43. Penn, "Chronic Illness: Trauma, Language, and Writing," 43.

44. Penn, "Chronic Illness: Trauma, Language, and Writing," 42.

45. For Frank ("Just Listening: Narrative and Deep Illness," *Families, Systems & Health* 16, 1998) "illness is 'deep' when perceived as lasting, as affecting virtually all life choices and decisions, and as altering reality" (197). What matters is the patient's perception of their illness: they believe their illness will always be present (197).

46. Frank, "Just Listening," 201.

47. Frank, "Just Listening," 200.

48. Frank, "Just Listening," 281. Recall how Scharmer described the open mind, will, and heart as three instruments to be tuned from the Introduction.

49. Frank, "Just Listening," 282.

Index

Penn, Peggy, 229
Peterson, Eugene, 7, 8, 84, 208, 216
politics, 9, 10, 27, 32, 43, 54, 90, 95, 96
prayer, 11, 22, 33, 34, 36, 46, 47, 48,
   49, 53, 54, 65, 81, 89, 91, 92, 93,
   106, 125, 136, 137, 141, 142, 143,
   144, 146, 147, 149, 150, 151, 152,
   153, 154, 156, 157, 161, 162, 164,
   165, 166, 167, 169, 170, 176, 177,
   178, 214, 217, 220
preaching, 11, 34, 46, 47, 52, 53, 57,
   58, 60, 63, 64, 67, 68, 70, 71, 78, 81,
   144, 177, 198, 206, 211,
presencing, 4, 5, 7

reading, 7, 13, 34, 51, 71, 219
reconciliation, 95, 99, 100, 211, 223,
   224
Red Cross, 78, 79
representation, 224
Responsiveness, 95, 98, 99
Rogers, Carl, 225
Role of the Listener, 121

Sabbath, 45, 130, 209, 212
salvation, 7, 55, 58, 59, 61, 63, 65, 67,
   136, 148, 164, 178, 180, 188, 193,
   194, 196, 199, 200, 203, 207, 208,
   210, 212
Scharmer, Otto, 4, 5, 6, 13, 14
Schmemann, Alexander, 43, 56
Scripture, 7, 8, 9, 10, 11, 12, 20, 21, 47,
   48, 51, 52, 53, 54, 59, 60, 63, 64, 65,
   68, 70, 73, 114, 133, 136, 137, 139,
   149, 150, 152, 155, 161, 162, 170,
   176, 185, 190, 191, 192, 193, 194,
   195, 196, 197, 198, 199, 200, 201,
   202, 203, 204, 210, 213, 215, 216,

217, 228
Sheriffs, Deryck, 22, 28
silence, 30, 33, 34, 72
Simmons, Annette, *18, 26, 28*
sound, 3, 7, 8, 9, 10, 19, 27, 30, 31, 32,
   33, 34, 35, 36, 37, 52, 76, 79, 122,
   134, 145, 159, 201, 225
speech, 3, 58, 61, 63, 64, 65, 94, 99,
   177, 178, 188, 194, 229
Stephen of Muret, 188, 189
story, 28, 223
Stroup, George, 26, 28
Students, 103

theologian's vocation, 176
Theological Listening, 175
theology, 176
Theory U, 4, 5, 13
Theresa of Avila, 11, 156, 159, 160,
   161, 165, 166, 167, 168, 169, 171,
   172
transformation, 152, 180

urban trance, 19

Vanhoozer, Kevin, 14, 210, 215, 217,
   219, 220

Ward, Graham, 9, 14, 230
Watson, George, 148, 153
Weil, Simone, 11, 159, 160, 161, 163,
   164, 165, 166, 168, 169, 171, 172
Wesley, John, 48, 53, 54, 56, 97, 157,
   214, 219
Westphal, Merold, 8, 14
wisdom, 24, 184, 185, 197
worship, 41, 42, 47, 53, 55, 198, 200

Contributors

Nathan Crawford
Adjunct Professor of Religion and Philosophy at Indiana Wesleyan University.

David Drury
A minister of The Wesleyan Church and serves as Executive Pastor at College Church in Marion, Indiana.

Timothy J. Furry
Adjunct Professor at the University of Dayton and is pursuing the diaconate in the Evangelical Lutheran Church in America. He is also the Director of Adult Education and Local Outreach at Living Water Lutheran Church, Dayton, OH.

Anne Gatobu
Assistant Professor of Pastoral Care and Counseling at Asbury Theological Seminary.

Kenneth Gavel
Professor of Biblical Studies and Theology at Bethany Bible College in Sussex, New Brunswick.

Frederica Mathewes-Green
A wide ranging author and speaker. She is "Khouria" ("Mother") of the parish she and her husband founded, Holy Cross Orthodox Church in Baltimore, MD.

David Higle
Dean of Discipleship at Bethany Bible College in Sussex, New Brunswick.

Edith M. Humphrey
The William F. Orr Professor of New Testament at Pittsburgh Theological Seminary.

Daryl MacPherson
A minister of The Wesleyan Church, serving on staff at Whitewater Wesleyan Community Church in Cobden, Ontario. He is active in the ministry of Spiritual Direction.

Alan Mann
A writer, educator and theological consultant based in the United Kingdom. He is a Tutor for the Open Learning Department of London School of Theology.

Michael Pasquarello III
The Granger E. and Anna A. Fisher Professor of Preaching at Asbury Theological Seminary.

Aaron Perry
A minister of The Wesleyan Church and Pastor of Christian Education at Centennial Road Church in Brockville, Ontario.

Brent D. Peterson
Professor of Theology at Northwest Nazarene University.

Ephraim Radner
Professor of Historical Theology at Wycliffe College.

Stephen H. Webb
Professor of Religion & Philosophy at Wabash College.

CPSIA information can be obtained at www.ICGtesting.com
Printed in the USA
BVOW03s1524160916

462129BV00002B/246/P